# Democratic Education:
# Ethnographic Challenges

# the Tufnell Press,
London,
United Kingdom

www.tufnellpress.co.uk

email contact@tufnellpress.co.uk

**British Library Cataloguing-in-Publication Data**
A catalogue record for this book is
available from the British Library

*ISBN 1 872767 427*

Copyright © 2003,    Dennis Beach, Tuula Gordon and Elina Lahelma

The moral rights of the authors have been asserted.
Database right the Tufnell Press (maker).

All Rights reserved. No part of this publication may be reproduced, stored in a retrieval system, or transmitted in any form or by any means, electronic, mechanical, photocopying, recording or otherwise, without the prior permission of the publisher, or expressly by law, or under terms agreed with the appropriate reprographic rights organisation.

First published 2003

Printed in England by Lightning Source

# Democratic Education: Ethnographic Challenges

Edited by

**Dennis Beach, Tuula Gordon and Elina Lahelma**

## The Authors

| | |
|---|---|
| Anne-Lise Arnesen | Associate Professor, Oslo University College, Norway |
| Dennis Beach | Associate Professor of Educational Sciences, Göteburg University, Sweden. |
| Thomas Gitz-Johansen | Researcher, Department of Education, Roskilde University, Denmark. |
| Tuula Gordon | Fellow, Helsinki Collegium for Advanced Studies, University of Helsinki, Finland. |
| Janet Holland | Professor, Faculty of Arts and Human Science, South Bank University, UK. |
| Inger Anne Kvalbein | Associate Professor, Department of Teacher Education, Oslo University College, Norway. |
| Elina Lahelma | Academy Fellow, Department of Education, University of Helsinki, Finland. |
| Sirpa Lappalainen | Researcher, Department of Education, University of Helsinki, Finland |
| Sverker Linblad | Professor, University of Uppsala, Department of Education, Sweden |
| Elisabet Öhrn | Associate Professor, Department of Education, Göteburg University, Sweden |
| Thomas S. Popkewitz | Professor, University of Wisconsin-Madison, USA |
| Ulla-Maija Salo | Professor, University of Helsinki, Department of Home Economics and Craft Science, Finland. |
| Daniel Sundberg | Researcher, Department of Education, University of Växjö, Sweden |

## Contents

### Introduction

Marketisation of democratic education:
Ethnographic insights
*Tuula Gordon, Elina Lahelma and Dennis Beach* — 1

### Part I: From policies to classrooms

1. Comparative ethnography:
Fabricating the new millennium and its exclusions
*Sverker Lindblad and Thomas S. Popkewitz* — 10

2. Nation space:
The construction of citizenship and difference in schools
*Tuula Gordon and Janet Holland* — 24

3. 'Strong nordic women' in the making?
Gender policies and classroom practices
*Elina Lahelma and Elisabet Öhrn* — 39

### Part II: Construction of normality and difference

4. Constructions of an 'outsider':
Contradictions and ambiguities in institutional practices
*Anne-Lise Arnesen* — 52

5. Representations of ethnicity:
How teachers speak about ethnic minority students
*Thomas Gitz-Johansen* — 66

6. Celebrating internationality:
Constructions of nationality at preschool
*Sirpa Lappalainen* — 80

### Part III: Discourses and practices

7. The politics of time in educational restructuring
*Daniel Sundberg* — 92

8. Becoming a pupil
*Ulla-Maija Salo* — 105

9. Mathematics goes to market
*Dennis Beach* — 116

10. Changes in teacher students' knowledge by changes in technologies of freedom and control
*Inger Anne Kvalbein* — 128

Bibliography — 141

# Introduction

## Marketisation of democratic education: ethnographic challenges

### Tuula Gordon, Elina Lahelma and Dennis Beach

Liberal democratic politics have emphasised the importance of education in the development of a just society with equal opportunities for all. Researchers have often shared the hope that society can be improved through schooling, whether their explicit or underlying assumptions about equality have been about social class, gender, 'race'/ethnicity, sexuality or other dimensions through which inequalities are constructed, or a combination of any or all of these. Studies have demonstrated that equality has not been realised even when it was an explicit aim. Whilst equality has not completely disappeared as an expectation directed at schools, new politics and policies of education have emphasised accountability, standards and individual choice. Concerns for efficiency have been expressed, and through such concerns major changes in schooling systems have been justified.

Today new policies of restructuring, with tendencies like striving towards accountability and closer links between school and industry are prevalent in many countries and continents. There have been tensions between state control and market forces for some time (Whitty 1989). The writers of this book take issue with marketisation of education through an examination of the impact of changes that have been imposed on education.

The idea of democratic education emphasises equality, and a structural way of realising it has been through the comprehensive system without selection. Nordic countries have been a particular example of strong commitment to comprehensive education inspired by social democratic politics. However, these achievements too are now being undermined through educational restructuring. In this book the new education policies and practices of restructuring are discussed and challenged. We trace what happens in schooling when democratic education goes to market, or when, as members of the British Hillcole Group suggest, New Labour's rallying cry 'education, education, education' becomes 'business, business, business' (Allen et al. 1999). Nevertheless, as Dave Hill (1999) argues, it is also important to pay attention to discontinuities between New Labour and Neo-Liberal and Neo-Conservative education policies, as well as to the continuities.

This book uses ethnographic stories of action within theories of context to explore and analyse the impact of educational politics and policies on teaching and learning and on the perceptions of people involved in educational and schooling processes. These stories have been specifically crafted by a group of ethnographic writers in order to try to reveal, interpret and analyse particular elements of every day encounters in various educational settings, ranging from preschool to primary and secondary schools and teacher education. Each ethnography is guided by its own specifically identified theory. The theories used are manifold, ranging from poststructuralist, to Marxist, interactionist and feminist perspectives.

Several themes appear in chapters of the book. These are linked in various ways with each other, although most specifically through the particular context that is made articulate and to which each of the chapters speaks in some way. This context is that of educational restructuring. It is focused in the chapters in relation to developments in several OECD countries, the Nordic welfare states and the UK in particular. The chapters are empirically grounded in rich ethnographic data.

We suggest that ethnographic research can challenge inequity by contributing to critical analyses of social and cultural processes, practices and meanings in educational sites. The book addresses the concept of education restructuring in a number of concrete examples. Our argument is that ethnographic studies where the researchers participate in the cultures that they study provide a powerful critique of the effects of New Right policies on everyday life at school. Inequality is manifested in a range of practices despite efforts of those teachers who include equity in their aims.

We focus on how restructuring affects the supply of a high quality of education to all citizens as a democratic right, and on how spaces for democratic agency are currently being reconstituted and constricted. Ethnographic studies demonstrate New Right politics and policies in action and thus challenge New Right politics and policies in a particularly powerful way.

## Marketisation of education in welfare states

New Right politics and policies have spread from the US for example to Australia, New Zealand, Europe and Nordic countries. They have circulated widely for many internal and external reasons. Internal reasons consist largely of the alliance between Neo–Conservatism and Neo-Liberalism that provides a promise to many political interest groups, whether, in the context of education, they have been interested in maintaining standards and promoting the competitive edge of the nation state, or whether they are more concerned to marketise education (c.f. Ainley 2000; Hillcole Group 1997). The aim is to promote the cutting edge of the new increasingly hierarchical work force, capable of crossing borders in a globalising world.

Schools and students are becoming targets of more exact evaluation and competition. Competition and increasing opportunities for differentiation are meant to enable suitably inclined school students to increase their potential. Others are expected to provide the labour force that maintains the infrastructure of society and necessary services. The reasons for the spread of marketisation in education that are external to the New Right politics include the failure of social democratic education to deliver the just, equitable education it promised (Arnot and Gordon 1996; Kenway and Epstein 1996). The New Right has criticised social democratic politics for inflexibility, inefficiency and falling standards. Increasing choice and individualisation have been argued to offer advantages to children, and particularly middle class families have taken advantage of these. The increasing costs and inefficiency of the welfare state were argued to cause insurmountable problems. Individual liberty was emphasised in the US, the problems of the 'nanny state' were discussed in the UK, and the control exerted in the context of the welfare state was thought to thwart self-reliance and initiative of citizens in the Nordic countries.

The supply and availability of education, as a welfare service, is being politically, economically and legally restructured through the creation of quasi-markets and networks for controlling flows of services that extend capitalisation processes into and within the public sector. These dimensions of change can easily be seen as aspects of the complex processes of transfer and patterned interaction between agents, nodes of activity and sites of power in the movement of physical artefacts (such as commodity products), people, symbols, tokens and information across global time and space (Castells 1998,1999; McMurtry 1998; Lindblad and Popkewitz in this volume). They speak loudly now even in the former 'shop-window democracies' of the Nordic countries, in and to just about every domain of social life. Market rationality – particularly the concept of market competition – is important and markets are still seen as rational tools for controlling the provision of services. Competition between suppliers is emphasised.

Although many people stopped believing this idea long ago, education systems have previously been expected to promote social justice and liberation, with increasing social and personal advantages (c.f. Davies, Holland and Minhas 1992). These expectations are expressed in different forms, and means to realise them vary between countries and between historical periods. Capable, active citizens were to ensure welfare and progress in their own societies. On the other hand, education has also been expected to maintain the status quo, to ensure stability of societies and to integrate children and young people into the prevailing social system of distribution of goods and services. These aims are contradictory and tensions between them have been played out in various ways in different countries at different times (Donald 1992; Brosio 1994; Gordon, Holland and Lahelma 2000).

In the Nordic countries the development of welfare states and the establishment of comprehensive education were central projects aimed to ensure social citizenship. Social–democratic education policies in the 1960s and 1970s addressed social class and (particularly in Norway, Sweden and Finland) regional equality of opportunity. There were many silences in such policies, such as gender, ethnicity and sexuality. Such silences in their part contributed to the New Right challenge of failing standards. Standards, efficiency and accountability became catchwords that spread from one education system to another. Better standards, more efficiency and increasing accountability of course are not problematic in themselves, but if the policies allow for increasing inequality and polarisation, claims for general improvement can hardly be made (c.f. The Hillcole Group 1997).

The Nordic countries provide a particularly interesting location for exploring the advent and onward march of the New Right in education. These countries have had a far stronger commitment to social justice and to policies for ensuring equality than for example the US and the UK. Educational rhetoric still emphasises equality – although at times there are slippages and the rhetoric is forgotten. But a new rhetoric of accountability, standards and efficiency has begun to occupy the centre stage in politics and policies.

## Ethnographic insights

We argue that ethnographic research can provide new insights for challenging the triumphant New Right hegemony. Such studies move beyond the rhetoric to examine what is taking place in the daily life of educational institutions. Through ethnography we can discern both how promises have been fulfilled and how they have been broken. We can explore processes of differentiation and practices of new modes of control at the school level by listening to voices in the field, from teachers, school students and other staff working in schools. Ethnographers are able to explore what is changing and how, and what stays the same. In the words of Angela McRobbie (1996), ethnography can provide insights into the material matters despised in research that has been influenced by the most strident post–modern textual turns (c.f. Roman 1993; Hey 1996).

Ethnographic traditions, as editors of the *Handbook of Ethnography* suggest, 'are grounded in a commitment to the first–hand experience and exploration of a particular social and cultural setting on the basis of (though not exclusively by) participant observation' (Atkinson *et al.* 2001: 4). Increasing emphasis has been paid to writing of ethnographies after discussions on representation initiated by James Clifford and George Marcus (1996) and Clifford Geertz (1966). Indeed Stephanie Taylor (2002: 1–2) suggests that nuanced and non–reductive writing is an important distinguishing feature of ethnographic research. At the heart of ethnographers' writing today is strong reflexivity and a recognition of the responsibility of the researcher (Spencer 2001). Questions of power are often raised in ethnographic research, hence critical traditions such as feminism have incorporated ethnographic approaches (Skeggs 2001). Ethnographic research in educational settings has been practised across the whole of the previous century, but intensified greatly during the last four decades. Most of the research has been taking place in compulsory schooling, but other educational institutions have been explored too, such as pre–school and teacher education. Educational ethnographies first started in the US, but became increasingly popular in European countries too (e.g. Delamont and Atkinson 1995).

Although established as early as the 1970s, there has been a growing interest in ethnographic research in education in the Nordic countries since the mid 1990s. A Nordic network on ethnographic studies was founded within the Nordic Educational Research Association in the early 1990s and, with support from the Nordic Research Academy, it has organised successful symposia and postgraduate courses. The current book is initiated within this network and most of the authors are members of it.

For us, ethnographic educational research takes place in or on educational institutions through observation and participant observation (e.g. Delamont and Atkinson 1995; Gordon, Holland and Lahelma 2001). Researchers themselves are important tools in the research process, as they acquaint themselves with educational settings through immersion in the daily lives of the participants. In that sense ethnographers' selves are implicated in the process, as they observe, learn and understand local cultures through their own experiences in the field (e.g. Coffey 1999). The process of making sense of organisational aspects, practices, cultures, conflicts and commonalities challenges the ethnographer to understand cultures through learning them and remaining detached as well as being participants.

The methods used by ethnographers in their immersion in the daily life as well as their efforts to see beyond the intricacies of micro–processes include observation and participant observation recorded as field notes, collection of documents, informal discussions, interviews, photography and video recordings. The data is often qualitative, but quantitative data is collected in ethnographies too. In recent years the array of techniques has become increasingly widespread (Atkinson *et al.* 2001). Ethical issues are important in all research, but the ethnographic approach in particular demands sensitivity and reflexivity, as ethnographers, with their everyday experiences in the field, can harm individuals, groups or institutions (c.f. Murphy and Dingwall 2001).

It is the immersion in the daily life of institutions and their participants that gives ethnography a particular edge in obtaining insights into what changes and what stays the same in the context of educational politics and the politics of restructuring. The chapters in this book provide a looking glass into the tensions and contradictions New Right policies have introduced in educational institutions. Actors in the field experience frustrations about introducing changes and about controlling the direction of those changes. It is their voices that ethnographers try to hear and disseminate. However, most ethnographers do not simply tell a (more or less) gripping story about the field, with researchers themselves at the centre—they aim to analyse the practices they encounter, and endeavour to render them into analytical narratives that tell different stories than policy research or questionnaires and interviews. The aim here is to produce theoretically informed methodology (Willis and Trondman 2000). Although these are not necessarily better stories, we suggest that they are particularly poignant in demonstrating the organisation and practice of differentiation.

Ethnographic research has always included critical voices, including theorisation of tensions between structural constraints and human agency. Increasingly critical ethnographers have been interested in cultural critiques of dimensions of difference that are infused with relations of power. They have addressed traditional practices in schooling, gender differentiation, inequalities based on social class, ethnicity, able–bodiedness, sexuality and age. Whilst a great many ethnographies are conducted in the liberal humanist framework, many ethnographers adopt a more critical approach (Gordon, Holland and Lahelma 2001), hoping that their research can contribute to social change. In the tradition of this genre our aim is to challenge the forward march of New Right politics and politics by examining their claims through an exploration of practices and processes in educational institutions.

## Contextualised practices

This book aims at suggesting the usefulness of ethnographic research in analysing the impact of educational politics and policies into practices and processes of teaching and learning, as well as into perceptions of the people involved. We describe, analyse and interpret everyday encounters in various educational settings, such as preschool, primary and secondary schools and teacher education. We are concerned with the intentions, practices and reflections of teachers and students, and we are also concerned with texts.[1]

The authors of the chapters in the book draw on diverse theories; for example, poststructuralist, postcolonial, Marxist and feminist perspectives are common, and we are also inspired by critical, textual or material ethnography. Ethnographic data is used to introduce theoretical issues, for example discussions of temporality, as in the chapter by Daniel Sundberg, or spatiality, which is a theme of Tuula Gordon and Janet Holland, or the infiltration of education by market thinking and neo–liberal values, as in the chapter by Dennis Beach. The context for our analyses is primarily the marketisation of welfare and educational restructuring in the Nordic welfare states. The focus is, however, widened to England in the crosscultural perspective provided in the chapter by Tuula Gordon and Janet Holland, and to several countries in the comparative perspective adopted in the chapter by Sverker Lindblad and Thomas S. Popkewitz. The latter authors suggest for ethnographers the importance of seeing the global in the local, historicity of context.

The impact of the politics and policies of restructuring in constructing and addressing *difference* in school is one of the foci in several chapters. Sverker Lindblad and Thomas S. Popkewitz write about categories and distinctions that

---

[1] We extend our thanks to the following members of the senior group of the network who commented on the chapters in this book: Karen Borgknakke, Kirsti Klette, Staffan Larsson, Sverker Lindblad, and Fritjof Sahlström. We also extend our thanks to Cathrin Martin for organisational help. The network has been supported by the Nordic Research Academy.

order and differentiate individuals and groups, normalising particular types of people. These categories are provided not only in the sites of the school, they are also *globalised*, for example through international uses of statistics in educational reporting and expertise. This discussion provides a background for understanding the similarities in patterns that emerge in in-site ethnographies demonstrated in other chapters. Teachers and students construct the border between what is normal and ordinary, but these constructions are not only made locally. Anne–Lise Arnesen analyses how a grade–9 girl with special needs is defined and described by her teachers and constructed as an outsider in the school–for–all. Thomas Gitz–Johansen suggests that non-Danish ethnic background is represented within a general discourse of social problems when students are talked about. In both cases, families are brought into teachers' talk about children, and the idea of a normal Danish or Norwegian family is constructed through explicating what is not normal (messiness, lacking support for daughter's career, mother having several partners). As Elina Lahelma and Elisabet Öhrn argue, it is clear that what is regarded as normal school achievement for girls and boys differs.

Ethnicity, gender and social class act as categories of difference in school that can be *emphasised, negotiated or challenged* in every day lives, but they cannot be avoided. In her chapter, Sirpa Lappalainen demonstrates the flexibility that pre-school children have in making differences in relation to nationalities and ethnicities, and suggests that this is enforced rather than challenged in the official preschool. Policy analysis and case studies in secondary schools in Finland and in Sweden, discussed in the chapter by Elina Lahelma and Elisabet Öhrn, suggest that gendered and class patterns in informal relationships prevail; gender difference is also maintained through sex–based harassment. Daniel Sundberg argues that the possibility and capacity to act as self–regulated learners is easier for middle class students. The overall view that these chapters suggest is that, in the era of restructuring, inequalities are not necessary challenged in Nordic schools, but differences in relation to ethnicity, class, gender and special needs are maintained and repeated in teachers' talk and classroom interaction, as well as in the informal relations of young people.

Another theme that circulates in several chapters is the question of student *agency*. Whilst the rhetoric of restructuring emphasises individuality and possibilities for choice, the limits of agency are suggested in several chapters. Ulla–Maija Salo's chapter demonstrates how children in a Finnish primary school are positioned and position themselves as 'pupils' during the first weeks in the school. This position is acted and practised by students, and a border between 'school–like' and 'play–like' is made clear by repetition. School knowledge proves to be stronger, more serious and more certain than the children's knowledge. Tuula Gordon and Janet Holland bring the concept of physical space in schools and suggest its impact on students' possibilities of autonomous agency in schools' time–space paths. This analysis also provides a background to Daniel Sundberg's discussion of temporality in his chapter on the reform of the school timetable in

Sweden. The reform of the school timetable is one example of restructuring, and the author suggests the ambivalences of freedom and control that practices based on it demonstrate.

Sundberg's chapter suggests that the idea of the self-regulating learner, one of the *motif major* of the new wave of education reforms in recent years, is not easy to achieve. This issue is also considered in Dennis Beach's chapter on the teaching and learning of mathematics within the reformed Swedish upper-secondary education. He presents aims and ideas of individualised, free and flexible learning that teachers emphasise in their speech, and demonstrates that these ideals are far from the actual outcomes. Inger Anne Kvalbein, in her longitudinal study of teacher education in Norway, shows how the current trend of control has led towards a form of student freedom from the demands of strictly regulated education, but not necessarily to the development of processes of reflective knowledge in the teachers-to-come. These case studies demonstrate from different angles that the impact of education reform is rarely as anticipated. The expressed aims of policies of restructuring on individuality are not seen in the everyday practices and processes at schools.

*Nationality* as a silent backdrop of the rhetoric of multiculturalism is the third theme that is evoked in several chapters. Classroom observations and teachers' interviews suggest the prevalent strength of ethnocentricity in the Nordic classrooms. This theme is opened up by the analysis by Tuula Gordon and Janet Holland of the construction of citizenship in schools. They use the concept 'nation space' to explore how nation and nationality are culturally constructed and repeated as taken for granted, for example through the constant presence of flags and maps. The actual efforts to bring the ideas of multiculturalism into school practices may turn out to be, as in the case described in the chapter by Sirpa Lappalainen, celebrations of Finnish nationality because differences between different ethnicities are manifested more than similarities. Gender is used in the constructions of nationality (see e.g. Yuval–Davies 1997), and this also happens in schools, for example by emphasising the good position of women and thus suggesting the inferiority of some immigrant cultures, as in the chapter by Thomas Gitz–Johansen. In their chapter Elina Lahelma and Elisabet Öhrn dismantle the myth of 'strong Nordic women'.

Taken together the chapters in the present book demonstrate the *ambivalences and controversies* that seem to be prevalent in contemporary Nordic schools. Anne–Lise Arnesen suggests ambivalence in the ideology of school-for-all which 'locks in' children, because the school is compulsory, but simultaneously 'shuts out' some of them from meaningful learning. Controversies between the ideas of individual, self regulated students, explicated as an aim in the new educational policies, and the actual practices and routines in schools are demonstrated from different angles; in starting primary schools (Salo), as well as in restructuring schools' time–tables (Sundberg), teaching of upper–secondary Maths (Beach) or teacher education (Kvalbein). Ambivalence between the ideas of multiculturalism and nationality also exist in the schools (Gordon and Holland, Lappalainen). Although these chapters reveal some examples of successful intrusions of New Right ideology into schools, there also is evidence of patterns that do not change.

## From local back to global

Dave Hill (2001) argues that it is necessary to note the consistency in globalisation and restructuring in terms of the accumulation of resources and power. This is important in a book built around ethnographies, because there is a possibility that the ethnographic focus on small–scale everyday interaction misses the historical specificity of the lived moment and the embedded patterns of complex social phenomena. An ethnography that only attends to micro details will not adequately address the changing nature of work globally, nor the effects of restructuring on the quality of life, on learning or training. The ethnographic cases in the present book pay attention to micro detail. However, they do this in a way that does not suspend consideration of the broader contextual interests of the restructuring of service organisations.

Globalisation and restructuring are important means by which global forces and ideologies impinge directly (via for example the media, advertising, text books and so on) on the lives of national, regional and local populations where learning is formally (as in schools) or informally (as at the shopping centre) significant. They also represent processes by which global forces and ideologies influence the formation of education policy at national and local State levels. Teachers deliver a curriculum, select students and test for standards in line with local and national policies and are complicit in the neo–liberal education projects of globalisation. But there is always some room for creativity and resistant agency, as well as for sidestepping, negotiating and withdrawal (Gordon, Holland and Lahelma 2000). These dimensions for resisting the pull of the forces of globalisation and restructuring are focused on in the chapters of the present book. Though the spaces for oppositional activity may be squeezed quite tight, they can never be fully closed off (cf. Willis, 1999, 2000).

The present book addresses the concept of education restructuring in a number of concrete examples from the Nordic countries. It focuses in particular on how restructuring affects the supply of a high quality of education to all citizens as a democratic right, and on how the spaces for democratic agency are currently constituted and constricted within education.

# Part I: From policies to classrooms

# 1

## Comparative ethnography:
## Fabricating the new millennium and its exclusions

### Sverker Lindblad and Thomas S. Popkewitz

**Introduction**

Our thinking about ethnographic studies involves historicising them as a practice of late modern education. Education in late modernity is increasingly linked to international communication patterns and supranational organisations. As a consequence educational research needs to capture international tendencies and movements as part of the construction of local educational phenomena. In this chapter we discuss restructuring of education as a world movement through a multi-site study in Europe and Australia with a focus on educational governance, social inclusion and exclusion.

Restructuring is a concept derived from economics and changes from the mid-1970s and onwards based on changes in organisational structure and distribution of accountability in order to deal with increasing uncertainty in the environment (see e.g. Castells 1996: 153). Educational restructuring is inspired by economic changes in order to deal with the inflexibility of institutions and to improve their efficiency (Papagiannis *et al.* 1992). This restructuring is based on decentralisation and deregulation combined with new ways of managing autonomous schools. The transition from governing by rules and directives to governing by goals and results is vital in this process (Lindblad *et al.* 2002).

Our concern is with the cultural practices through which educational structuring is produced, and we focus on the systems of reason that construct the subjects of schooling—mostly students or teachers—in the transition in the governing of education (Popkewitz 2000a). By systems of reason we refer to the rules and standards for 'thinking about the objects of education'—the rules and standards by which teachers, state officials and policy documents order and classify what is to be considered as educational problems. They are neither logical nor 'natural' expressions of an individual's voice, but historically produced effects of power. Here we focus on categories and distinctions that order and differentiate individuals and groups. Such distinctions are vital in the constructions of traditional ethnographic studies, where 'the foreigners', 'the others', as well as differences between cultures are of primary concern. There are two reasons for this interest. First, education is the construction of the person; the citizen in a nation, the child redeemed through education, or the competent and competitive worker (Hamilton 1990; Hunter 1994; Popkewitz 1998b). Second, ongoing discussions in ethnography embody categories of kinds of people that educational practices are acting upon in order to produce strategies of inclusion. We ask in what ways, and with what rights does the ethnographer deploy these distinctions and categorisations of human kinds? And how do the distinctions in use locate the identities of those who are included and excluded (Denzin and Lincoln 1994; Eisenhardt 2001)?

## Ethnographic studies in a globalised world

Recent theoretical modes of interpreting changes and interaction in societies (e.g. Castells 1996) have introduced different ways of thinking about the meaning of the local as it is portrayed in ethnographies. The slogan *the global is in the local/ the local is in the global* is applicable here. To consider the talk of teachers in Helsinki, Stockholm, Madrid or New York is to consider interacting networks and supranational authorities and organisations such as the European Community or the OECD who mobilise particular ways of reasoning about and engaging in educational matters. This means that the sites of ethnographies are neither only local sites nor are the actors made visible through the speech of the persons speaking. That is, the local cultures are not necessarily performed by the situated actors and cultural practices are not only situated in specific observable contexts.

The relation of the global and local is illustrated in the international uses of statistical reporting of education that we discuss later, and also in the circulation of the writings of the American John Dewey and the Russian Lev Vygotsky in the national reform pedagogies (Popkewitz 2000a and 1998a). Dewey and Vygotsky are indigenous foreigners in that the names and discourses that they symbolise in pedagogical reforms seem as without a history—universal values and categories in which the child becomes a lifelong learner and a problem solver in order to cope with a changing world. This history without a history includes imported cultural practices that bring into the local context particular notions of an autonomous individual, and quality assurance measures as facts that no longer seem alien across the different national and local contexts. Schooling can be viewed as something that emerges within a world system where the local practices or ways of living lose their obviousness, and the way of living is getting stranger, since the expertise of such practices is somewhere else.

This globalisation of expertise that circulates as seemingly without a home poses new sets of obligations to the interpretive qualities of ethnography. Sensitivity to the historicity of context and to the ways in which systems of reason circulate is necessary. The issue of governance requires that the 'context' of education cannot be only about particular events and the talk of participants, but also about the discourses that circulate to create the narratives and images of the educated subjects and those who are placed in spaces outside the norms of inclusion.

## Globalisation, restructuring of education and governance

Globalisation is a concept used to portray new patterns of economic and cultural relations. Hirst and Thompson (1999) present an empirically based critique of discourses that state that we now have a new kind of globalised economy, where international processes and interaction subsume national economies. They also suggest that the rhetoric of globalisation has an important role to play in politics:

> The nation state has ceased to be an effective economic manager. It can only provide those social and public services deemed essential by international capital and at the lowest possible overhead cost.... The job of the nation states is like that of municipalities within the state ...to provide the infrastructure and public goods that business needs at the lowest possible cost. (Hirst and Thompson 1999, pp. 261-2.)

Based on such discourses, education as a public good is placed in a difficult position. What matters is only the survival of the community and corporations under economic laws of competition.

Education and schooling can be regarded as international movements with similar characteristics across the world (Boli and Ramirez 1986) in which the emergence of popular schooling was part of the creating and maintenance of national states. From this point of view it is not surprising that educational ideas and reforms have a strong international character. This is further underlined by the work of organisations such as UNESCO or the OECD. On the other hand, education is part of the internal work in seemingly autonomous nations. The relation between nations and world systems is evident in supranational organisations that appear as constraints in national activities, as they have no authority or legitimisation to deal with education policy in their member states. Yet, in both the United States and the European Union (both 'federal' systems), decentralisation of education is coupled with the harmonisation of education merits and competencies, demanding international cooperation on education (Nóvoa and Lawn 2002).

Of special interest is the governance of education that brings the global and local as overlapping concepts. First we have, as pointed out by Hirst and Thompson (1999), transitions from government to governance. The institutions of the sovereign nation-state carry out government. Governance in turn is a function carried out by a range of institutions and agencies—public and private—in order to regulate activities. This range of networks is more visible with new relations of centralised and decentralised governing of schools in formerly strong welfare states such as the Nordic countries. There is an internal relation between these aspects, since a transition from government to governance presumes that we have some identifiable norms to evaluate the outcomes of actions by different agencies and to control their work from behind.

The second aspect deals with changes in policy making linked to matters of secularisation and scientification in modern society. As noted by the Swedish Commission on Power and Democracy (SOU 1990:44), policy-making is becoming more and more about negotiating facts. Thus, the production of facts and the power to frame and negotiate them is vital for the governance of educational systems. The third aspect of Governance relates to the systems of reason that order and classify the distinctions about the child. Governance, in this sense, is the construction of the right classifications and sorting devices for charting a course of action. By the end of the 18th century, this governing linked the 'freedom and will of the individual' and the 'political liberty and will of the nation' (Cruikshank 1999). This linking of the will of the individual with the political rationalities of the nation is changing with new supranational institutions such as the European Union.

Restructuring of education can be regarded as a response to discourses on globalisation based on the three aspects of governance. Contemporary education restructuring places great emphasis on a transition from government to governance. One of the significant features of modernity is that power is exercised less through brute force and more through secularisation and scientification of knowledge that order 'objects' through which action is produced. Thus, the governance of educational practices needs to be located in the systems of reason that coexist with transitions in institutional changes, such as deregulation and decentralisation combined with a change in governing from rules or directives to governing by goals and results. This change is completed with 'new manageralism' (Lindblad, Johannesson and Simola 2002) as well as contrived professionalisation (Lindblad 1997), as new intentions in the 'making' of the histories of the nation, the 'self' and 'the other' are constructed.

The governance of schooling and education is highly critical in the joining of questions about what knowledge and practices are necessary for social and economic access, and what subjectivities are to be produced so that individuals can participate and act in productive ways. Hamilton (1999) reiterates a question of modern pedagogy in European traditions of didactics and pedagogy and argues that curriculum is a vision of future brought into the present. Rejecting the instrumental, short-term question 'What should they know?' that is often found in Anglo-American discussions of curriculum, Hamilton suggests that the central question of curriculum is 'What should they become?'

Schooling is about the types of individuality that are possible in the society. The cultural practices of schooling fabricate sets of capabilities and capacities that normalise particular types of people. This approach brings us back to interpretive qualities of ethnographies of schooling, to 'actors' in ethnography and to problems of inclusion and exclusion (see Arnesen and Gitz-Johansen in this volume). The actors are not only those who participate as assigned speakers (teachers, school leaders, students), but also the institutional settings in which that speech is enacted, the policy statements of schooling, and the global circulations of ideas, narratives, stories that intersect with the possible speech in and about schooling. We suggest that systems of reason through which speech is organised and objects of schooling are made legible and administrable are also 'actors', and we argue that rules and standards of reflection are principles that order action.

## On making of the case in an Ethnography: The event is not the case

Our study of social inclusion, exclusion and governance departs from the existing studies of world systems and traditions in the sociology of education, in both its concreteness and its broadness. The concreteness is related to our focus on the European Union and to our emphasis on interviews with multiple layers of policy texts and actors in the political, as well as educational arenas. The focus of existing studies is broadened by including detailed discursive analysis in order to consider how educational knowledge describes and explains phenomena as social 'facts'. Importantly, this strategy enables us to investigate how institutional rules and the systems of reason in schooling differentiate and divide. This is central when relating issues of governance to social inclusion and exclusion.

### Sites/informants and the data of the ethnography

The national cases consist of three Mediterranean states—Greece, Spain, and Portugal—and three Nordic welfare states under reconstruction—Finland, Iceland, and Sweden. To this are added the UK cases England and Scotland, with a recent neo-liberal history similar to that of Australia. The final case is Germany, with links to Eastern and Western Europe. Developing modes of interpretation with which to order the phenomena posed a methodological challenge as we needed to search for comparable data among sites with different cultural and political relations, as well as different languages. The theoretical basis of the study provided a background against which to judge equivalencies as 'the informants' changed. The studies were carried out with a set of researchers from different contexts and data sets.

We think about 'actors' in two senses. First we refer to people that we talked to in order to understand the culture of schooling. Second, we refer to the discourse networks through which principles of actions and participation are made possible and understandable. In this later sense of actors, the texts produced in the educational system bring intent and purpose to action. It might sound odd to speak of actors in ethnographies as non-animate objects (governmental texts and statistical reporting), because the 'dogma' of educational ethnographies is to study 'the natural attitudes' and 'meanings' of people in context. Statistics are cultural artifacts that also provide interpretative lenses that shape and fashion the problems of education. In this sense they are actors as they circulate among different layers of the educational system and order, classify, and place boundaries of the actions taken. Texts of policy, research and other cultural practices intersect with and provide ordering principles as individual people engage in action and participation. Ethnographies need to account for the different sets of actors: the descriptions of the national educational systems, the narratives of educational restructuring, and national and international statistical reporting. The more conventional notion of actor is embodied in our interviews and surveys in which people 'talk' about education and its subjects. We conducted interviews with school actors in different local sites: head-teachers, teachers, school nurses and so forth in compulsory and post-compulsory education (n = 360). In addition, we carried out surveys among adolescents in five cases—Finland, Sweden, Portugal, Spain and Australia, directed to samples of students (n = 3008) in their final year of compulsory education. Our interviews with teachers, school leaders and ministry officials focused on their professional practices and reflections.

We endeavour to identify 'ways with words' on governance and social inclusion/exclusion in education systems as discursive organisations. The variety of data that we collected enables us to consider the standards and rules of reason that circulate among institutional layers to shape and fashion the objects of reflection and action in educational affairs. For example, while teachers worried about different things than some of the system actors, the distinctions and classifications that ordered the world of schooling, teachers, children, learning, and inclusion/exclusion formed a grid to give shared intellibility to the problems and solutions of education.

## Education governance and social inclusion/exclusion: Making Human Kinds

Our attention is on how the categories and characteristics of people fabricate particular kinds of human beings placed outside the maps of what is viewed as normal and reasonable. We are concerned with the 'thought' of education that travels among participants, statistical reporting, and policy statements. We ask what kinds of cultural, social and pedagogical categories are formed to narrate a child, parent, teacher and family who stand outside the normal and are classified as deviant.

Overlapping networks of people and texts fabricate subjects. They are fictions to think about children as particular kind of humans in order to construct action by educators. These fictions order and simplify the world so that judgments can be rectified through appropriate planning. The fabrication of inclusion/exclusion are the subject of policy, school programmes and research that rescue and remediate the individual who has fallen outside the norms and values of schooling.

But the fictions also 'make' human kind. Categories such as children as 'problem solvers' or 'at-risk' become determinate classifications that have distinct chronological, physiological and psychological characteristics that can be applied to many people (cf. Arnesen in this volume). Profiles are 'built' of the 'good' child and the child who fails. These ordering principles appear as the impersonal management of the capabilities and capacities of people who are to become autonomous learners (cf. Sundberg in this volume). We argue that the notion of problem solving is an amalgamation of social, economic and cultural qualities that overlap and come together as a narrative and image of the child. This making of human kinds is neatly summarised by Lisbeth Lundahl (2000) who analyses Swedish policy texts on education governing and social exclusion. She states:

> The majority of the selected policy texts explicitly include students (teachers, parents etc.) that are motivated, alert, inquiring, self-governing, flexible, responsible, and well articulated as needed and desirable in society and in the labour market. One may conclude that a need of special persons rather than special competencies are stressed stronger than earlier, and that this simultaneously creates new forms of exclusion in education and in the labour market, probably only partly based on class, gender and ethnicity distinctions. (Lundahl 2000, p 192.)

In Lundahl's description two different human kinds are mutually fabricated: qualities and characteristics that 'make' a normal child, and characteristics of the child who stands outside that normality and becomes classified as deviant and in need of correction in order to be brought in line.

Problems of marginalisation and exclusion are repeatedly expressed in relation to social problems of 'lack of discipline' in the community, unemployment, dysfunctional families (single parent, teenage pregnancy) and educational attainment. For example, the various actors (respondents and texts) talk about the breakdown of discipline as producing behavioural problems, and lack of common values and integration are seen as important elements in social exclusion. There is, for example, a belief in Iceland that declining discipline and order produce social and cultural disorganisation and the loss of tradition. The declining discipline is seen as preventing integration, solidarity and cultural reproduction. In Spain, school failure is viewed as bound to children with special needs who do not have basic 'human' and Christian values. The Swedish respondents relate the problem of exclusion to societal changes that have produced dissimilar children and a negative image of society. In consequence there is a suggested need to reassert discipline at school and in the home in order to prevent dissolution and chaos.

Embedded in the distinctions about social change and children are divisions that inscribe a continuum of values about normalcy and difference/deviance. These distinctions and divisions, however, are best understood as forming particular human kinds, through interrelation of external social/cultural distinctions and internal pedagogical qualities that are calculated for governing groups and individuals. We found great similarities among the nation states; social structural and demographic numbers concerning social segregation of class, ethnicity, race, poverty, rural/urban, crime, are related to other populations' groups of deviancy, such as children and families 'at risk'. The 'older' classifications of individuals and groups by socioeconomic status and poverty are woven together in educational planning with categories of ethnicity, gender and race. Many, but not all of the newer categories, are correlated implicitly through talk about an ethnic or minority group in contexts of social problems of 'lack of discipline', unemployment, and family (cf. Gitz-Johansen, this volume).

The external categories are themselves transported into the school to form and interrelate with the internal categories that divide students. The 'older' structural categories of poverty and class as well as the more recent categories of ethnicity, gender and race are correlated with new distinctions of deviance in pedagogy that makes for a practical cause-effect relation. A practical relation of magnitudes is established in the statistical reporting, for example, between the excluded from the school and the individual who is poor, unemployed, suicidal, and a drug and alcohol abuser, as well as through educational performance indicators, such as a grade repeater, a drop out, truant, illiterate, and a bully. The weaving of social, cultural and pedagogical categories is part of the 'common sense' of what is wrong and in need of rectification in schooling. The external and internal pedagogic categories construct groups and individuals designated by social planning for rescue or redemption in the name of progress. The excluded students, for example, are transient students who enrol for short periods of time, children with behaviour problems, and are 'at risk'.

In some instances, the teachers and policies do not speak of particular groups but of problems of social stability and moral disintegration. The talk on the family and the community involves norms of the dysfunctional family that the school is to remediate (see Gitz-Johansen in this volume). Without naming groups, 'everyone' knows who is being talked about when discussing the breakdown of discipline or family. They are often perceived as the new immigrant families and children in the school system that need discipline to produce social harmony. In Finnish and Icelandic school policy, for example, there is continual discussion about the need for instill discipline, tradition, and social harmony, with the immigrant as the unspoken subject of these remediation strategies of pedagogy.

The new categories of education have the seemingly objective and detached criteria of science but are moral and cultural categories placed into the theories and research strategies of the education sciences, including interpretative methods. Income and economics (workless households, poor households) are placed in a grid as its categories are related to health (such as low birth weights), social stability (family environment such as divorce, divorce where husband is unskilled, and the 'lone mother' and teenage births). Other indicators of social disorganisation and cultural breakdown are also introduced as categories to think about programmes for correcting the pedagogical problems of school failure. For example, statistical categories of income and family are related to categories of criminality, youthful offenders, families under stress, street living, African Caribbean boys, special needs pupils, drugs, bullying. These social categories of deviance are related to educational categories, such as pupils at risk, disaffection, education achievement, exclusion from secondary school, truancy, eligible for free school meals, speaking a foreign language such as English as second language (cf. Alexiadou, Lawn, and Ozga 2001: 36).

In the previous discussion of the characteristics of the child and family who are deviant, there are two important aspects that we wish to draw attention to in current educational reporting about social inclusion and exclusion. One is the construction of finer and finer distinctions about who the child and family are that require attention and remediation, that is, where the finer set of distinctions of deviant human kind are targeted as the psychological and cognitive characteristics that schools and social programs are to change in the remodeling of the child.

What were previously, for example, classifications about social stratification are now mixed with categories of cultural and social characteristics of race, ethnicity, and family.

Second, particular human kinds are produced for state and educational intervention. The various categories in educational reports and statistics about 'the conditions of education' function as actors to organise thought and action. Patterns are formed through the categories, distinctions, and magnitudes reported. These patterns about who is the individual who does not succeed in schooling produces particular human kinds in which to think about, organise, programme, and to evaluate the inputs and outputs of educational systems. We call it a human kind as the different categories and distinctions overlap to think about the capabilities and characteristics of the deviant child and family. The various categories also need to be seen as producing a practical causality that is determined through the textual relationship in which the various categories and distinctions are thought of and acted on as belonging together.

We can also identify the changing categorisation of the problem of inclusion and exclusion in educational statistical reporting to changing governing practices. The shift is from governance by rules that focused on input approach (what social classes achieve and stay in the educational system, or money spent on national educational systems) to governance of education as an output approach by goals and evaluation, with the implication that the results of education are emphasised. This shift can be related to other changes in the relations of centralised and decentralised governing practices of education (see, e.g. Kallos and Lindblad 1994; Popkewitz 1998b).

## Realigning the individual, the social and agency

The new standards and rules generated for action and participation involve particular principles of self-governing. One relates to individualisation in pedagogical reforms. The second is a fatalism that prohibits possibilities for resistance. A general pattern in the texts produced in different contexts is an individualisation (see Lindblad and Popkewitz 2001 for cases and discussion of case studies) that embodies normalisation of the child. The child who is a lifelong learner is different from the child who lacks the characteristics such as discipline, moral character or cultural norms that are deemed important for success. The 'good' student across the countries is flexible, problem-solving, collaborative and perpetually involved in a self-monitoring and active 'lifelong learning'. The quality of child is one that embodies an entrepreneurial logic.

Individualisation has different qualities among the different contexts of the study. The Finnish case, for example, discusses individualisation as the movement from the citizen to a particular self-responsible individual. Whereas previous reforms placed the individual in relation to concerns about the citizen who contributed to the collective, social development, today's reform does not point to citizens improving society, but to the ethical education and to the role of the pupil as an active learner and the development of talent. The student becomes an active, rational subject who uses services offered by the school. This new individualism relates to cooperation in an international world where human rights are not related to generalised solidarity but are embodied in the qualities of the individual in a constant state of flux. The Portuguese case emphasises a new individualism as well, focusing on civic responsibility as tightly linked to individual interests and 'learning rhythms'.

The new management strategies for governing education overlap with new remediation strategies for including the child. There is a shift in the principles governing teachers' actions from the social situation to a pedagogical focus about student knowledge and attitudes. The fabrication of the teachers involves characteristics that relate to the individualisation of the child. In the Portuguese and Swedish cases teachers are agents of change as reflective professionals. The new teacher can be understood as a 'counsellor', a 'reflective facilitator', who is directed by goals established in advance and by procedures for assessment, evaluation and measurement of outcomes, rather than processes. A darker side is presented in the Greece and English cases where teachers are to be held accountable for the performances of the educational systems. Families and children become agents of change. Families in England, for example, are given new responsibilities and home-school 'contracts' that relate to homework assignments for children and their behaviour and performance in school. The reordering of the family-child relations embodies a *pedagogicalisation* of the parents where they take on the responsibilities of the school in the cognitive/moral development of the citizen. This differs from previous child-rearing values (Popkewitz, in press). The parent becomes a surrogate teacher and the home environment is brought closer to the pedagogical norms of the classroom. In this way the individualisation project is brought back to the family from the education system. These are not only changes in education governance but also constructions of new education projects. The teacher, the child, and the school administrator are constructed as having not only the right knowledge but also the right personal traits, dispositions and social and cognitive competencies that are thought of as necessary for the future.

In our interviews with politicians and administrators, we asked, 'What do they perceive of changes in education governance?' and 'How do these actors reason about such changes, their rationales and implications for social integration and exclusion?' In all of the school systems, system actors were experiencing a need for change and fatalism about change. The expression of fatalism had certain characteristics that can be related to individualisation. Globalism of the changes was taken as inevitable in national school systems. In Iceland, this was expressed as the attempts 'to tame the change' that was considered wild. In many instances, the respondents felt that the changes were authorless and appeared as the product of anonymous forces of society. The fatalism appears as the outcome of a reasoned course for progress and there is no course of action to prevent it.

The Greek study suggests that concepts of egalitarianism/equity and democratisation of education that dominated the discussion in the 1980s were revised in the 1990s. The new discourses linked education to modernisation in a globalised society, and the needs of economy and society of knowledge through a holistic reform in education. The phrases were banalities or *topoi*, assumed to be known by everyone, but with no points of reference or specificity other than their mobilising of a seeming consensus about change.

Another anonymous face was that of the European Union as a generalised object used to explain the purposes and directions of local actions. In the Greek context, the European Union was symbolically positioned in relation to the political regime. System actors located the source of change symbolically as 'the European Union' making demands for changes in the education system. These changes, it was believed, would provide a counterpoint to the political system where state clientelism exists.

The German case talks about intertwined or conflicting tendencies between internationalisation and indigenous tendencies. In Germany, internationalisation was reported as important to make its schools comparable to others in the EU. While the European Union stood in the narratives as a convenient fiction in which system actors could justify local practices, there is also an author to these fictions. The official discourses function as a mobilising agent that gives direction and purpose to actions. As Nóvoa (2001) argues, the official principle of subsidiarity is expressed as it relates to education in the European Union. The language of harmonisation of rules and regulation is not politically allowed in official discourses, while changes are in fact being harmonised through regulatory ideas that serve the same function. The process occurs through words that reorient and edit the past.

## Changes and continuity in governing inclusion and exclusion.

We have thought about ethnography as the production of a culture through interrelating different sites of data—interviews of different populational groups, policy texts, and other documents about education—to consider the principles generated to make the objects of schooling known, comprehensible and capable of action. We have sought not to make the distinctions between texts and context. The focus on the new discourses of school restructuring at the management, institutional and pedagogical level suggest that the cause of exclusion is the inner characteristics of the child, as opposed to earlier classification which focused on systemic factors of poverty and social class. Individualisation and decentralisation, when combined with other changes, produces a regression toward the mean that is expressed as a levelling of pupils and special teaching. At the same time, the assessment procedures increased differentiation of pupils and increased centralisation through tests and grade criteria. This makes alternatives and resistance more difficult.

The categories and divisions that are constructed in order to seek a more inclusive society contain their own irony. There are increased and finer national and international distinctions and elaboration of policy statistics. The expansion of categories that differentiate the external social characteristics of the excluded student and the expansion of the categories internal to the institutional ordering of the school have two implications. One is that they embody images and narratives of deviance. The other is that the kinds of people that are targeted as socially excluded are produced through new sets of distinctions and differentiations that overlap the external and internal categories that are practically related as governing principles in educational discussions. Thus, we can reach a counterintuitive conclusion to the problem of governance.

## Concluding comments

We have discussed an ethnographic approach that has the ambition to provide a way to interpret globalised aspects of education. Our notion of ethnography is based on international cooperation, working in a number of sites through talking and observing different kinds of agents that construct education today.

When comparing this study of schooling with a work of one of the authors in the early 1980s, there are some similarities and some differences in methods and theoretical 'entities' that we want to address here, in order to think of an ethnography concerned with the mutual relation of the global and the local. The 1980s study was of a U. S. programme for primary school reforms that were used around the country (Popkewitz, Tabachnick and Wehlage 1982). The aim was to understand the culture of schooling through comparing different sites. An array of sources was used for constructing the data of the case of educational reform. It was comparative in the sense of seeking to understand the differences and similarities in the cultural norms and practices among schools located in different geographical locations in the U. S.

Both the 1980 and 2001 studies used theoretical entities in order to make comparisons possible. Comparison requires theoretical 'tools' in order to be able to select what constitutes related data in different social contexts that are comparable. Culture and the notions of ethnography are themselves 'theoretical' concepts even when seeking to provide a deep or grounded 'description'. We think of theory in a non-positivist sense of orienting sets of ideas and ways of thinking about phenomena (see Popkewitz and Pereyra 1993). Here we are interested in the narratives and images that governed the construction of the child who was included and excluded across sites. The notions of narrative and images emerged from our interest in discourses and knowledge. But it is important to also recognise that the actual categories (the particular human kinds of deviance, the individualisation and fatalism, for example,) were constructed through an interaction with our ways of seeing and the phenomena that we studied.

Recognising the relation between data and theory brings us back to the ways in which ethnographies construct or assume 'the case'. It is important that ethnographies do not reify and naturalise the particular events and utterances of participants as to what constitutes 'the case' of schooling—for example. This involves the interplay of multiple actors—some present and some not visible but participating as a horizon in which particular events are given intelligibility. In the previous and current study the case was theoretically defined—one was as a problematic of the cultural patterns that underlie educational reform and the other was educational governance and social inclusion and exclusion. The theoretical orientations ordered the discussions about what to collect data about (that is to transform the events and daily 'talk' into data for interpretation) and how to look at narrative patterns from the data themselves. To say this, however, is not to ignore the dialectical interplay of theory and the phenomena at-hand, but to recognise how particular theory functions as an epistemic position in which to orient and order what is important to think about and classify in ethnographic studies.

If we bring these different ideas about theory, data, and interpretation back to the discussion about ethnography, there is the need to think more broadly concerning what constitutes the actors in the study of the culture of schooling present in the early study. Our current approach is to think of the local and the global as in an interplay and overlapping—the circulation of global discourses and planetspeak in local sites that moves from Ministry documents and local teachers talk about individualisation and the 'fatalism' of reforms, the importance of the circulation of human kinds that move among international agencies and research communities that seem to have no national ties and ministry and school participants. These 'actors' are *participants* in the generating of the norms, values and distinctions that produce a continuum of values about normalcy and deviance.

While phenomenological lenses are important to ethnographers, the issues that underline globalisation and restructuring require thinking about the multiple actors that are present in any speech act of schooling. Bakhtin provides a simple but elegant articulation of this complexity:

> 'Language is not a neutral medium that passes freely and easily into the private property of the speaker's intentions; it is populated—overpopulated—with the intentions of others. Expropriating it, forcing it to submit to one's own intentions and accents, is a difficult and complicated process'.                    (Bakhtin 1981: 294).

There is no ethnographic context without systems of coding and structuring through which the objects of reflection and action are mediated.

# 2

# Nation space: The construction of citizenship and difference in schools

## Tuula Gordon and Janet Holland

### Introduction

The process of constructing citizenship and difference in schools is complex and multilayered. We draw connections between analyses of citizenship, nation, education and space, exploring how spatiality is implicated both at the macro- and the micro-level. The concept of space is used to link nation space and school space with examples from an ethnographic study to illustrate how this plays out in practices and processes in secondary schools. We deal, first with nation space, second with school space, and third nation space in school.

This work is based on the project 'Citizenship, Difference and Marginality in Schools—with Special Reference to Gender'[1], where we examine the impact of neo-conservatism and neo-liberalism on education politics and policies and explore processes of restructuring in education in Finland and Britain. First we elaborate concepts of citizenship in the context of an increasing concern for individualisation and differentiation rather than equal opportunities in educational politics in these two countries. Second we examine the curriculum to illuminate the development of educational policies and differences and similarities between the two countries. The project is based on an ethnographic study of four secondary schools in Helsinki and London. Practices at school are explored through comparative, cross-cultural, contextual and cooperative ethnographic research. We have gathered data on teachers, students, the pedagogic relation, textbooks and teaching materials, lesson content, youth cultures, school-home relationships, space and embodiment (Gordon, Holland and Lahelma 2000a, Gordon *et al.* 1999). We focus on aspects of regulation and emancipation and trace these by exploring the process of 'making space'.

### Citizenship

The concern with citizenship has directed our attention to nation space (Gordon, Holland and Lahelma 2000 a and b). The homogeneous 'nation', through constructions of neutral 'citizenship' and abstract 'individuals', masks social

---

[1] Other members of the project in Finland were Pirkko Hynninen, Elina Lahelma, Tuija Metso, Tarja Palmu and Tarja Tolonen. Nicole Vitellone and Kay Parkinson worked with Janet Holland in London. Anne-Lise Arnesen in Norway has conducted similar research

differentiation. The development of modern nation states has been explained through the social contract in which 'individuals' became citizens through a voluntary contract to maximise their own self-interest. Abstract notions of citizenship produced by the nation-state disembody citizens (cf. Westwood and Phizacklea 2000).

This presupposed differentiation of the state of culture and the state of nature (cf. Pateman 1988). Connected to this division are oppositions such as mind and body, reason and emotions, rationality and irrationality, abstract and concrete, public and private, male and female. Predominant meanings and practices in the state of culture are characterised by the hegemonic masculinity of Western, middle-class, white, heterosexual, able bodied maleness (cf. Connell 1987). Social groups, particularly women and minority 'racial'/ethnic groups, which are thought to be more closely connected to the state of nature, are marginalised as 'the other'. Others are not powerless—there are different ways in which they can have and take power—but power is not invested in them.

Citizenship, based on abstract notions of individuals, is mediated at the school level through the concept 'pupil' through which children and young people are abstracted from their social locations (Gordon 1992). In school processes their differences are typically understood through 'natural' attitudes. A compulsory state system of schooling has been important in the construction of Western nation states, and schooling has played a crucial role in the preparation for citizenship. In Britain the decision to extend education to the 'lower orders' was made, after considerable debate, in order to integrate them into the democratic system through educating them about rights and duties, and one explicit aim was to limit the spread of socialist politics. Schooling as a national project has been particularly clear in Finland, where the developing national education system was invested with the task of strengthening the national culture and maintaining an independent nation status and national identity in a vulnerable geo-political location. Despite its apparent universality the concept of citizenship is exclusive as well as inclusive.

## Nation space

The space of a nation state is not a pre-given container but a product of historical processes (cf. Brenner *et al.* 2003). We differentiate between physical, social and mental space, and between school space and nation space (cf. Gordon, Holland and Lahelma 2000a). We focus on nations as bordered territories, as organised sets of social relations, and as mental constructs. Every society, Lefebvre (1991: 31) notes, 'produces a space, its own space'. Nation states are geographically and politically inscribed; they occupy particular territories with mapped borders. At this level space is conceptualised as a three-dimensional grid (cf. Smith and Katz 1993). Borders constitute and construct the physical ground of a nation, construct their territoriality and separate them from other nation states. Physical nation space is often taken for granted, but is a construct created, produced and reproduced (and also contested, as recent events in Europe and elsewhere have illustrated). To capture and understand this we consider nation space as also social and mental.

Nation state is constituted as social in a range of practices. The physical, geometric space of a nation cannot exist without practices that assert and reassert it. Lefebvre (1991) notes that 'physical space has no 'reality' without the energy that is deployed within it' (13). Michael Billig (1995) suggests that through social practices nation states become as if self-evident. He refers to 'flagging' of the nation as a process whereby the nation state becomes a entity—flags, national news, national weather forecasts and other such practices produce taken for granted 'banal nationality'. Nation space implies the existence of a market as well as armies in readiness to defend the borders of the nation state. Space is socially constructed, but it is also a dimension through which and over which social relations are constructed (Keith and Pile 1993; Massey 1993, 1998). Production of space constitutes and concretises social relationships; everyday life is localised in particular spaces and places (cf. McDowell 1999).

Nation space is also imaginary and symbolic; it is a mental space constructed through representations and images of a common past and shared present. Guarding its borders is a masculine project connected to evocations of a fatherland (or motherland) to be protected—along with the women and children in it. Bhabha (1990) argues that nations are narratives which have lost their origins in myths of time, the mythical origins nevertheless provide a context for national iconography. In this sense nation space becomes a mental construct that is embedded with emotions (McClintock 1995). Yuval-Davis (1997, 2003) notes that since discussions about nation and nationalism often take place in the public sphere, women are less visible in those debates, but gender relations are fundamentally implicated in nationalist thinking, for example in constructs of motherhood.

## Education as a national project

Education as a national project operates differently in different national education systems. In Finland, the production of a nation has been an historically framed project in a country that achieved independence from the Soviet Union in 1917 – the Finnish state has been constructed close to a super power, between east and west, in a complex geopolitical location. The education system was given the task of producing a homogeneous, united nation, balancing between constraints of its geopolitical situation and its historical interest to develop as a Nordic welfare state. The UK, on the other hand, is an old world power, a former empire with a history of colonial conquest. At the same time Britain has been a more heterogeneous country with a long history of ethnic diversity. The process of constructing a nation is less evident in British educational history. The relationship between Englishness and Britishness is complex and ambivalent, and has become perhaps more so, or more examined, in a period of devolution of power to constituent countries of the UK.

In our discussion nation space and school space are linked. In previous decades, theorists suggested that social relationships in education replicate the hierarchical division of labour in production (Bowles and Gintis 1976). This was called the correspondence principle. Spring (1972) argued that schooling is a tool of the corporate state. These analysts accord a central role to the state, but it is not clear what the mediations between economy and education are, and how capitalist schooling operates. Whilst such correspondence analyses were mechanistic, it is interesting to pursue the possibilities and limitations of using the idea of correspondence in a more flexible, less deterministic way, taking account of the cultural context.

We argue that schooling is a national project, but what happens in schools is not reproduction in such a neat way that education can be studied merely by focusing on educational politics and schooling as a product of the state. How processes of relations of power are practiced in everyday life at school is important in developing a more dynamic approach that combines material, social and cultural processes in an analysis of differentiation and marginalisation, in a way that also makes it possible to discern and analyse the agency of teachers and students. Schools are microcosms of social relations in society (Gordon 1986) but these social relations are also constructed in people's practices. National educational systems are purposefully created. In that sense what happens in school space is connected to nation space, but it is not determined by it. Correspondence in our analysis is a heuristic device through which spatiality is seen as central in both producing links between national state and school system and at the same time altering and changing those links to produce discontinuities as well as continuities. The concept of citizenship, produced in the nation state and in the school is crucial in our analysis. We have discussed the gendered route through which young people come to occupy the space of an adult citizen through being positioned as a student in the official, the informal and the physical school (Gordon, Holland and Lahelma 2000c). In the following sections we illustrate the links between nation space and school space that our analysis of the physical school and its spatial praxis indicates.

## School space

In our ethnographic study we distinguished between three layers of the school: the official school, the informal school and the physical school. These layers are intertwined, but making distinctions between them allows us to analyse many aspects of the school that often remain invisible. (Gordon, Holland and Lahelma 2000a) At the official layer we began with the curriculum in schools. We focused on classrooms and lessons to indicate processes of differentiation in lesson content, textbooks, teaching materials and methods and classroom interaction. We constructed a picture of the disciplinary apparatus of the schools: rules and sanctions. We outlined hierarchies among students in the classrooms, and formal hierarchies among teachers.

At the informal layer we expanded our analysis of classroom interaction to include interaction among students in other areas of the school, between teachers and students beyond the instructional relationship in the classroom, among teachers, and between teachers, students and other groups working in the school (office staff, caretakers, domestic staff). School rules are contrasted to practical application in concrete situations. Informal hierarchies among teachers and students are outlined, and compared and contrasted to official and formal hierarchies.

Processes of differentiation and formation of subjectivities are further illustrated by outlining their embodied and spatial components. In the physical school focus is on the possibilities and limitations school buildings offer for the teaching and learning in the official school, and the interaction and hierarchical differentiation of the informal school. Rules about movement, about the use of different spaces and about talk and noise are contrasted to informally sanctioned and forbidden practices of students (cf. Tolonen 2001). Spatial dimensions of social interaction in schools have often been neglected in educational research (see, however Delamont and Galton 1986; Fielding 2000). The school as a physical space provides a context for the practices and processes that 'take place' there. But the physical school is more than a context; it is an aspect in the shaping of these practices and processes producing differentiation. Decisions about the use of space involve decisions about location and movement of bodies in specific areas of the school, as we have suggested (Gordon, Holland and Lahelma, 2000a, c).

School buildings form a physical, built backdrop to the teaching and learning in schools. They embody pedagogical principles and assumptions about how teaching and learning is organised. As pedagogic thinking alters, school buildings also incorporate these changes. The spaces of the schools reflect prevailing societal expectations of the education of children and the construction of citizenship. We can see these elements in the four schools in our study.

In Helsinki the newer school, Green Park, blends into its environment in the suburb without clearly distinguished borders. The schoolyard continues smoothly into a park. City Park is clearly delineated, and the borders of the schoolyard are formed by the nearby houses. Green Park is more horizontal than City Park, less imposing. Green Park is built with fair materials and the corridors are light with lots of windows, in contrast to the dark corridors in City Park.

Green Park was built during the beginning of a recession in Finland. Clear guidelines with tight cost controls for building were given by the National Board of Education. The efficient planning of Green Park was partly ill-founded, as the school is already too small to cater for all the local students who wish to attend. There are not enough classrooms for each subject teacher, and some of them must use whichever classroom is vacant. Ironically in the older City Park there has been scope to renovate areas; for example the textile area has been enlarged, and areas in the basement and attic have been reconstructed to enable new and different uses.

The research schools in London provide a similar contrast, one old and one relatively new. Oak Grove has two buildings on the same site, the 'old' building (built in the 1960s), and the 'new', finished within the last few years. During the research, yet more building adjustments were being made to the old building. Access to the new building is within the confines of the old, with a ground floor entrance across an outdoor space that also gives access to the dining hall and gymnasium, and an elevated passageway linking the two first floors, and crossing the outdoor space. In the entrance of the school there is a display of photographs showing the physical changes to the school over the period of building, from the top of a nearby high-rise block of flats. The second school, Woburn Hill has an old, dark, elongated building to which bits have been added at different times

Teaching and learning in Finnish secondary schools is more teacher centred than in British schools. In Green Park, new thinking about education is, however, embodied in more extensive storage space and facilitation of the use of a broader range of teaching aids. Green Park also has more specialised classrooms, for example for computer teaching. City Park was more clearly built for chalk and talk type of teaching. In Oak Grove, the two buildings stand in contrast to each other, and to styles of pedagogy and the construction of the student. The old building has long, low and relatively dark corridors, and classrooms furnished and organised in a traditional style, with tables and chairs for the students in rows or blocks, largely facing the teacher's desk at the front. The new, brighter and lighter building has a central spacious classroom encircled by a corridor, with further classrooms on the outer rim of the building. Here surveillance and observation of classroom activities and students is easy for anyone walking in the corridor. The classrooms are activity rooms, for technology (which includes cooking), computer work, dance, music and art. The spaces within classrooms are such that the students can move around, using the modern and specialised equipment as appropriate to the tasks of the particular lessons, although always under control of the teacher. Some spaces are forbidden to students—typically where supplies are stored and kept. In Woburn Hill, these two styles intermingle. Many of the original Victorian classrooms are small and cramped, crowded with old wooden desks which constrain movement; the new additions and reconstructions are lighter, brighter and more spacious, often containing expensive specialist furniture and equipment. More movement is possible, particularly in relation to certain activity based lessons, but again still under control and surveillance from the teachers.

While the school building is usually a physical 'given', recent building works have created a contrastive space to the old building, and the physical school in Oak Grove and in City Park has a more fluid aspect. During rebuilding in Oak Grove, spaces—classrooms, halls, the library, the gymnasium—have been reassigned functions; corridors become narrower, parts of the school expand outwards, eating up outer space, and parts are inaccessible while building takes place, shrouded, and boarded. In City Park, the school yard was filled with building materials whilst alterations were taking place, and the students were allowed to leave the school area during every break—a concession which they valued very much and longed for afterwards. These disruptive changes in the structure of the school offer new opportunities for student resistance, place new demands of control and discipline on the staff, and construct different relationships between teachers, students and the physical space. These different relationships and practices contribute to a reconstruction of the social space of the school.

Physical space becomes socially constructed on the basis of current pedagogic thinking, and assumptions about hierarchy and distance. However, for the teachers, administration, other staff and school students using the building it is 'already there', presenting 'an appearance of stability and persistence' (Soja 1985, 94); this stability becomes fragile when alterations are made. The school is a physical entity that enters into the activities and processes of those located in it. In these activities and processes the physical space becomes shaped by social praxis.

## Social space in school

Though physical space provides limitations for teaching and learning, ways in which it can be used are also subject to organisational decisions. An important task for schools is to formulate a curriculum of the body and to organise the time-space paths of school students (Giddens 1985; Gordon and Lahelma 1996; Gordon, Holland and Lahelma 2000a and c). Time is important in determining the use of space. In the course of the day corridors are filled with people at some times; at other times they are empty (cf. Tolonen 1995). Doors are locked and unlocked, opened and closed, punctuating the temporal ordering of the school day. There are times when you are not allowed to be in the corridors and times when you must be there. There are times when you cannot go outside to the schoolyard, and times when you must go out.

The school timetable is a device for organising compulsion and exclusion in relation to space—it states when you are required to be in music, computer, or biology or some other classroom, and when you are not allowed to be there. The school rules include regulation of the use of space and embodiment. School rules vary in their detail, but typically include stipulations about movement in the corridors, specification about when school students are allowed to leave the school area, thus linking space and time. Rules relating to the appropriate appearance of school students are typical in Britain. In Oak Grove there was a constant struggle on the part of teachers to maintain school uniform, with multiple sanctions available for its enforcement. As well as space and time, embodiment is regulated, although the signs of this regulation are less obvious in Helsinki schools (see Gordon, Holland and Lahelma 2000a and d).

The teaching and learning of rules are emphasised during the first days in Finnish secondary schools (Lahelma and Gordon 1997, Gordon *et al.* 1999). After that, considerable energy is exerted by teachers to ensure adherence to these regulations. Considerable energy and inventiveness is also expended by school students to avoid compliance. If the use of space is carefully controlled, then an easy form of visible resistance is to disregard it. But resistance or evasion of rules is also a quest for autonomy. Routinisation of time-space paths removes a considerable amount of day-to-day decision-making from school students. Yet at the same time the western emphasis on individuality encourages distinctiveness and independence. It is not surprising that students are likely to resist the state of dependence they are reduced to in the school. The time-space paths are manifestations of power relations in schools. For the students, trying to hide in the corridors or going to the nearby shop during breaks when you are supposed to stay in the schoolyard is a means of exercising agency through evasion (and possibly resistance). A hole in the fence through which students escaped to the forbidden shops was a constant focus of critical attention and attempted control by teachers, both physically at the fence and verbally in assembly and classroom.

Gender differentiation is embedded in spatial relations, and boys (but not all boys) are likely to use more space than girls (although not all girls). This is consistent with cultural expectations; hence teachers, without endeavoring to do so, control the use of space of girls more than that of boys (Gordon, Holland and Lahelma 2000a). A mobile, noisy girl is more likely to catch the attention of a teacher than a spatially and vocally active boy.

Customs and expectations backed up by various informal and formal disciplinary measures structure what happens in classrooms. Lessons in classrooms are typically characterised by student immobility. Students try to break this immobility by going to the toilet, to their lockers or to sharpen their pencils, and the negotiation about whether these movements are possible or not during the lessons are typical and begin during first encounters with new teachers. Some teachers' pedagogic practice facilitates both negotiation and movement, and others' do not (Fielding 2000). Seating arrangements are organised in complex interaction between students and teachers and contests and negotiations take place in the first lesson with any teacher. Generally students choose their seats, although some teachers use seating as a form of control.

Where movement is allowed it is regulated by teacher control, with rules about what movement is permissible. An important rule about movement and the body in schools is that of contact. There should be no physical contact between teachers and students, and in particular no contact by the teacher that could be interpreted as aggressive, violent or sexually motivated [2] This is a sensitive issue from both student and teacher perspective in the UK, but not much discussed in Finland. There has been rising student violence towards teachers coupled with an increased awareness of student and parental 'rights' in the educational context in the UK. This can create the paradox of a teacher who has been threatened, or even struck by a student, and who has responded by physical restraint and the removal of the

---

[2] There has been a recent relaxation of this strict ruling of no teacher contact with student in the UK.

student from the classroom, being reprimanded or disciplined. Whilst the guidelines in operation at the time of the study seemed clear, in practice these interactions are fraught with difficulty for the teacher.

## Mental space in school

The journey into adulthood and the status of citizenship and the construction of independence is fraught with complexities for young people. Their responsibilities in personal decision-making and in the construction of their own lives is emphasised in individualistic cultures but their scope for doing this is limited, particularly in schools. Although the process of teaching and learning is negotiated and contested and students are active participants, their personal autonomy is limited. Teacher centred classroom practices and often fragmented curricular knowledge constitute a considerable incursion into the autonomy of students.

If social space is limited and immobility becomes unendurable, there are different ways of escaping. The first is not coming to school at all—truanting. The second is coming to school but not adhering to the routinised time-space paths. The third is redefining the use of the space by grooming, using make-up, eating and drinking (all strictly forbidden by the rules and requiring dexterity and subterfuge if to avoid discovery). The fourth is trying to stretch the contours of one's limited space physically—by tapping your pencil, drumming your feet, throwing items across the room, scraps of papers, often with messages, pencils, rubbers and other small pieces of equipment, often with the excuse of lending it to a fellow student. The fifth is stretching the limits of one's space in one's mind. Whilst sitting at her desk a student, in her mind, may be far away, inhabiting wide vistas with endless possibilities. We do not use 'she' accidentally. Facial gestures and body posturing of girls in classrooms indicate that they engage in this activity more frequently (Gordon and Lahelma 1996).

The students' attempts to create autonomy or resist control are often related to inappropriate use of equipment. This can involve playing with it, inventing elaborate games, unassociated with its correct use. A simple example is to play computer games rather than engage in the assigned activity on the computer; another is to act out sports and ball games with kitchen equipment, for example, playing 'ice hockey' with brushes when you are supposed to sweep the floor. Girls were more likely to employ elements of female/feminine culture to subvert the classroom processes, or resist its impositions (items of make-up, or with which to groom—nail varnish, hair spray, combs and brushes (cf. Hey 1997).

Students may be engaged with the official agenda in a classroom—the teaching and learning process. They may be engaged in the informal agenda of student-teacher and/or student/student interactions, constructing and reconstructing the 'teacher's' lesson into something different. They may be engaged in a physical agenda of extending the space round their bodies. Or they may be involved in a project of 'flight in the mind', a process of evasion and escape. Teachers are more tolerant with students' 'flight in the mind' than with their more visible and audible escape. It is partly for this reason that boys are reprimanded more in classrooms than girls.

Whilst New Right education politics emphasises the individual and active citizenship, our analysis suggests that in the physical school the spatial and embodied autonomy of the students is generally narrow. It is difficult for them to cultivate a sense of agency and autonomy, if processes and practices encountered in the school are carefully controlled.

## Nation space in school

The analysis of nation space frames our exploration of how nation and nationality are culturally constructed. In the schools we examined the ingredients of homogeneity in iconography, associations and cultural representations and ways in which nationality appeared as a taken for granted frame (cf. Billig 1995). We also looked for arenas and narratives of plurality. We tried to disentangle possible narratives of exclusion, expressed through hegemonic constructions and iconography *as well as* possible narratives of inclusion expressed through multiplicity and elasticity. The universality of geography as a subject in the school curriculum suggests that physical space is meaningful in the education for citizenship. In geography, nation is presented through maps as a physical space with strict borders, and maps appear in biology, showing lakes, climate and vegetation. The regularity with which maps are presented in history lessons also emphasises the nation-state—maps of territories that are attacked, invaded and defended. In history the nation-state also appears in relation to social relations and as a social space. In Finnish lessons, for example, maps show how people that use Finno-Ugrian languages have moved to the west. Maps of different countries typically hang on the walls in foreign languages classrooms, demonstrating the relationship between languages and geographical territories. All of these contribute to the banal construction of nationality as a self-evident backdrop.

Compared with the UK, Finland is a relatively homogeneous society with a history of restrictive immigration policies, although recently the number of immigrants and refugees has increased, providing new challenges (as well as opportunities) in education. The UK, with its history as a colonialist empire, multicultural educational policies and school practices have a longer history, albeit not unproblematic (cf. Troyna 1993, Gillborn 1993 and Gillborn and Gipps 1996). In Finland the vast majority of school students are white, and Finnishness was mostly taken for granted in our research schools. Being Finnish appears as a process of constructing a national identity, as a narrative mental space. Music lessons include Finnish pop (Suomi-pop) and traditional Finnish music, in history lessons the national poet's (J. L. Runeberg) life is discussed.

Teachers refer to being Finnish as entailing 'lack of confidence', shyness and silence thus producing 'stigmatised Finnishness' (Apo 1996) where being Finnish is placed at the taken for granted centre, even if it is criticized.

> We Finns don't have a very friendly basic nature. In the newspaper there was an article about changes in the workplace. Service enterprises have to teach manners to their employees. What's wrong with us Finns when you have to teach that. Ability to co-operate is needed in working life.
> (TG fieldnotes)

The national identity is emphasised by flags and the national anthem during special occasions, such as Independence Day festivities. Despite the stigmatizing talk being Finnish appears as a shared emotional affiliation worthy of celebration. Finland is constructed as being outside the framework of colonialism, and activities that can be interpreted as part of general colonial trends assume a different inflection when practiced by Finns are discussed differently.

In relation to these constructions other nations and nationalities become absent others, defined as more skilled, flexible and vocal, as exotic, but also as poor and hungry. When the absent others, either as culturally superior or socially inferior, have become more present (through immigrant or refugee status), in the constructions of being Finnish they are defined as not-Finnish, foreigners, strangers.

A snapshot illustration of this is provided by the iconography of Finland produced by school students when they were asked in interviews to provide an association for the prompt 'Finnish'. They included the Finnish flag, lakes, sauna, trees, wood, Lapland, Santa Claus, sports, alcohol and sausage. Such metaphors for being Finnish provide little opportunity for the integration of absent others who have become present. In so far as the representations are masculine (such as beer consuming sausage eating men) they also marginalise women (Gordon 2002). Associations to the prompt 'Finnish' produced exclusive associations such as 'blond' and 'blue-eyed', but there were also associations that are more inclusive, although within the context of the nation space, such as 'all those who live in Finland'. In one English school, the 'other' is a constant presence, in that many nationalities are present in the school, and the school has a developed multicultural policy and ethos. When asked in interviews, all teachers and students responded that it was good to have so many nationalities, you learned about and to live with many different types of people. They endorsed the school's policy, implicitly or explicitly (the latter largely in the case of the teachers). When pressed further, some agreed that tensions and difficulties could emerge in this 'melting pot'. Researchers observed in the school that 'cussing', verbal attacks by students on students, could be based on 'otherness', and took place between different nationalities and ethnic groups. Cussing usually occurs between two students, one attacks, and the other reacts to the verbal taunt. Teachers either ignore or are dismissive of this type of interaction, various teachers have called it 'childish', 'stupid', 'immature', 'silly and funny', 'juvenile', 'daft' and 'pathetic' at different times. Cussing occurs between boys, between girls and between boys and girls. Students have referred to cussing as 'clever', 'cool', 'nasty', 'bad' and a 'joke'. One young woman said: 'I was at an interesting cussing contest' and added: 'if someone cusses well it's really cool to watch. It's boring when people say the same things when cussing'.

Given the mix of nationalities and ethnic groups in this English school, and the positive multicultural approach, there are many images of different nationalities both around the school and in classrooms, in posters, artwork and in the curriculum. In Religious Education (RE) videos portray the religious beliefs of different cultural and ethnic groups, in Arts students are invited, for example, to use images from India in their work, in Geography the countries of the Economic Union are discussed and a video of a holiday in Spain shown, and around the school posters depict some of these countries as holiday destinations. Some of these representations can be used to fuel the cussing process, as when an image of a man and a donkey working a plough in Spain were used to insult a North African student about his father being a peasant. This was certainly recognised by the student as a serious affront, since he made a formal complaint. In other instances the response is more ambiguous, for example in an art class about images from India, one boy went to dance an imitation Indian dance in front of an Asian student (male), and the rest of the boys enjoyed a joke at his expense. These constant images of 'otherness', and the presence in the school of multiple 'others' can also bring out strong differences of opinion. In a Religious Education lesson, for example, a Muslim student (male) put forward the view that

> It's important for everyone to believe in a religion—to have an understanding of creation. It is OK for everyone to have different beliefs and values. You can still be friends with someone from a different religion.

to be countered by a white, British male response:

> It's not OK to have different religions because it causes arguments. Everyone should be the same religion, preferably Christian. (JH fieldnotes)

While there were many images of different cultures and religions in the school, there was no one assertive image of British culture. This was the invisible backdrop against which 'otherness' was portrayed. When asked in interviews, people who identified themselves as British, often with some difficulty with the identification, also had difficulty in describing what they meant by it.

> I feel more British than Indian, well more English than Indian. I know that at home I would say that I was English – er, Indian, sorry. But when I come to school I feel English.  (Rita, JH interview)

In the other English school, although it too was multi-ethnic with a different mix of cultures, the ethos was oriented towards producing academically (and for some musically) successful individuals, who would potentially take up a place as a citizen in the elite of the society. This was a position with which parents and students concurred. Often students would not, for example, take lessons or exams in their own language, or if they did so, would do it outside the framework of the school. The lived experience of diversity was there, but not highlighted in the ethos and practices of the school.

In Helsinki schools banal nationality was constructed, but we have also observed situations where exploration of nationality moves beyond iconographies and stereotypical narratives. For example in one music lesson the subject was samba.

> The teacher draws Latin America and says that it is an enormous region, and there are lots of different cultures. We choose examples from here and there. Now samba, in the spring salsa. There is also reggae, calypso, Argentinian tango. Pinja: Does reggae come from there [pointing] Teacher: It's from Jamaica. City music. (...) The teacher explains that before a carnival people make instruments themselves in Brazil. He shows various instruments [and explains the rhythm]. (TG fieldnotes)

In Arts lessons ethnocentricity and racism were addressed in discussions. For example when the teacher and students had been to a modern art exhibition, where one the exhibits consisted of glass box filled with Finnish passports, the following discussion took place:

> Leo asks what the idea behind the passport item was. The teacher explains that when the artist was in Helsinki he wondered where all the foreigners [in Finland] are. It is in opposition to politics on immigration.
> (TG fieldnotes)

In a mother tongue lesson when school students did presentations on novels that they had read, an intensive discussion about 'us' and 'them' developed with several strands in relation to absent and present others. Seeds for a more inclusive, rather than exclusive construction of being Finnish in relation to other ethnicities as well as in relation to gender were present. The students were active but the teacher also facilitated discussion. Education's task of promoting social change, and the definitions of critical citizenship and autonomous individuality fed some of these strands.

In observations in the school, the school ethos and ideology of multiculturalism in Oak Grove was not always so apparent, as indicated by the social interaction of cussing described earlier. A discussion in an English lesson explored nationality, citizenship, and the rights of the other. The students were about to start reading a novel about a young girl living through the troubles in Ireland. It was a fantasy but it had many elements of the reality of life in Belfast during the troubles, although the reading took part during an IRA ceasefire. To introduce the book the teacher initiated a question and answer session on what the students knew about Northern Ireland. Amongst the group they collectively had the information that some people in Northern Ireland did not want to be part of 'our country', that the IRA were using bombs to make this point, but that others, protestants, loyalists, who did want to be part were also using bombs, and that most of this violence took place in the capital of Northern Ireland, Belfast. They were not too sure why British soldiers were on the streets in Belfast, or were not prepared to volunteer any views they had on it. When a slogan painted on a wall appeared in the novel 'Give them their rights not their last rites' the students could volunteer a number of human rights—freedom of speech (right to say what you want to say), religious freedom, and the right not to be bullied at school, in the street and home—but were unsure about 'rite'. The teacher led them to the answer. The teacher took the opportunity of introducing information about religion, rights, and deprivation of the rights of citizenship experienced by Catholics in Northern Ireland. The discussion was facilitated by the teacher, who introduced, or elaborated potentially contentious material in relation to the British role in Northern Ireland, but in a clear and apolitical way. The students were engaged and interested, and variably informed about the particular and more general issues raised in the debate.

## Conclusion

Official, informal and physical practices at school included complex processes constructing gendered and racialised otherness as we have illustrated here and elsewhere. Conceptions of individuality and citizenship, despite immersion in a taken-for-granted narrative of neutrality, are constituted as male, as suggested in the introduction. This creates a complex interplay between race, gender, ethnicity and nationality, in which, however, masculinity and the exercise of male power is a dominant feature. This is not to deny of course that other processes, involving more fluidity and diversity, are at work in this context, including co-operation, negotiation and resistance. New Right politics do not constitute practices of control that are totally determined. The 'correspondence' principle is too mechanistic to capture everyday life at school with its practices of diversity as well as differentiation.

Space becomes a place through human practice and exercise of agency in the context of hierarchical spatial organisation. Thus spatial praxis is a continuous project in schools. Both school students and teachers are constantly involved in an (often) unarticulated 'politics of location'. In order for people to practice their rights and duties as citizens they are expected to operate as independent, autonomous individuals. The way in which schools organise space, time, movement and talk, the way students respond to this are socially differentiated. We have used examples of these processes from our ethnography of four schools to link nation space and school space through the concept of citizenship in the context of the nation state. We have pointed to correspondences between physical, social and mental space in nation space and in school space, arguing that this is not a simple, mechanistic correspondence, but involves the interaction of complex material, social and cultural dimensions which must be included in the analysis. Breaks and tensions in the correspondence provide those spaces where more inclusive practices of the production of citizens can take place.

Similarly, exclusive conceptions of nation states and nationality can be questioned and challenged in school practices. However, in the context of neo-liberal and neo-conservative policies this is not easy. We have adopted a cross-cultural approach, whereby we are particularly interested in tracing practices of schooling across two societies, rather than simply comparing them. This has provided an opportunity to trace the multiple ways in which nation space and school space are intertwined. Whilst Finland has a more democratic education system in terms of state provision, in the UK school based democratic practices are further developed. Weakening of the welfare state, particularly obvious in the UK, but an ongoing process in Finland and other Nordic countries too, poses difficulties and tensions for inclusive education based on principles of social justice. Whilst multiculturalism characterises educational politics and is incorporated in policies, at the same time some extreme practices of racism are prevalent in the UK and the Nordic countries. New Right politics do not provide a sufficient framework for democratic education.

# 3

# 'Strong Nordic women' in the making? Gender policies and classroom practices

## Elina Lahelma and Elisabet Öhrn

### Introduction

'This is how strong Finnish women grow: they survive being teased! 'This was an ironic comment from a teacher in a Finnish secondary school during a lesson when some of the boys were observed constantly nagging about the activities of some of the girls. Taking this comment as a point of departure, we set out to discuss contemporary research and discourses concerning the schooling of girls, concentrating on gendered patterns in school achievement and in official and informal relationships in the classroom. Our context is Finland and Sweden, two Nordic countries often regarded as 'model' countries in terms of gender equality; several indicators such as women's participation in the labour market and day-care facilities suggest that the position of Nordic women is good.

Educational policies in relation to gender in schools are intertwined with changes brought in by restructuring (e.g. Apple 2001; Arnot and Gordon 1996; Gordon, Holland and Lahelma 2000a). The neo-liberal wing of the New Right puts forward strong arguments supporting choice, competition and autonomy, and has brought markets into education. This has weakened the politics of equal opportunities that have been central in the social democratic policies of Sweden and Finland from the 1960s onwards. Moreover, restructuring has brought an emphasis on the problems of boys in the educational agenda, because their school achievements tend to be poorer than that of girls', on the average. The neo-conservative wing, on the other hand, has emphasised traditional gender differentiation, and essentialist views on sex differences are on their way back.

This chapter draws on a broad range of research, but will make special use of a Finnish ethnographic study on secondary schools in Helsinki—the project 'Citizenship, Difference and Marginality in Schools with Special Reference to Gender'[1], a comparative, cross-cultural study of secondary education in Finland, with similar work conducted in Britain (Gordon, Holland and Lahelma 2000a; see also the chapter by Gordon and Holland in this book). The study traces the trajectory of educational policy from the macro level of the broad social context in which it is generated, through an analysis of curriculum documents and to the micro level of its realisation in the classroom. The final stage is an investigation

---

1  Tuula Gordon acted as director of the project. It was funded by the Academy of Finland.

of processes in schools, as well as the practises of teachers and 13 to14-year-old students, in an ethnographic study of two secondary schools in Helsinki. We also use ethnographically grounded life-history interviews of the same young women and men at the age of 17 to 18, conducted by Tuula Gordon and Elina Lahelma in the project 'Tracing transitions: a follow-up study of post-16 students'[2].

These results are related to a Swedish study 'Gender, power and resistance' (the resistance-study) carried out by Elisabet Öhrn in two secondary classes in grade 9 in the 1990s (Öhrn 1997, 1998)[3]. This research was concerned with gender and power relations in school, with particular focus on students' strategies for gaining influence and resisting subordination in the school environment. This project followed a previous one (the interaction study) focusing on student-teacher interaction in seven 9th-grade classrooms (Öhrn 1990, 1993) and attempted to deepen its understanding of power processes and the ways students may draw on various rules and resources in order to pursue their interests.

When using data from the Finnish and Swedish studies, we do not aim to present comparisons but aim rather to suggest that similar practises and processes are to be found in both countries, although educational policies and debates seem to differ somewhat between the countries.

## Gender onto the agenda of research and educational policies

From the late 1970s there was a growing body of research on gender and education in the Nordic countries. Typically, these early studies argued that boys initiate and receive more teacher contact than girls, although patterns seemed to some extent to vary between school classes (Wernersson 1977), between students with different social backgrounds (Bjerrum-Nielsen and Larsen 1985) and between educational levels (Hjort 1984). The overall pattern of female subordination through classroom organisation, teacher attention and textbooks was largely in accordance with the one described in international literature (see Öhrn 1990).

Nordic research on gender and education at the turn of the century presented a less uniform picture of gender relations in classrooms and schools as compared to the earlier studies. Local variations of gender patterns due to subjects, situations, classes and contexts were demonstrated (Öhrn 2002). Some commentators have even taken these variations to indicate that girls are now 'stronger', more active, extrovert and independent than previously (e.g. Frimodt-Møller and Ingerslev 1993; Lähteenmaa and Näre 1992; Schultz Jørgensen 1990). But this picture is full of contradictions. Contemporary research also points to oppressive classroom practises with teachers interrupting especially girls' performances in the classroom (Lindroos 1995), extracting services from girls in order to help and support boys

[2] Lahelma's work in this study is funded by the Academy of Finland, and the University of Helsinki, through support to the project *Inclusion and Exclusion in Educational Processes* (Lahelma 2001-04).
[3] The study was funded by The Swedish Council for Research in the Humanities and Social Sciences.

(Gulbrandsen 1994) and considering boys to possess more genuine talent (Arnesen 2002).

Looking at educational policies and debate we note that in various countries during the 1990s voices have been raised in favour of focusing more on boys' situations and achievement in school (for this discussion, see e.g. Epstein *et al.* 1998; Kenway and Willis 1998). This is partly connected with the strong emphasis on achievement tests instituted by restructuring policies. These have shown that boys obtain, on average, lower grades in core school subjects. Worries about boys, however, were presented in Finland already in the 1980s when the first nationwide statistics on school achievement were published (Lahelma 1992). This discussion reappears regularly, and in administrative texts measures to support boys have sometimes been presented as measures towards gender equality.

A fairly recent Swedish report from the National Agency for Education makes references to the international debate on boys' underachievement as it concludes that boys in Sweden are getting lower grades than girls and also achieve less well than girls when it comes to civic – moral competencies.[4] This is contrasted to the earlier emphasis on the fortunate position of boys when discussing equality between the sexes in Sweden, and the claim is made that 'we must dare to ask whether boys are now becoming the losers of the school system' (Skolverket 1999, p. 145, present author's translation). However, there has not been a media debate of 'boys' underachievement' in Sweden equivalent to that in, for instance, Britain or Finland. This may seem somewhat surprising, since girls in Sweden achieve well academically and have done so for a long time. Moreover, from the 1960s onwards they have been found to outscore boys in comprehensive school by attaining higher grades in languages and mathematics than might be expected from tests (Emanuelson and Fischbein 1986). Paradoxically, the fact that this is such a well-established gender pattern might actually help to explain why there has not been such a fierce debate. The pattern of girls receiving higher grades was identified during a time when the gender debate focused largely on girls' disadvantages in school and thus, might not have been seen to threaten boys' positions in the way it would in relation to today's gender discourse. Besides, grades might be said to have lost some of their importance as selection instruments into higher education during the 1990s. The Swedish scholastic aptitude test now provides an equivalent alternative into higher education and one that has been shown to favour male test takers. Some have taken this to indicate a fair relation between the sexes when it comes to making it to the university level; boys benefit from the scholastic aptitude test, girls from grades (Svensson 1998). In Finland, grades or achievement in the matriculation examination as such do not have much importance in the competition for entry into the most popular fields of higher education – particularly among women (Lahelma 2002a).

---

[4] The underlying theme being related to a fear of boys' attraction to anti-democratic movements and organisations (see Öhrn, 2001).

In spite of the recurrent public discussions on boys' problems in school, gender seems a more muted category in Finnish than, for example, British and Swedish educational policies and documents. The myth that gender equality has already been achieved has led to 'gender neutral' policies that do not challenge self-evident, dichotomous assumptions about gender difference (Lahelma 1992; Gordon, Holland and Lahelma 2000a). In Sweden gender has been more frequently on the agenda, but from somewhat changing ideological standpoints. The Ministry of Education published a report in the early 1990s entitled 'We certainly are different' (Utbildningsdepartementet 1993), that was strongly criticised by researchers for essentialist views and emphasising the need to learn about sex differences and to adhere to them when developing teaching strategies for gender equality. Gender reappeared in a program of measures (Utbildningsdepartementet 1994) suggesting that educators should take sex differences as a point of departure when organising education. This poses as a shift within Swedish educational policy, with its former stress on the need for all students to face the same conditions for achieving gender equality.

## Understandings of girls' success

As demonstrated above, there are various tendencies towards a re-emerging focus on boys and their situation to be found both in Finland and Sweden, as well as internationally. Related to this is an emphasis on achievement that is associated with changes of de-industrialisation in contemporary society—forcing growing numbers of young people to achieve well within education for longer periods of time—and a neo-liberal emphasis on competition and individualism. In terms of grades, girls as a group are achieving well in contemporary education. However, ethnographic classroom research points to prevailing contradictions and ambivalences concerning girls' achievement in school. Attempting to highlight some of them, we now turn to our empirical studies to discuss school achievement and teacher-student relations in the classroom.

Although gender at school is rather muted (or maybe because of that), assumptions concerning dichotomous gender differences prevail in perceptions of teachers, girls and boys, as well as parents. Girls' school achievement is often regarded as one of the self-evident 'truths' of school. Equally self-evident seems to be the perception that girls' success is not, after all, especially valuable. Valerie Walkerdine and her colleagues argue that middle class girls' educational success is neglected also in research, where it seems to be regarded as 'healthy normality' (Walkerdine *et al*. 2001, p. 164) against which all other performances should be judged. Boys' (assumed universal) lack of interest in studying, on the other hand, is sometimes celebrated as 'healthy idleness' (Cohen 1998). One example of this kind of hidden attitude is demonstrated by an extract from field notes from the first parents' evening of a Finnish secondary school, in which the head teacher explains, accompanied by parents' understanding laughs and contented smiles:

'Girls, they would come to school even if they were not compelled to. Boys, those starry eyed young rascals would not come voluntarily' (Field diary). Another example is from an interview of a teacher:

> Boys do not have the patience for systematic work (. . .) But then, on the other hand, especially among boys there are many who are so talented that whatever goes down well with them. (Female teacher)

Judgements of talent are interesting from a school perspective. They seem not to have a direct relation to grades. A student may well be considered talented without achieving well or achieve well without being seen as talented. Furthermore, the Swedish interaction-study (Öhrn 1990) shows teachers as being unsure of how to interpret what seems to be students' academic interest. Some suspected that the seemingly interested students might only be concerned with getting good grades. Another interpretation was that maybe they were only accommodating to school expectations. Such doubts were primarily voiced in relation to girls, whilst boys were more likely to be considered either to have or to lack interest in a subject:

> It is difficult to tell with this girl whether she is interested or if she is only sort of doing well because she is used to doing well. She does whatever she is expected to do. I don't know if she is particularly interested.
> (Male teacher)

Gender difference in achievement is often taken for granted by students. They may suggest in the interviews that girls work more dutifully, raise their hand more often, listen more carefully and know more than boys. Sonja in the Finnish study achieves well at school, and is aware that girls help one another (Gordon, Holland and Lahelma 2000b). She understands why teachers often help boys:

> It's possible that boys don't learn, kind of, so quickly. They kind of need to shout for the teacher more on the maths lessons. And the girls in most cases turn to me and Milla[5]. (Sonja)

Sonja thought that boys do not learn as quickly as girls. Some boys, however, would not share this opinion. They do not necessarily have respect for the well achieving girls (or boys). For example Otto, at the age of 17, remembered Marjaana, who always got the highest grades: 'But she also worked like crazy ... I don't know, reading was the only way that she could have achieved so well'. At the age of 18, however, Marjaana herself remembered that she did not study especially hard in secondary school, but achieved on an adequate level.

There were several high-achieving girls in the Finnish research schools who were active during lessons as well as in out-of-school activities and hobbies. Tuula Gordon (2000) has called a group of this kind of girls 'Bold, Brainy and Beautiful'.

---

[5] Milla was interviewed by Tuula Gordon.

In a class with a considerable female majority, this group was vocal and liked by most of the teachers. However, in staff-room discussions as well as in interviews, some teachers expressed worries about the situation of the boys in a class with such strong girls. During the lessons, teachers often controlled these girls' vocal interjections.

In another class some of the high achieving girls were rather quiet. During the lesson they did not often speak unless spoken to, but they participated actively in the periods when teachers asked questions. Marianne and Riina were close friends, and both were hard-working and talented girls. In a joint interview at the age of 18 they related a long discussion with a male teacher during the class trip, just before leaving secondary school. They had expressed to him their hesitations and worries concerning which upper secondary school to choose, and the teacher had told them about the important values of life: 'leisure, happiness, love, friends and all'. From this long discussion with their favourite teacher, the girls learned – as they argued – that school is not everything, and that one need not always be the best. We leave open the question, whether Marianne and Riina should have learned much earlier that 'school is not everything', or whether a suggestion to curtail their efforts to success was beneficial for these girls with rather ambitious plans for further education.

These examples suggest that girls' achievement is an ambivalent and even controversial issue. Moreover, worries about boys' low achievement might leave in the shadow those girls who do not achieve. As Sonja above argued, girls who have problems tend not to get the teachers' attention as easily as boys, who – according to repeated extracts from the field notes in the Finnish study – are often more quick to 'shout' for the teacher than girls.

Many of the high-achieving middle-class girls in the Finnish study were publicly active and confident in school. This coincides with results from other Nordic countries indicating that it is primarily the academically well-integrated middle-class girls who manage to position themselves well in the classroom (see Öhrn 2002). The situation of working-class girls – especially if low-achieving – seems more problematic. They are found to be more silent, or silenced, in class than other girls and there is some indication that this increases as they proceed through the last years of compulsory schooling (Staberg 1992). Also, some of them seem to be estranged by the kind of social relations taken for granted, where students have to compete with one another (and thereby jeopardise relations) to get high grades (Berggren 2001). Some of the girls in the Finnish study had severe problems at school, but they were nice and quiet in the lessons, or skipped regularly – their problems turned out to remain invisible and were not necessarily addressed by the teachers. One of these girls was an immigrant, and her problems reflected her lack of knowledge of the Finnish language, whereas another was a working-class girl who had severe difficulties in her private life.

Working-class girls who display resistance in the class, also appear particularly at risk of being stigmatised as troublesome. As teachers in the Swedish interaction-study described individual students, working-class girls were more often than others mentioned because of their negative behaviour in class. They were said to be either disruptive or lacking in attendance. Also, the few students who were singled out by teachers as verbally abusive and confrontational were all working-class (low-achieving) girls, who were said to act in ways that were difficult to handle, as in the following case:

> When squeezed into a corner [this girl] becomes her own defence attorney and starts using her verbal machine-gun. [...] When I have to accuse her of something as her form-teacher, and she gets into this defensive position and starts shouting things, I feel really sick, it makes me nervous.
> (Male teacher).

Girls who publicly confront teachers seem to violate expectations of acceptable femininities in school, and also to pose as threats to authority; using 'machine-gun' as a metaphor for a girl might suggest that this male teacher regarded her behaviour as masculine, which made him 'feel really sick'. Conflicts with girls were held by teachers in this study (Öhrn 1998) to be more difficult to manage.

The heightened risk for girls of being stigmatised when criticising authority calls for sensitivity when trying to wield influence. Aggressive behaviour is – both in its overt and sublimated forms – in accordance with dominant masculinities (see Connell 1987) and thus does not jeopardize the boys' identities to the extent that it does the girls'. Girls have to be cautious. How this might be done was demonstrated by some girls in the resistance-study. The girls in question lived (as did most of their classmates) in a working-class area. During the fieldwork there was an incident in class in which a long-planned school trip suddenly risked being cancelled, since the class would not get permission to leave when planned. The girls in the class started a process where they, after thorough discussions, arrived at a common definition of the situation and a strategy for handling it and eventually confronted the teacher held to be responsible. There will be more said about this process in the next section and a detailed description can be found in Öhrn (1998). The point to be made here is that the girls in question, in spite of an upset discussion where a teacher was publicly confronted, as well as other instances of open criticism during fieldwork, were not generally seen as troublesome by teachers, but even received some sympathy. In this respect it is worth noting that the process was orchestrated with sensitivity to school rules; the girls were asking teachers for permission before discussing with their classmates, where they were using scheduled class council time when confronting the teacher, and they did not bring the subject up more than once in class before resuming to private student negotiations for solving the case.

We have suggested that girls' achievement is an ambivalent issue in everyday life at school. For high-achieving middle-class girls, their achievement seems expected rather than valued – by teachers, parents and themselves. Moreover, because of complex entrance criteria, good grades are not necessarily decisive in the competition for higher education. On the other hand, low achieving girls are easily forgotten, if they are quiet and well behaved, or stigmatised, if they are not. Focus on boys and emphasis on traditional gender patterns in educational discourse do not make the situation any easier for these girls.

## Students' informal relations in school

School is certainly not only about studying and learning. When young Finnish women and men were invited to remember their secondary school, enjoyment and anxieties in peer relations seemed to be most vital in their memories (Lahelma 2002b). School students make connections and emphasise differences with each other during the lessons and breaks, on special occasions and in school-related activities. Henna was a rather high-achieving girl whose memories from secondary school were related to the informal aspects of school life:

> Always when I went to school I got cheerful. (. . .) And when I was sick, then I was like, oh, what has happened now. What kind of gossip and all. (. . .) You belonged to the group and it was kind of a clique. (Henna)

In secondary school, gender is a strong divider of informal relations – although not all the time. Girls and boys might make gender divisions explicit by sitting in single sex groups and avoiding the other gender; they might challenge each other verbally or physically; and they might demonstrate heterosexual interest, curiosity or fears in many different ways. There are situations in school when gender is not a relevant divider, but such were not typical in the secondary schools that were followed in the Finnish study (Gordon, Holland and Lahelma 2000a; Tolonen 2001).

A great deal of learning about what it is to be a young woman takes place in the context of informal relationships. Girls' relations with one another seem very important to them, although often controversial and filled with ambivalence (Gordon, Holland and Lahelma 2000b; Tolonen 2001; Hey 1997). The support that girls give to each other in the official school environment is for them the most important aspect. If they are not getting enough attention and energy from the teacher, girls can help each other. Moreover, their cooperation makes the classroom a more pleasant place for them and helps them to broaden the space that they are using, facilitates their vocality and gives their bodies more scope. Friendships make school days more fun – though particularly in the informal spaces, girls also play out their differences and engage in exclusionary practises, marginalisation of some girls or some types of femininity (Gordon, Holland and Lahelma 2000b; c.f. Hey 1997).

The importance of social relations for establishing a strong position in class was demonstrated in the Swedish resistance-study. As mentioned previously, this study showed 9th-grade girls in a working-class area to actively influence school issues through negotiations and confrontations with teachers. When explaining their readiness to challenge authority, the girls in the class stressed the importance of their interpersonal relations. The girls had known each other for a long time, most of them met frequently out of school and they felt safe in each other's company.

> Don't know really, but like girls, us girls, there are some of us who always hang out together, so like, you're not afraid to do something embarrassing, 'cause there's no one to be embarrassed towards. (A girl)

Shared experiences meant that there was a solid base for acting in school. The girls emphasised the importance of knowing each other and each other's opinions for speaking up in class (see Gordon, Holland and Lahelma 2000b, p. 21 for similar findings). Awareness about the opinions of the others meant knowing what kind of student support to expect in classroom conflicts. This was also implied during observations as the girls were seen to confront authority by acting collectively, in a process with someone starting and others following. Some boys indicate – as the three boys below – this to be an oft-used strategy among the girls in their class:

> *Boy 1:* Usually there are a few who start objecting at once. Who agree something's wrong.
> *Boy 2:* Yeah, it's mostly the girls who like, object. Then the rest start bringing stuff up.
> *Boy 3:* Yeah, they're go... the girls are good at latching on to each other's opinions like. If a girl thinks something's wrong, 'Yeah, that's what I think' like that.

The girls in this class believed in collective action as a prerequisite for exercising influence in the school. So did their male classmates, but in this class they did not manage to form groups that could accomplish such actions. Consequently, this case should not be taken to demonstrate a gender difference in behaviour, but rather to highlight the importance of interpersonal relations for confronting authority in school. It is worth noting that the collective actions of the girls relied on small-group activities. As the girls prepared for the dispute mentioned earlier, they formed temporary groups that dissolved and reformed into new ones in a process allowing for numerous interactions. Through this process the girls got to know each other's views and also managed to arrive at a description cohesive enough to serve as a basis for action. The vital ability and importance of networking as seen here is particularly interesting considering the descriptions made elsewhere of girls' small group interactions as almost detrimental to public group actions (see Öhrn 1998).

Girls' friendships are important not only in their relations to teachers, but also in their relations to the boys in their classes. Although girls' and boys' separation in the informal arenas of the school is evident, they are expected to stay in the same small spaces for several hours daily. Secondary school classrooms are sometimes filled with gendered play-acting and name-calling. It is not always regarded as disturbing by the girls or boys themselves; some of the young women relate 'fights' with boys in positive terms, especially in their memories (Lahelma 2002b). Sometimes it is difficult for an observer to interpret what is going on within the informal agenda. For example Elina's notes reveal an interpretation that the following process during a lesson of home economics started as a joke, but was turning towards a conflict when the teacher finally intervened.

> Sami waves a towel towards Riikka. Matti play-acts kicking her. Teacher: 'Matti, get away!' Sami and Riikka continue, Inka comes along, starts to play-act a fight with Sami, Riikka goes away. Sami and Inka start to scuffle with fists, laughing. Then it seems that the fight gets more serious. The teacher realises it only when it has continued for a while. She comes: 'Heh, Sami!' They finish[6]. (fieldnotes)

Whilst the line between play-acting and harassment is sometimes difficult to draw, data from the Finnish ethnography (e.g. Lahelma 2002b) suggest situations in which some of the young people were systematically harassed. Boys were harassed by other boys and, more seldom, also by girls. Girls were sometimes harassed by boys, as in the case with Hannele, a quiet working-class girl whose school achievement was not very good. She did not have close friends in her class. Class room observations suggest that she was occasionally harassed, but it was only when she was interviewed at the age of 18 that she reported repeated harassment by a male classmate:

> I don't know whether he meant it as a joke, or whether he was serious. Well, I think he was joking, but sometimes it really disturbed me, because it was practically every day. (Hannele)

Hannele did not want to reveal the name of the boy. Now she had, however, turned out to be a determined young woman who suggested that she would not let the boys rule any more[7].

Adolescent girls in Sweden consider themselves subjected to boys' teasing and criticism in school, as Berggren (2001) also suggests. In particular, they find it hard to counter the kind of deprecatory, sexualised remarks that boys inflict upon them. The girls seem to devote a lot of time and energy to trying to avoid boys' labelling. There are some indications that this is becoming a more severe problem as the girls move into secondary school. The secondary girls in the study considered their positions *vis-à-vis* boys to be weakened as they moved into secondary school and they felt that the secondary boys grew in toughness through their liaisons with older boys and teachers. The girls relied heavily on their relations to each other in order to endure schooling and preserve self-respect. As in the

---

[6] Riikka and Inka are girls, Sami and Matti boys.
[7] A detailed description can be found in Lahelma 2002b.

Finnish study, a friendship group afforded a defence and was vital for the girls as it provided intimacy, security and long-term relations that offered far more stability than relations to young men.

Girls are vulnerable because they can be insulted at any moment by sexist comments, and 'any moment' could be a situation that has begun as play-acting and joking but which can turn into harassment. To react powerfully and negatively against what is 'just joking' is to show oneself to be humourless (Larkin 1994; Phoenix 1997); the response of Hannele above was that she tried to ignore the harassing boy. Therefore the situation also remained invisible. Sex-based harassment as a form of social control has material effects on all girls, including those who have not experienced it personally (cf. Kenway and Willis 1998). Sexist comments and other forms of sex-based harassment, then, constitute a way of maintaining and policing gender boundaries (Steinberg, Epstein and Johnson 1997). Competition between masculinities can take place by performances of control and harassment of girls.

Sexuality seems to be almost taboo in schools, and relations and enactments of power that are involved are seldom questioned (see also Holland *et al.* 1998). Therefore, sex-based harassment is not easily regarded as a gender issue by teachers either. It is often seen as a part of normal relationships, as an 'adolescent mating dance' (Kenway and Willis 1998, 108; see also Mac an Ghaill 1994). Gendered conflicts are often regarded as natural in secondary schools, and some boys' harassing behaviour taken for granted because of the 'difficult' age (Aapola 1997). Teachers sometimes interpret disputes between girls and boys in these terms, as evidence of heterosexual attraction; the young women do not necessarily have the same interpretation (Lahelma 2002b).

The situation is ambivalent also for those students that seem to have more power than others. Someone who is able to exert control in the informal group of fellow students, may be in a vulnerable position in the hierarchies of achievement in the official school. Furthermore, the stress on formal education in contemporary Nordic societies might mean that it is hard to neglect achievement when developing alternative hierarchies. Research on male working-class counter-cultures has pointed to some boys' rejection of academic work as 'female' and in contrast to masculinity, based on manual labour (e.g. Kryger 1990). Their resistance in school has been seen as developing from a culture in opposition to the ideals of academic schooling and authority. However, as argued by Weis (1990), present processes of de-industrialisation threaten both the male working-class jobs and a kind of masculinity based on it. In Sweden and Finland formal education has become more important also for this group of boys. This is likely to have a bearing on the kind of alternative hierarchies developed at school. The Swedish resistance-study (Öhrn 1998), showed boys being tired of school but still planning to go on to upper-secondary education in order to eventually get a job. To achieve that, they needed good grades from secondary school. Grades were often considered by students to be instruments of power in the hands of teachers, and in order to get access to the best grades, one had to act in certain ways. To protest in class for instance, was generally considered as risking good teacher relations and, especially, grades.

## Conclusions

We have presented some of the complexities concerning the presumed 'strength' of the girls. Through examples of ethnographic studies conducted in Sweden and Finland, we have discussed gendered patterns in school achievement and in official and informal relationships in the classroom. We have tried to dismantle the monolithic understanding of girls at school as either (too) strong and powerful (as the 'failing boys' discourse suggests) or powerless and discriminated against (as some of the earlier feminist studies argue).

We have contextualised our analysis in the era of the restructuring of education, with its focus on achievement and traditional values, and have suggested that there is less emphasis on trying to promote women's and girls' positions than in the previous era. This change takes place in Nordic countries which politicians tend to celebrate as model countries of gender equality because several indicators of welfare suggest the good position of Nordic women, as compared with women in some other countries. This is also taught to Finnish school children, for example in the sections on gender issues in textbooks (Lahelma 1992, Aapola, Gordon and Lahelma 2003).

In our ethnographic observations as well as interviews we have met 'strong' young Nordic women who are successful both in the official and in the informal arenas of the school. But their success is full of ambivalences. Valerie Walkerdine and her colleagues (2001) suggest that, in today's British society, the success of middle-class girls constitutes a serious threat to the academic hegemony of boys from professional families. In Sweden and Finland, girls' success has long traditions, but the entrance criteria for higher and further education address high demands, and even sacrifices, for young women if they wish to perform. The emotional costs of achievement might be high as well; success is expected but not necessarily valued, and sometimes (though not always) trials to achieve academically take time and energy from other fields of life.

Drawing from memory-work with young middle-class Finnish women, Elina Oinas (1998) has suggested that these women, influenced by the disembodied Nordic version of the gender equality ideology of their mothers, had adopted a 'non-sexy', 'smart' femininity, thus emphasising a contrasting image to that of 'sexy' working-class girls. Ambivalence regarding their own sexuality might make these young women still more vulnerable to the sexualisation that takes place in school. Raija Julkunen (1997) has suggested that sexual harassment is a way of counteracting the current challenges to male hegemony. Recent statistics demonstrate that the percentage of Finnish women who reported having experienced sexual harassment has increased during the last few years (Melkas

2001). It is difficult for girls to develop the capacity to control their own lives, if their autonomy in relation to their own bodies, and the space surrounding them, is curtailed (Gordon 2000; Gordon, Holland and Lahelma 2000c). The celebration of 'gender equality' while simultaneously neglecting power-relations blurs and silences gendered hierarchies and practises of sexualisation aimed at girls and women.

Drawing from their study with young girls, Walkerdine and colleagues (2001) argue that class in England still makes a difference in girls' school experience (see also Skeggs 1997), regardless of the fluidity of boundaries or transformations in economics. In Swedish and Finnish research, issues of class are less often focused than in England, but still some startling class differences are to be found within the groups of young women that we have worked with. There are classed patterns in school achievement, life perspectives, dreams for the future, and resources available for young women (Gordon and Lahelma 2001). The quiet working-class girls who do not achieve at school are the most invisible persons in the classroom – easily in the margins of the ethnographers' gazes as well, which concentrate more on the visible and audible (Gordon, Holland, Lahelma and Tolonen 2002). Those working-class girls, on the other hand, who are visible and audible, are at risk of being dismissed as difficult by teachers, as the Swedish examples suggested.

We now return to the comment of the teacher at the beginning: 'This is how strong Finnish women grow: they survive being teased!' Many of these girls have various ways of acting and influencing within the school; they not only 'survive being teased', but negotiate, resist and talk back, achieve and are popular in informal relationship. But a position like this is easier for some girls than for others. We have argued that social class is still important in order to understand such processes, but we have also paid attention to the importance of girls' friendship relations (see also Gordon, Holland and Lahelma 2000b). We wonder what resources, if any, the myth of the Strong Nordic Woman provide them with.

# Part II: Construction of normality and difference

# 4

# Constructions of an 'outsider': Contradictions and ambiguities in institutional practices
### Anne-Lise Arnesen

## Introduction

Contradictions and ambiguities in everyday life can often be traced to formal relationships and social and discursive practices. I examine inherent contradictions in school with a focus on the ways in which teachers perceive, construct, and manage 'outsiderness' and 'otherness' in their everyday social and discursive practices. Four concerns are central: the content of school and classroom practices; teachers' perceptions and constructions of student identities through social and discursive practices; student perspectives, experiences, and participation; and the tensions between inclusion and exclusion in school.

The chapter focuses on Helen, a girl of 14, and intends to demonstrate how formal procedures and processes operate through the way she is constructed by her teachers as an 'outsider', not fit to attend the local school. Her problems are almost entirely referred to in terms of inadequate home environment and individual pathology and vulnerability. My analysis suggests that there is evidence of negative factors in school that might at least partly account for her situation. These include a lack of flexibility in the curriculum, inadequate individual support, and actual problems of bullying and teasing among her class mates that are insufficiently dealt with by the school. I use data from an ethnographic project 'Difference and marginalisation in schools—with special reference to gender and social background' (Arnesen 2002).

Establishing a disjuncture between individual problems and school contexts seems to be a more general feature of discursive practices in schools (Arnesen 2002), particularly evident in schools in which the 'normal' is defined in terms of 'the traditional' school with limited possibilities to individualise and include a diverse student population. I argue that 'special provisions' in this type of contexts are locked into contradictions that in the wider context may be seen as stemming from tensions between the public education's democratic ends and bureaucratic means (Skrtic 1991, 1995). The effect may be that students, contrary to intentions, are left vulnerable, stigmatised and excluded (Sætersdal and Heggen 2002).

## A school for all

In order to situate this study in its proper context, it is necessary, first, to describe in brief the structures and dynamics of the larger social milieu in which the school is situated. In recent years, school reforms in Norway have transformed the educational agenda in a number of inherently contradictory and ambiguous ways. The reforms have introduced new ideas about diversity, professionalism, responsibility, and knowledge. The rhetoric of the Norwegian curriculum underlines the idea of a 'school-for-all' embracing diversity, inclusive community, humanism, and democracy[1]. The notions of social community and inclusion, however, are contested by ideas of schools as functional instruments for global competition and adaptation to a changing market (Beach in this volume). Such ideas have become increasingly influential and have gradually permeated debates about education and policy formation. Despite the influx of these new ideas into official educational philosophy, there are a number of indicators showing that schools are resistant to fundamental changes. Schools and classrooms often appear to be impervious to change and continue to feature traditional pedagogy and curricula that restricts processes of individualisation and inclusion (Arnesen 2002; Carrington and Elkins 2002; Lindblad and Popkewitz 2002).

One way of framing the tensions between ideas of inclusion and practices of exclusion is to trace the formal relationships and social and discursive practices of the actors in school. These often become apparent in the contrast between the official policy of a school-for-all and the 'normal' school discourse that prevails when problems arise. The normal school discourse involves traditional practices favouring the majority of students. Such practices are based on a curriculum from which some students are excluded. Despite reforms, this notion persists and is reinforced by established institutional procedures for dealing with students having 'special needs'. Traditionally, applications for remedial and often scarce resources for some students set in motion procedures for mapping the needs of each person, often involving individual diagnostics and close follow-ups. Those identified as requiring special attention are often subject to massive identity transformations and surveillance by the school. These interventions are presented as providing support according to the special needs of the child so identified. However, it has been shown that special provisions within an unchanged curriculum do not necessarily benefit either students or teachers (Carrington and Elkins 2002; Fisher *et al.* 2002).

In several individual cases of intervention to assist students in my study, it was found that provisions were often coincidental, lacking in planning and direction,

---

[1] Legislation (Ministry of Education 2000) and the National Curriculum (Ministry of Education 1997) state that all students are entitled to a schooling that takes into consideration individual differences. They have the right to go to their 'local school' and be part of a 'social community', and any special measures and provisions have to be based on agreement between the parents and the school. The social community has a central status in the National curriculum (L97) as the basis for learning and development and for becoming a citizen in a democratic society.

and inadequate for meeting what was regarded to be the 'needs' of the student (Arnesen 2002). One explanation for this may be the belief held by many teachers that some students naturally 'do not really belong'. This notion, as discussed by Hvinden (1994), often leads to half-hearted efforts to bring about changes that could make a positive difference in a child's school performance, and a number of measures have been initiated in the name of 'integration' and 'inclusion' into the mainstream. There is, for example, first, the 'pull-out' model, in which students in need of special support, who are mainly taught in regular classrooms, attend a special group outside class for a few lessons a week; and second, the 'in-class support' model, in which the students are kept in regular classrooms and schools. However, several studies have documented that both these models may produce the opposite effect (Carrington and Elkins 2002; Englert et al. 1992; Lavers et al. 1986). This is especially so when they are not accompanied by a reconstruction of teaching and learning strategies across the curriculum emphasising greater individualisation and flexibility, and taking into account the diversity represented by students in the classroom (Dyson, 1994).

## Helen in the school context

Helen was a ninth-grade student at Central Park School, an inner city school with a majority of students from a working class background and with an ethnic composition of 50 per cent of the students with non-Norwegian family backgrounds. Helen's family background was white working class. The school had a written policy aiming to meet all student needs. The school's deputy principal attempted to summarise what this meant by stating:

> We aim to take care of the minority students, the cleverest students, the weakest students, and those who may drop out because they do not fit into academic work. (Interview).

Yet despite the legal requirements to provide inclusive education, very few changes had been made in the operations of Central Park School in order to meet this standard. Those who did not fit into academic work were mainly included in regular classes, but sometimes taken out for a few hours a week for remedial teaching or for gaining in-class support provided by a specialist teacher. Some of these students were provided with full-time support for various periods of time in what were called 'projects'. Others, like Helen, were placed in special care homes (*omsorgshjem*) for shorter or longer periods of time during which they attended nearby regular schools. In these cases, the child's home school still had primary responsibility for her/his education, and such arrangements outside the school or classroom were not meant to be permanent.

Helen's school class was regarded by most teachers and students to be a 'problem class' in which a number of students were the object of much teasing, but it was also regarded as a 'clever' class in terms of academic performance

(Arnesen, 2000a). After observing the class, I concluded that it had many faces, sometimes sociable and industrious and sometimes messy and full of conflicts. As far as I could tell from observing her, Helen never took part in any academic or social activities during lessons. The overall teaching pattern in her classroom was traditional: a new theme was introduced on the blackboard for about half the lesson, and then followed by individual desk work (Lindblad and Sahlström 1999). In the classroom, students were expected to work independently or together with their neighbour, and they were to receive individual help if needed. The main model was based on a common theme and progression.

When I started my fieldwork, Helen had just returned for the second time from a special care home. Back at her local school, she followed her regular class, sometimes with a supplementary teacher. A few hours a week, Helen was taken out of class to work with a remedial teacher. What follows is a condensed version of my observational field notes of a mathematics lesson attended by Helen. Present in the classroom were 27 students, 3 teachers, and myself. The head teacher was Erik, the regular teacher of mathematics; the remedial teachers were Maria and Nafissa. At this point, I had been observing Helen's class for about a month. The lesson was based on an inclusive model in that it provided extra teachers to assist students with special needs (Maria), and bilingual children whose first language was Urdu (Nafissa). The students as usual were paired off. Helen, however, sat by herself at the back of the classroom near me.

> The lesson follows a procedure, which seems to me after a month to be typical at this school and in this class. After having waited for everyone to be attentive, Erik starts with the day's theme: the difference between $(-2)^2$ and $-2^2$. My immediate reaction is that this seems to be a very abstract theme to present for the whole class. The majority of the students seem to follow by writing down what the teacher presents on the blackboard. Pauline (one of the students identified for me by teachers as very bright) interrupts to ask Erik if the test they took a few days ago will be returned. Erik says no, and proceeds working with the problem on the blackboard. Maria and Nafissa stand beside Erik during the lecture (apparently they are waiting to assist students after he has concluded his introduction). As Erik concludes his presentation, he asks, 'Has everyone understood?' No one answers. He then tells the students to proceed individually with the tasks from page 71 in the red book and from page 89 in the blue. Most of the students find their books and start. A number of the students indicate that they need assistance, and Nafissa and Maria go from one to the other.
> 
> (Field notes)

Maria is assigned to provide remedial help to Helen and Tor. During the first minutes of the individual deskwork, she turns to Helen.

She sits down in front of her. Helen has no books on her desk. Later, I found that she did not have them. Maria, however, has the textbooks and shows Helen where to start. Maria reads from the book, repeating Eric's introduction, and shows Helen the problems she is supposed to solve. As Maria starts to write in Helen's workbook, she whispers to her as she proceeds. No one seems to notice. Helen sits in what seems to me to be a frozen and tense posture. She shows few signs of being attentive or listening. As Maria continues, Helen's body language suggests that she is not following. Maria spends about five minutes altogether with Helen before she moves on. Helen does nothing after Maria moves on and this continues the rest of the lesson. She just sits still, occasionally looking down at her desk and around the classroom. Maria spends the rest of the lesson period with other students (those with no defined special needs) and does not return to Helen. (Field notes)

The pattern described was typical of mathematic lessons in this class,[2] except for the number of teachers attending. On the surface, it seemed to be a model lesson. Most of the students actively worked during the entire period, despite the abstractness of the task. There was very little noise, and the atmosphere was relaxed. At the end of the period, Erik gave the class his approval of their work, saying 'You have been extremely good today. Let's take a break'. However, as indicated by field notes from this and other mathematics lessons, several children] did not do much work. Most probably, this was so because they did not get the help they needed or did not understand the problem at the outset. Of course, there could be other reasons for their inaction. Field notes from other lessons support this picture of a number of children doing little or not at all the tasks that they were supposed to do. However, if they did not become noisy or make trouble, they were left unattended by the teachers (Arnesen 2000a, 2002). Maria, it should be noted, was supposed to attend to the special needs of Helen and Tor. As she later put it to me, her reason for not staying long with either of them was to prevent stigmatisation. She thought that sharing her time with other 'normal' students would prevent that from happening. The result was that Helen might not have got the help she needed.

---

[2] I observed the class in the following subjects: mathematics, natural science, Norwegian and social science. The pattern varied from one context to the next. However, in the lessons I observed, no real attempt was made to introduce differentiated content or working methods that would take into account the diversity in the class (e.g., abilities, social background, ethnicity, gender). In fact, lessons in which discussions and dialogue were practised most often resulted in excluding even more students from active participation (Arnesen, 2002: 228ff). Teachers' concerns, empathy, and willingness to engage with particular students were of great importance for the individual, but these might not necessarily result in a general improvement in the provision of education.

## The teachers' descriptions of helen

The following analysis draws on 'institutional ethnography' inspired by Dorothy Smith (1987, 1990a, 1990b) and is informed by critical discourse analysis (Chouliaraki and Fairclough 1999). My aim is to analyse the accounts and discover how institutional relations emerge directly or indirectly from the texts (Arnesen 2000b). Consequently, my focus is on those material, conceptual, and discursive structures that come to light from the teachers' construction of Helen.

The teachers were asked to describe their class, and then each of its 28 students. They could focus on whatever came to mind and was important to them. The interviews yielded accounts of teachers' experiences of the school and of their class as a community as well as how they perceived the social relations of the class. The following analysis draws from interviews with three of Helen's pastoral care teachers and three regular teachers. These interviews were conducted at the school in the spring of 1997 during a free period or after-school time. As already noted, Erik is Helen's head teacher as well as her mathematics and natural science teacher. Marie is the Norwegian language teacher as well as occasional remedial teacher. Julie is social science teacher. They have known Helen since she began in the secondary school one-and-a-half years ago. Ruth, the pastoral care teacher, has known Helen since she was a student at primary level in the same school.

The head teacher, Erik, emphasised in the introduction to his account of Helen that her home was a mess. He described her as 'isolated from the surrounding world, inside herself. You don't get a word out of her'. He was concerned with her situation. Initially, he had assumed that her condition might stem from sexual abuse because 'she is so terribly self-effacing'. Acting on that assumption, he reported her situation to the multi-professional team meeting *(tverrfaglig møte)* and held a meeting about her with the local Child Protection Agency *(Barnevernet)*. In Helen's case, Erik reported that school subjects and academic work were not of paramount importance. He stated that Helen 'must learn to live with and be among other people', but did not elaborate on what this meant in practical terms. Erik was very concerned about Helen's absences from school. According to him, Helen attended school for only 3 weeks in eighth grade before, as he put it, she disappeared. The pastoral care teacher had tried to get in touch with her home without success:

> We write, send messages and report when she is absent. We hear nothing more. You never succeed in getting into contact with them (the home), you never get in. Her mother does not let you enter. They have no phone. You could stand there and bang on the door; it was not opened.
> (Erik, interview).

Erik occasionally met Helen on the bus on his way home from school and once had asked her whether she was going to come to school or not. Helen then told him that she was about to change schools. Erik reckoned that as far as he knew,

Helen had not attended any other school during her absence from Central Park School. When he asked her where she was going on the bus, Helen told him that she was going to meet a girl friend in town and showed him a CD she had brought with her. Helen did not tell him about what she and her friend were going to do. Although Erik did not think that drugs were involved in Helen's case, he regarded her as a 'pitiable and wretched little creature'.

Erik went on to recall that it eventually was decided by the school that it was impossible for Helen to continue living in Central City, and they managed to get Helen's mother to agree to send her away to a special care home where she had been before. He reports that Helen was there for a time until

> suddenly, one day, she was standing at our door. She was going to start again at our school. Suddenly. Without any warning. Nothing. She just stood there. (Erik, interview).

The school had already received extra resources for special education for her, but as Erik put it, they 'never got around to organising anything before she was gone again'. This same pattern repeated itself when Helen once more returned.

The social science teacher, Julie, in describing Helen, concluded that her attendance in class did not work. According to Julie, Helen just sat there. She described her as pleasant and smiling girl, but suggested that this did not help her situation. Helen seemed to come and go and was present for only a few lessons.

The Norwegian language teacher, Marie, mentioned Helen in describing Jorunn, one of the other students. Marie described Jorunn as very social, and a sign to that effect was her willingness to help Helen and look after her. Marie thought Helen was easy to forget when she was present, and described her as someone who does not say a word. In addition, Marie viewed Helen as a girl having special resources who had attended a special school. She viewed Helen's home background as rather turbulent, and believed that Helen's mother kept Helen at home to help her look after the younger siblings. She concluded:

> So it is a rather tragic case; she is more absent than present in school. So it is quite hard to follow her up. (Marie, interview).

The pastoral care teacher, Ruth, was not directly involved with Helen's academic situation. Her job was to follow up Helen's social situation and to maintain contact with the Child Protection Agency and Helen's family. On a few occasions, however, Ruth had included Helen in the art class she teaches a few lessons a week. As pastoral care teacher, Ruth possessed more information about Helen's background situation than did the other teachers.

Ruth first became aware of Helen when she was on a home visit to check up on Helen's brother, who had been absent from school for some time. She talks about Helen's home condition in an episodic and non-chronological way. Helen's father died when she was 12. After that her mother had two more children with two different fathers. Ruth reports that the Child Protection Agency was involved with the family. According to her, the agency was not very efficient. Yet where they failed, Ruth succeeded, and she recalled how she managed to get a signature to apply for a place for Helen to stay during summer holidays:

> I managed to do it by marching into their place ... getting some kids to show me where they lived, and taking the lift up .. and the doorbell was kaput. And [I] stand on their doorstep. The mother's fourth husband who is the father of the fourth kid is present. He is there. Mother is not home. She used to sit at the bingo. But then I say to him that he has to be the man in the house and provide the signatures that Helen needs from her mother in order to get help. And the next day the mother turns up with the signatures to the headmaster. So then it worked somehow. (Ruth, interview).

Ruth emphasised that Helen's mother did not manage to follow up on agreements, despite her apparent willingness to do so. In the course of working with Helen, it turned out that her mother as a child had been to the same special care home.

> So it is the evil circle, you know. Then perhaps you cannot expect more. There is never anyone who does anything to break it. And that is what is wrong ... . She is so frail, you know, so ... when she returned, we saw how frail she was, and then I remember ... her mother knew me from my contact with the brother, so she said 'I will come and talk with you about Helen', but she never turned up. They want so much to do something, but do not manage. (Ruth, interview).

Ruth felt that neither the school nor the Child Care Agency was able to provide support that would make a difference for Helen. Once, Ruth had assigned Helen to be her assistant when she taught in a class of fifth-graders. Although frail, according to Ruth she enjoyed very much being together with younger children.

> It was safe for her. Then they chatted a bit in the corners, and I left them in peace. I think that was good for her. But she never confided in you ... Oh, no, she was not open enough. But she could answer questions about whether she would like this and that. But at the start of her special caring home period, she was not able to say as much as yes. She said, 'Yes. No'. She never knew the right answer. She was so delicate. So in that respect they have worked real good. Really. (Ruth, interview)

Ruth indicated that Helen seemed to have benefited from her stay at the special care home. After being asked to review the process from the first time that Ruth had become aware of Helen as a problem, she recalled the following events: Helen was ill all the time, and often 'forgot to bring an absence note, since there was no order at home. That's how it started'. Furthermore, like her brother, Helen performed very poorly in class, a fact that according to Ruth may start a negative process, 'so that is probably a weakness in the family. Her mother is not very smart either. I don't think so. But that is how it can begin'.

An additional point that Ruth made was Helen's misunderstanding and misinterpretation in social interaction with classmates. When I asked her to elaborate on this, we had the following exchange:

> Ruth: And then there are difficulties, misunderstandings in terms of someone laughing in the wrong place. But that is impossible to control. Certainly, kids ought to be robust, to be as confident and secure from home to be able to put up with it (teasing). Because ... you have to survive in this society. But of course, no one should sit laughing at you with spite, but it happens when that is the situation and it is not at all certain that they laughed at her, but she believes they do. Anne-Lise: Do you remember a special episode to that effect? Ruth: No, not really. But I can imagine that ... later on it was told that ... some of the students had commented on her clothes and things like that. None of us thought she looked strange in the way she dressed, so I think that she is vulnerable rather than they are being spiteful. Really. And you know, when you have no self-esteem at all, then it is a very bad mixture and... Anne-Lise: Mm, yes...? Ruth: So. .. she is vulnerable and easily gets hurt whatever you do.     (Interview).

Ruth may be right in both her observations; of Helen as being vulnerable and the teasing not intended to harm. However, in the context she is constructing the image of the normal kid as someone who is robust, confident and secure, leaving Helen as a deviant.

Here Ruth is addressing problems in the school environment and seems to make judgements about Helen's behaviour in light of what she thinks is required of normal students in school.

## Institutional analysis

The accounts about Helen are the main basis for the analysis of how the social construction of students as deviants is a particular discursive practice that involves a complex process of definition in which actual events become transformed into documented forms that consolidate what is considered normal (see also Lindblad and Popkewitz in this volume). Research communities provide concepts and frames of reference that become part of professional training: Curricula, policy documents, professional literature, teacher handbooks, evaluation forms, grading procedures, and contact books between home and school that constitute and maintain 'theory' in terms of the conceptual lenses through which teachers conceive and assess their work and their students (Popkewitz, 1998b). According to Smith (1990a), they are part of procedures for reporting and framing what should count as success and failure, high and low achievers, normal and deviant students, and where to set the line between a student's right to be included or not.

My analysis puts a lens on the social organisation unveiled by the text. Each interview contains bits of information about Helen, as the teachers perceive her, as well as the discursive resources they draw on. The tellers in this case are the teachers. I did not interview Helen, since she had left before I interviewed other students. However, she is still the main character in the text. In addition to the tellers and the interviewer (me), we are presented with other actors in Helen's environment. These include a fellow student, Jorunn, who helped her in class; Helen's family, including an older brother, mother, father (deceased), two younger siblings, and Helen's mother's last husband; younger students Helen liked to be with; and 'some of the students [who] had commented on her clothes and things like that'. The text shows us that the institutions that were involved in Helen's school history were designed to assist children who need special help: the multi-professional team, the local child protection agency, a special care home, and the school itself.

As a researcher, I am part of the text and provide direction by my questions in the interviews and the decisions I make regarding the form and the context of the text. I am well aware that there are many alternative ways to interpret the interviews and to present the text. My role is as an active participant influencing how the tale is told. I am a person positioned between what actually happened and the account of it. The text is a construction by the way the interviews are conducted, transcribed, and presented. The readers conduct a further level of construction as interpreters of this text (Smith 1990b).

In the analysis below I look at the case from the perspectives of the institutional construction of deviance and authorisation of versions.

## Institutional constructions of deviance

Any procedure used to map children is based on assumptions about objectivity and truth. Teachers and experts are supposed to introduce facts upon which proper interventions may be based. Smith (1990b) asserts that actual events are not facts, since what is seen to have occurred in actual events always depends on whose version counts most. It is the use of proper procedures for categorising events that transforms them into facts. In this respect, there are several ways of analysing the teachers' accounts of Helen. One is to examine the texts in detail in order to reveal how the teachers position Helen and other actors in the text. Here emphasis is on what is said and what is left out. Ethnomethodologists (e.g. Garfinckel 1967) focus on commonsense methods and interpretative procedures that we routinely use to classify aspects of our experiences and establish connections between them (Miller and Glassner 1997). How persons are assigned to categories of deviance can be analysed by *contrasting structures* or distinctions that 'cast some circumstances, behaviours or persons as normal, natural or preferred and cast others as abnormal, unnatural or undesired' (ibid. 28).

We find a typical example of this at the end of Ruth's account. She is contrasting Helen with normal children in a way that confirms her behaviour as inappropriate and deviant. Helen's reaction to teasing is disqualified as abnormal. The teacher's version is not just composed of straightforward statements about teasing, but involves reality-creating activities through which Helen's behaviour is assigned to have moral and cultural significance. This involves assumptions about normality and deviance. Normal children should be robust in order to be able to survive (cf. Lahelma and Öhrn in this volume). Helen appears to lack this characteristic of normal robustness.

Another way of designating behaviour as deviant is to focus on certain aspects of the person in a way that produces a cumulative effect. Here, a number of witnesses provide similar messages, adding to the image of Helen being deviant. Their pictures are formed on the basis of what they have experienced of her through direct contact and what they have heard about her from various sources, not least from informal talk among themselves in the staff room, and more irregularly from meetings with special staff and experts. They seem to have been kept in the dark as to progress and changes in her current situation after a period at the special care home. Helen is thus kept within the discourse of deviance.

All teachers focus on different aspects of Helen, and their accounts are constructed from pieces observed in different contexts and at different times. Opening up the texts for examination does not always make clear what comprises the problem and what is at stake for the school. Is it a question of lack of care and even abuse at home? Poverty (no phone, broken doorbell)? Lack of confidence to cope socially? Vulnerability (cannot endure teasing)? Low school performance? Yet taken together, the teachers' accounts suggest alternative images of Helen: she is also described as pleasant and smiling, able to have a conversation with her head teacher on the bus, have friends, and enjoy being together with younger children.

To report on and categorise students is a complex work of construction in which certain information and 'truths' are disseminated and become internalised as the official version. Dorothy Smith (1990a) describes the task in more detail:

> The categories, coding procedures, and conceptual order sanctioned for use in the context of formal organisation are a linguistic and methodological specification of organisational (or professional) structures of relevance. The objects, environment, persons, states of affairs, and events thus given reportable status are themselves constructed in the everyday organisational practices realising the enterprise. (Smith 1990a: 96)

Significant information is left out of the accounts about Helen concerning the context in which she is physically placed: the classroom, the activities, and the school environment. The teachers' accounts focus primarily on Helen's disabilities and dysfunctional home environment, rather than on problems in school. This may be because to obtain extra resources for special help requires 'hard' evidence of special needs for individual students (Ministry of Education 2000). What strengthens a school's chances depends on the extent to which it can present the problem as a case of individual pathology in terms of a medical diagnosis, or as in this case, bad home conditions combined with inadequate resources for tackling problems. With this emphasis, the connection between her problems and the school context tends to be severed. However, if we combine certain indications given in the texts with additional information about the school, we see how this context might have an actual and significant bearing on her situation and school problems in addition to her problems at home.

Since the school and her classroom were sites where bullying and teasing were everyday experiences among many students, this alternative perspective allows for different interpretations of Helen's behaviour. Her anxiety about school and frequent absences, her muteness in the class situation, and her tendency to isolate herself make sense in the light of her school life as I observed it. However, such problems are seldom taken into account when 'problem' children are being identified, categorised, and otherwise mapped. Whatever factors are introduced or omitted in teachers' accounts establish Helen's place in the stories told about her and her family as well as in written expert records based on these accounts. And these follow her into the future as documented personal history (cf. Smith 1990a).

## Authorisation of versions

Smith (1990b) asserts that for any set of actual events, there is always more than one version that can be accepted as what has happened. It is the teller's privilege to define the rule or situation and to describe the behaviour. The concentration of problems generates urgency and also provides a basis for understanding why the normal school cannot cope. The authorisation of any particular version requires that the accounts are taken to be objective in terms of covering the actual events and to be truthful about, as in this case, Helen's situation. The reporting and recording at various levels and the procedures around these activities contribute to accepting, promoting, and incorporating certain matters and excluding others. The teachers and agencies involved in these accounts possess a particular mandate and interests that may colour the issues being discussed as well as those not discussed. For instance, absence (truancy) itself is counted as a matter of great importance and a sign of serious problems whatever the cause. In this case, Helen is seen as a problem both when she is absent and when she is present. The school may in effect shut her out as the procedures and lack of flexibility in the system fail to fit her in, either to the mainstream or to the special provisions set up by her school. Dismissing her by defining her as an outsider while no real alternatives exist only adds to the risk of further exclusion when she is at school. The authoritative version is based on the institutional organisation of dealing with problems in school.

Alternative versions from the involved parties, such as from Helen or her mother, are not seen as bearing sufficient authority to define what is at stake. In the manner in which these alternative voices are presented, they are assumed to be incapable of understanding what the 'real' problem is. Helen has become a 'case' for the experts. The effect is that the 'normal' teachers, although feeling concern and pity for her, may end up opposed to what is formally required. They remain unable to relate to her since she has become someone beyond their direct responsibility.

## 'Locked in' and 'shut out'

Phil (2001) claims that professional practice is conducted within the content and structure of government reforms instructed by a government discourse on education. She states that Government rhetoric draws legitimacy primarily from an argument for social justice and expert professional judgement (ibid.: 27). Special education is according to Phil 'seen as good, just and provided on the basis of professional judgement by qualified experts' (p. 21). However, according to Nilsen's (1993) empirical study on the extent to which teaching is adjusted to the individual child's needs and capabilities, this is in fact very limited. Whereas the Norwegian school has changed dramatically during the last fifty years in terms of 'including' all children between 6 and 16, many of its teaching practices have not changed. The traditional school is still alive. In principle, all students can be conceived of as being 'locked in' by the mere fact that schooling is compulsory. But since schooling is taken for granted and many children today may have rewarding experiences in school (whether from the official curriculum or at least from meeting friends), they can experience inclusion and belonging there, at the same time as they occasionally feel imprisoned (Gordon, Holland and Lahelma 2000a; Lahelma 2002c). Those who may be seen as really locked in are those who cannot compensate for 'failure' with friends and who do not succeed in or benefit from their schooling. For these students, the school may represent a double bind in which they are trapped. Many do no academic work or are occupied with routine work and meaningless activities that do not enhance their learning (Edvardsen, 1998).

An individual's right to schooling adapted to his or her capacities and abilities initiates selection procedures that are defined by the normal-school logic and designed to obtain scarce resources for remedial teaching (e.g. individual diagnostics and close follow-up of individual students). Those who are identified as in need of special attention are subject to identity constructions by the school, leaving them in some cases more vulnerable and subject to stigmatisation and total exclusion than before, when alternatives to schooling existed.

To define deviance and to decide how and when to intervene in individual cases is a process that has no absolute criteria for what should count as problem behaviour or pass as normal. To formally accept certain events or observations as 'facts' and to state that an individual has behavioural problems involves complex conceptual work (Smith, 1990b: 15). This includes collecting observations of the individual at different points in time, and in different situations separated in time, and organising them according to the recipes or authoritative accounts of what types of problems are implicated.

Teachers use the concepts that are available to them to deal with students' problems. In this example, Helen has come to represent a special case that illustrates how school transforms such problems as anxiety, disaffection, failure, conflicts, and violence into individual pathology. Teachers are confronted with increasing demands to deal with a variety of problems and an increasingly diverse student population. They have a heavy workload and, in many cases, limited means to realise the claim of a school-for-all. However, limited resources and lack of flexibility and effective ways of dealing with problems were seldom addressed by the teachers. The rhetoric of the inclusive school and a school-for-all may, according to Haug (1999) in reference to special education discourses, function like rationalised myths about evolving realities. The secondary school in Norway has not been redesigned or changed in order to include all. Quite a number of students do not fit, drop out or fail in school for various reasons. 'Individual needs' is a rhetoric that may conceal that special provision will often be a compromise between adequate help and available means. To explain failure as an individual problem can be seen as a culturally legitimate way of resolving contradictions in today's schools.

# 5

# Representations of ethnicity: how teachers speak about ethnic minority students

### Thomas Gitz-Johansen

### Introduction

The Nordic societies have never been ethnically homogeneous, as each society has included ethnic minority groups such as the Germans in Southern Denmark, the Sami population in Sweden and Finland, and the Swedish and Russian minorities in Finland. However, since the middle of the last century these countries have experienced the arrival of new immigrant and refugee groups and today many areas, especially around the larger cities, face a situation characterised by significant ethnic diversity. One place where the challenge of ethnic diversity has become apparent in recent decades is the school.

Nordic school systems have traditionally operated within the boundaries of the nation state, communicating the national identity through subject areas such as geography, literature, history, and language (see Gordon and Holland, this volume). The presence of new ethnic minority groups is forcing schools to develop strategies to cope with the new ethnic, linguistic, cultural, and religious diversity. To a large extent, the educational response to diversity depends on how minority students and the notion of diversity itself are conceptualised by policy makers, teachers, and other educators. In the Danish context, on which this chapter will focus, the teachers in primary school have extensive freedom to choose their pedagogical methods as they see fit. This means that it will largely be the teachers' understanding of ethnic minority students that will decide what the educational response to the new diversity will be. Little research has been done on this issue in Denmark. So far, studies on ethnic minorities and schooling have mostly focused on language acquisition (Gimbel 1992; Holmen 1993; Holmen and Normann Jørgensen 1993) and on how students negotiate ethnic and national identity (Jensen 1998, Mørch 1998, Staunæs 2003). In the UK, however, a rich ethnographic tradition has developed around the study of ethnic minority students' schooling and the role of teachers' stereotypes in this regard (Mac an Ghaill 1988, Troyna and Hatcher 1992, Wright 1992, Connolly 1998, Connolly and Troyna 1998). A major finding of these studies is that teacher understandings of, and attitudes towards, ethnic minority students are important for these students' identity and for their educational careers. It is therefore essential to explore teachers' attitudes and expectations. This is the question at the centre of the present chapter.

The data presented here was collected within research about how ethnicity is represented in everyday interaction and pedagogical programmes in the case studies of two Danish compulsory schools.[1] The research is based on fieldwork in two classes in each of the two schools over a period of three years; a kindergarten class, where the students were typically six years old, and a third grade class, where the students were typically nine years old. The research aimed to cover the first six years of school in the two schools; that is, from when the children first enter school and are faced with its social and institutional setting, to the point when their identity as students has been further developed (Salo, in this volume, describes the process where children first enter school and gradually make sense of school and their role as students). The main intention is to show how the meaning of students' ethnicity is negotiated in interactions among students, in the interaction between students and teachers, and in the social and pedagogical context that schools provide. Both schools are located in the vicinity of Copenhagen. They are characterised by drawing their students from a neighbourhood with much rental housing, a relatively high rate of unemployment, and a relatively large proportion of foreign citizens[2] compared with the national average. The proportion of minority students in the four classes varies from 25 to 60 percent.

Participant observation in the classroom, playground, corridors, staff-room, and other school locations has provided the majority of data. However, the analysis in this chapter is based primarily on informal talks with teachers and school administrators during the fieldwork. This method resembles what Spradley refers to as 'the ethnographic interview' (Spradley 1979) and what Burgess calls 'interviews as conversations' (Burgess 1984:101-122). This method has the advantage of enabling the researcher to speak with the informants in the field about pedagogical and other issues while immersed in the everyday context where they appear. Instead of asking the informants to relate abstractly to their daily context or, alternatively, asking them to recall specific situations, the in-the-field interview enables one to speak about matters directly at hand. This helps to minimise the risk of what Bourdieu refers to as 'imposition': the academic and journalistic habit of requiring informants to relate to questions that they have never considered in their daily practice (Bourdieu 1999: 207-26). The conversations were recorded in a notebook directly afterwards, while still fresh in memory. In taking these records, the emphasis was on recapturing the general flow of the conversation and the negotiation of meaning in the conversations (see e.g. Emerson, Fretz and Shaw 1995 on writing and interpreting ethnographic field notes).

---

[1] The material derives from the research project 'The School as a Cultural Meeting Place' funded by the Danish Humanistic Research Council. In charge of the project are Associate Professor Linda Andersen and Professor Jan Kampmann, both at Roskilde University.
[2] The term 'foreign citizens' is here used to refer to citizenship, which is the categorisation used by the municipal authorities when producing demographic statistics about the municipalities.

## Representing cultures

In the analysis of the interviews or conversations use was made of the concept *representation*. Stuart Hall uses this concept in his work to theorise ethnicity as a discursively produced cultural identity (e.g. Hall 1996). Hall defines the concept as follows:

> Representation is the production of the meaning of the concepts in our minds through language. It is the link between concepts and language which enables us to refer to either the 'real' world of objects, people or events, or indeed to imaginary worlds of fictional objects, people and events. (Hall 1997: 17)

Within Hall's constructivist understanding of representation is the process by which real or imaginary phenomena are put into words. Inspired by Foucault's concept of discourse, Hall does not take representation to be a conceptual mirror mimicking the 'real' world of objects, people, or events; rather, the process of representation is the discursive understanding and organising of phenomena and thus also produces these phenomena. The Norwegian political theorist Iver Neumann employs a similar definition in his discussion of representation as a point of departure, but he then elaborates his definition: 'I will ... use the concept representation to specifically refer to the most important clusters of reality claims that constitute a discourse' (Neumann 2001:33, my translation). According to Neumann, *identity* is such a reality claim:

> Persons and groups exist as bodies, and as spoken facts in the political space – as representations ... Thus, the study of identity should not only be a study of material phenomena such as territories and bodies, but must also be a study of representations. (Neumann 2001: 127, my translation)

Equipped with the concept of representation as defined by Hall and Neumann, I investigated how teachers represent (and in a sense produce) the students' identities, paying special attention to representations of cultural identity (ethnicity).[3] An implication of working with the concept of representation is that when I write, for example, about *problematic students* it does not mean that I see these students as problematic myself. Rather, it refers to the teachers' representation of some students as being problematic. Likewise, the concept *normal* does not refer to any kind of average or typical situation, but to the teachers' representation of what they see as normal (for a more thorough discussion of the concept normality in relation to schooling, see Lindblad and Popkewitz in this volume). This is an

---

[3] A researcher who has worked with ethnicity from a perspective similar to mine in a Swedish context is Pirjo Lahdenperä (1997). Lahdenperä does not use the concept of representation as an analytical tool, but works with a related method of textual analysis inspired by Foucault's concept of discourse.

important point. My aim is to identify and characterise the way teachers create such images. It is not to contribute to this imagery myself.

A central concept in the following analysis is that of *ethnic minority*. Hence, a few words on the sense in which it is used are in order. Following Stuart Hall, I use the concept of *ethnicity* to signify a cultural identity. This means that the concept will be used to mean a culturally produced and reproduced image that defines a group and not an essential property of a cultural or territorial group. When ethnicity is conceptualised as a matter of cultural identity, representation is moved to the centre of attention as the procedures through which cultural identities are produced:

> Perhaps instead of thinking of identity as an already established fact ... we should think, instead, of identity as a 'production', which is never complete, always in process, and always constituted within, not outside, representation. (Hall 1997: 51)

I investigate how such identities are produced by teachers and applied to the students. This is not to say that students do not play a role in producing their identity, but this analysis will limit itself to the teacher perspective.

The second part of the concept *ethnic minority* is here used to signify that the majority/minority issue is a matter of who has the power to represent what and who is normal. Helen Krag, the founder of minority studies in Denmark, defines majority/minority as follows:

> I usually define minorities as groups in society that do not have the power to decide what is normal. ... [A] dominant group is a group whose norms not only count as normal for themselves but also for others.
> (Krag 1992: 305)

Combining these two definitions, the concept *ethnic minority* signifies a group of people who are defined and who define themselves in cultural terms and who do not have the discursive power to define what counts as normal in society. Also, being defined as a minority often means having a limited means of representing oneself and thus often being represented by the majority and from the majority's own perspective. Here I explore what it means for minority children to be represented by majority teachers.

## Teachers talking about problematic students

Setting out to do fieldwork, I entered the schools with the intention of investigating how ethnicity is constructed in the early school setting; I was prepared to pay special attention to ethnic or 'racial' stereotypes such as depicting certain ethnic groups as slow learners or coming from backward cultures. After spending some time in the field, I had recorded hardly any instances of such stereotypes. The teachers generally did not refer to the children's ethnicity or cultural background when accounting for their behaviour in school. Only the occasional comment about Arab children's different musical background, the competitiveness of Turkish boys, or the different body culture of ethnic minority children provided this scarce evidence of the teachers' discursive representation of 'the ethnic other' (Hall 1992). At one point I wondered if the teachers were really as 'colour blind' as they claimed to be when they spoke about how they viewed the students as individuals and not as belonging to different groups. However, reading through my field notes, it struck me how certain words often seemed to recur when the teachers spoke about their students as 'behaviourally problematic', 'socially weak', or 'understimulated'. Curious about this representation, I started looking into the reasons teachers provided for their viewing certain students (minority and majority) as problematic.

One of the most common explanations for the perceived problems was an idea of the neighbourhood as a perilous place for a child to grow up in. The danger lay not so much in the risk of physical violence, but was perceived in a more subtle way as detrimental influences to the child's personality. Already during my first meeting with the staff and leaders of one of the schools, I was presented with a picture of the neighbourhood as producing a certain kind of child:

> I am having a meeting with the kindergarten teachers. We are discussing doing observations in a nearby after-school institution, and I am telling them about an earlier research project in which I participated. In this project I followed some bilingual children in a nearby day-care institution. One of the kindergarten teachers tells me: 'The children in this institution are the same kind of children that you find in the day-care institution you followed. It's located in a council housing area'.

In this quotation a connection is established between the teachers' conception of the neighbourhood and their understanding of the children in the day-care institution as a special kind of children. Generally, this 'kind of children' is not seen as very resourceful, although some of the teachers may find this a charming 'kind' of children to work with:

> The teacher tells me that she thinks we should have selected a school in another part of the town for our research. In this school they have a whole different kind of children, she says. They live in private houses, she tells me. She has done teacher training in a neighbourhood like that, and there the children were more egocentric, but they and their parents were also more resourceful, she says. She tells me that when she gave these children a message to bring home for their parents, the parents would react on it immediately, and the children had more prerequisites for going to school than the children in the school where she is currently working and where I am doing my fieldwork. However, she says that she prefers to work in a

school like the one she is in now, as she likes to work with this type of children.

This teacher represents the children of the neighbourhood in which she is now working as less suited to school than children from a wealthier neighbourhood where she has worked earlier. In the field note extract, she discusses how she perceives the neighbourhood to have fewer resources in comparison with the wealthier one and describes the children of the latter as being more resourceful and being able to do more things by themselves. This neighbourhood is located north of Copenhagen and is generally considered to be the wealthiest neighbourhood in the country. The teacher relates the resources of children at school to the neighbourhood and implicitly to social class. This means that however charming this teacher finds it to work with the children in the present neighbourhood, she is placing a label on them collectively as less resourceful and potentially rather problematic participants in a schooling context. Also, a head of department in one of the schools refers to the neighbourhood when explaining the school's problem with some children:

> I talked to the head of department during break. He tells me that the school has some children with very problematic behaviour. Sometimes the teachers call him to the class if some of the children are wrecking the classroom or have to be pulled away from each other. He tells me that they have more problem-children than other schools, as they have students with very diverse backgrounds. They have many children from council housing areas. Many of these parents have had bad experiences with school themselves which they transmit to their children. It is the social inheritance, he says.

In addition to the representation of the local community as a 'danger' to the children's development and schooling, another important image in the teachers' collective representation of the children is 'the family'. Often, the children's families are represented as weak, unresourceful, and stricken with social problems. Here, the concepts of 'weakness', 'unresourcefulness', and 'social problem' cover a wide range of issues: divorce, unemployment, and, as seen in the following extract, lack of linguistic competence:

> The class is working by themselves. Meanwhile, I am talking to the teacher. She tells me that with regard to reading, it is a very difficult class. She attributes this partly to 70% of the class consisting of bilingual students and partly to the fact that the Danish children come from what she calls linguistically impoverished homes. I ask her what she means by 'linguistically impoverished', and she replies that it is connected to the social class that generally inhabits the area.

Here, the image of 'linguistically impoverished homes' is introduced as an explanation of the difficulties the teacher experiences. The general meaning that can be read from these extracts is that resourcefulness in relation to schooling is a matter of the students' social background. Furthermore, social background is taken to be a matter of which kind of area the students live in. In this teacher's view, coming from a family in council housing areas makes one a certain kind of student; conversely, a child coming from an area of privately owned houses is expected to be an altogether different kind of student. The two 'kinds' of students are represented through almost binary oppositions: one is seen as well adapted to school, and the other as problematic in a school setting. One is represented as coming from 'resourceful families', and the other from 'linguistically impoverished homes'. As the students in both schools for a large part are characterised by the teachers as 'social housing children', they are primarily associated with the negative side of the binary.

Another interesting remark in the last extract is how the teacher regards the percentage of ethnic minority students in the school as problematic in itself. I will return to the issue of how ethnicity is represented shortly, but proceed for the moment to characterise the discourse that is drawn upon by the teachers in their representation of the students.

## Social inheritance

The teachers generally worry about some of the children on account of the influence of their neighbourhood and their families. As one head of department expressed it earlier, 'it is the social inheritance'. In a Danish context, the concept of *social inheritance* is widespread when it comes to explaining individual conformity. The term originates from a 1967 Swedish study of the background of a group of what the study calls 'delinquent boys'. This study may not be the origin of the term, but it caught major interest by capturing a common thinking of that time. The study traces these 'delinquent' boys' background over two generations and concludes that delinquency is inherited and accumulated through generations and transmitted through the families' behaviour and values (Jonsson 1967). As the concept has become popular in both scientific debate and everyday discourse, it has taken on at least three different meanings in the way it is used (Ejrnæs 1999). In one version the concept signifies a relatively high risk for some children to develop social problems as a result of growing up in a delinquent environment. Another version is the idea that parents' social and psychological problems are transmitted in such a way that the children will develop similar problems, and the third version uses the concept to emphasise children's unequal possibilities in the competition for education and jobs as a result of their family background.

If we look at these three meanings of the concept, the first two focus on explanations in the family and environment where children grow up and supposedly acquire problems. These uses of the concept 'social inheritance' can be characterised as *individual* explanations, which put the blame on individual weakness, dysfunction, laziness, or unwillingness to behave properly. This approach has been criticised as 'blaming the victim' (Ryan 1986) as it tends to develop a social-pathology (Baratz and Baratz 1974) of the individual while legitimising the institutions in which the individual is immersed. The third meaning can be characterised as a *structural* explanation as it turns the attention away from the individual, family, and local environment and instead focuses on selection according to social and cultural background by educational institutions and the labour market.

The individualising versions of social inheritance are the ones often found in the social system where social workers treat families and individuals according to their perceived dysfunctions. From the empirical examples given here, it appears that this version flourishes as a discourse in at least part of the early educational system. The teachers pathologise the students on behalf of perceived dysfunctions in their social background, which is a rationality characterising the individualising explanation. They do not draw on the structural version of the social inheritance theory, as they do not question the schools' (and thus their own) role in producing educational problems. In the next section I move on from the discussion of how students are represented as social problems in school to how ethnicity is represented through the individualising discourse of social inheritance, thereby associating ethnic minority students with social and educational problems.

## The question of ethnicity

So far, my argument has been 'colour-blind'. Talking in terms of social problems presents itself as a socially engaged and expert-validated way of relating to what the teachers perceive as problems in class. This discourse does not have the prejudiced and discriminatory ring that is dangerously near when one is talking about ethnicity or 'race'. But the question is still whether ethnicity is not still there underneath or within the social-problem terminology? Let us consider the following extracts and how they collectively demonstrate how ethnicity is discursively connected to social problems in a school context. First, an extract that tells us something about a teacher's perception of families with Arabic descent:

> The teacher tells me that she despairs over the parents of the bilingual students. According to her, they have no ambitions on behalf of their daughters. Only the parents of Suleyma have some ambitions for her, but, as the teacher explains, they are not typical Arabic parents. They have an orderly home and are functioning well. Generally, the teacher is desperately in doubt as to what to do with the bilingual girls.

It is characteristic of the way the teachers discuss ethnic minority families that they are represented in terms of what they lack and in an implicit comparison with an unspoken image of 'normal' Danish families. This tendency is especially clear when it comes to language ability, where bilingualism often is represented as a threat to the students' development of their Danish language and thus their ability to do well in school. However, as can be seen in this extract, ethnic minority students are sometimes assumed to be problematic for other reasons than their bilingualism. For instance in the previous extract the teacher represents bilingual families ('bilingual' is used by the teachers more or less synonymously with immigrant, foreign or ethnic minority) as lacking ambitions for their daughters, which she finds highly problematic. Then she comes to think about an Arab girl in the class, Suleyma, whose parents she finds quite supportive of their daughter. This family, however, is then represented as being atypical of Arab families; they are orderly and function quite well. The 'typical Arab family' is represented through an opposition with this well-functioning family. In other words, the typical Arab family is represented as being unsupportive of the daughters' careers, somewhat dysfunctional and unorderly (whatever is meant by these terms). Another teacher portrays children and families with Turkish descent in a similar way:[4]

> During lunch break I am talking to the teacher who is overseeing the schoolyard. She is also a teacher of a kindergarten class. She tells me that last year she had a class of students (who) just stood there and looked at her, and had to be helped getting started and needed assistance for all sorts of things. She has the general impression that it is mostly the Turkish children who lack resources. They need help for everything and come from families with very few resources.

In this field note extract, the teacher explains how she perceives last year's class to have been exceptionally unresourceful. She found this to be the case for most of the class, both minority and majority students. However, as she points out, she generally perceives the children with a Turkish background to be the most unresourceful in relation to life and work in school.

While not generally complaining about some students' affiliation with a language other than Danish and a country other than Denmark, this affiliation is seldom represented as a resource by the teachers. More often the teachers worry about language development, when minority students speak their mother tongue and not Danish with their parents. This attitude is expressed in the next extract, where a teacher represents a girl's connection to another country as a hindrance to her educational development:

---

[4] The two schools in the study are characterised by different proportions of the various ethnic minority groups. Thus, one school has a relatively high number of children with a Palestinian Arab background, and the other school has more children with Turkish and Turkish/Kurdish backgrounds. Also, in one school it is primarily the children and families with an Arab background that receives the teachers' problematising attention, and in the other school this attention is primarily reserved for the Turkish/Kurdish children and families.

The teacher tells me that she is worried about Hatché, a Turkish girl, who has been falling behind lately, and she doesn't know what to do about it. She attributes it to the fact that in Hatché's home her family has only the approaching vacation in Turkey on their minds.

Earlier, I discussed how teachers represent minority children. It is relevant then to consider how majority children are represented, thereby to explore whether there are any pronounced differences. In this regard, what is perhaps the most striking is how little 'Danishness' is represented directly. Little is actually spoken about what it means to be Danish, and the teachers do not represent Danish children as a group but rather as individuals or differentiate among them according to social class distinctions, as was discussed previously. In consequence, Danishness is mostly represented indirectly through what it means to be non-Danish. In this way, Danishness becomes almost invisible as the normal or typical mode of being in school, which need not be made explicit (for an analysis of the construction of nationality in a preschool context see Lappalainen in this volume). In the field notes I find few direct representations of what the typical student is like:

After the last session I talk to the two teachers. We talk about which of the children we have chosen to pay special attention to in our fieldwork and later to have interviews with. The primary teacher of the class thinks that it is a bad idea to choose Jens, who is a Danish boy. She gives the reason that Jens is a child with a lot of personal problems. She thinks that it would be a better idea to choose the Danish boy Henrik as, according to her, he is a completely normal boy with a good sense of humour and lots of personal resources to share with other children.

Here, the most interesting thing for the purposes of this chapter is to note how the teacher talks about a boy whom she perceives as problematic, as being untypical for Danish children. Instead, she proposes that we choose a boy who she sees as 'normal' and characterised by a good sense of humour and lots of personal strengths. During my fieldwork, I did not experience Henrik as a 'normal child' in the sense of being average or typical. Rather, he appears to personify an ideal of how a school child (or perhaps 'school boy') should be, according to the teacher. The way I experience Henrik is that he is the boy with the most school-adapted behaviour in the entire class. He seems to do well in all subjects (perhaps especially in physical education when they play soccer) and I do not see him having any arguments with the teachers or other children. Furthermore, he generally does not act egoistically, and this is a behaviour that is generally highly approved by the teachers.

So, what we have here is the teacher's picture of the normal (Danish) child. He is well behaved, socially minded, and good at his schoolwork. Even though the students, as has been argued above, are often represented as problematic with reference to their social background, the teacher's representation of the normal student is a very well functioning boy according to the norms in school. When the three examples are considered together, it becomes apparent that 'normal' Arab and Turkish families are portrayed as lacking resources, which generates problems for their children's performance in school. Successful Arab and Turkish children are seen as exceptions, the typical Danish boy is recognised by his qualities and competencies in school and the problematic Danish boy is seen as an exception to the norm.

When one compares the extracts about ethnic minorities with the foregoing discussion of social background, a similarity appears between how families from social housing areas and ethnic minority families are represented. They are both represented as special kinds of families that are characterised by their problems. A difference is that when ethnic minorities are spoken about, problems are expected to be the normal condition. It can be argued that ethnic minorities from the council housing neighbourhoods are viewed as doubly problematic as both their social background and their ethnicity are expected to act against their adaptation to the school code. It can also be argued that the teachers perceive problematic behaviour of ethnic minority children as a more fundamental problem. Danish problematic children are explained with reference to a divorce in the family or not getting proper parental guidance from home (cf. Arnesen in this volume). These are more individualised explanations that make the child's behaviour in school correspond with knowledge of the specific family. Problems for Danish children tend to be explained in social, psychological, or neurological terms. Ethnic minority students, on the other hand, are viewed as coming from backgrounds that lack cultural and language resources.

## The question of gender

I have argued that ethnicity is represented within a discourse of social inheritance, which tends to problematise the ethnic minority students and their background.[5] One question is whether all ethnic minority students are problematised the same way or whether differences can be identified. My observations suggest that the social pathologies connected with boys and girls often have a different content. Boys more often than girls are problematised as a danger to order in school (for an in-depth discussion of school achievement in relation to gender see Lahelma and Öhrn in this volume). This may be especially true for ethnic minority boys, as is exemplified by one teacher's representation of the five Turkish boys in his class. He perceives these boys to be troublemakers in that they often get into fights and often behave in a competitive manner that

[5] Researchers in educational ethnography have for some time argued in favour of combining different perspectives in ethnographies. The now classical focus on class has been expanded with gender and ethnicity (Mac an Ghaill 1988, Mirza 1992, 1997) and lately also sexuality (Kehily & Nayak 1997, Steinberg *et al.* 1997) and disability (McDermott & Varenne 1995); the sociology of childhood now argues for the inclusion of generation (Alanen 2001) in the numerous and growing number of perspectives that vie for the attention of ethnographers and social researchers.

invites conflict in the schoolyard. The following exchange is an extract from an interview where I talk with a teacher about the Turkish boys in his class:

> *Interviewer:* What do you mean by the Turkish boys' behaviour?
> *Teacher:* They probably have difficulties feeling empathy ...
> *Interviewer:* How is that expressed in relation the Turkish boys?
> *Teacher:* I guess it is more difficult for them to contribute to solving conflicts in the situation. [We begin to discuss whether the Danish boys are part of this problem.]
> *Teacher:* Mathias and Janus [two Danish boys] are not part of these conflicts. What other Danish boys are there? Finn is not participating either ...
> *Interviewer:* And Niels?
> *Teacher:* Niels is not doing it either.

As a response to this alleged problematic behaviour, the teacher has experimented with pedagogical techniques, directed at stimulating the Turkish boys' empathy, so that they do not cause so much conflict or at least become capable of resolving conflicts in a manner more acceptable to the teacher. During the fieldwork, the teacher offered the following explanation for what she experienced as problematic behaviour:

> If one is raised, as I imagine Turkish boys are, to show off, like 'I can do it and I have to be first and best', then it is very much in opposition to trying to understand others' feelings. It must be incredibly difficult.

The teacher attributes the confrontational attitude of the Turkish boys to the way they are brought up and thus to the family culture. However, the teachers do not display this anxiety about anti-social behaviour in relation to minority girls. They do worry about these girls, but their anxiety tends to have a different content than the concerns about the minority boys. Consider, for instance, the earlier extract (page 6) in which a teacher expresses concern about what to do with the minority girls. This teacher is worried about the academic achievements of these girls, except for the girl Suleyma, who is emphasised as an exception. The teacher describes in an interview how she first became worried about these girls:

> I simply discovered that they did not pay attention but were sitting and doing other things. Sometimes they were almost sleeping, and appeared to be in a world of their own.

The anxiety this teacher expresses is not primarily concerned with social behaviour (as with the ethnic minority boys). Instead she expresses a concern about participation. Whereas the boys are represented as too active or active in the wrong way, the girls tend to be represented as too passive in that they are not participating enough in the teacher-initiated activities in class. In the Danish school system it is highly valued to speak up and participate actively in class discussions. Personal opinions, original ideas, and creative solutions are important cultural capital in the classrooms if presented in the right manner and followed by the right kind of reflections. Some of the teachers do not see the minority girls acting in this way, which causes them to express worry about them being understimulated at home, discouraged by their families from having educational ambitions and generally being socialised into a dominated and silent role in the family and subsequently in school.

## Effects of representation

Apparently, the habit of representing minority students in terms of deficits is not isolated to the two case schools. Tove Skutnabb-Kangas (1990), a researcher in multilingualism, describes how minority children are often described in terms of what they are supposed to be lacking. This perspective assumes that minority children have deficiencies and proposes these deficiencies as the explanation of the children's possible problems in school. These assumed deficits can be both linguistic and cultural in nature, but they are always a description of the child in terms of what he or she lacks in comparison with a conception of the ethnic majority. Skutnabb-Kangas claims this to be a dominant perspective on minority children in the mainly monocultural and monolingual educational systems of Scandinavia. In another study, by Fabienne Knudsen, exploring how the issue of immigrant integration is discussed in Denmark, the conclusion is that immigrants are usually viewed as problematic persons:

> In most cases [immigrants] and their integration in society are talked about as a problem, and the source of the problem is identified within the immigrants themselves. Their culture and traditions, their religion, their lacking language competencies etc. ...stand in the way of their integration. (Knudsen 1998:5)

In sum, it seems as if perceiving minorities as problematic and locating the source of the alleged problems within their background is not isolated to the two case schools, but is far more general.

The discussion so far has only been concerned with representation. One might ask about the importance of this, perhaps arguing that representations alone can do little harm as they are, after all, only words. But representations are not as innocent as that, as they can have real (i. e. non-discursive) effects when embedded in institutional settings such as a school. Representations are connected with how we view others and thus with our expectations about them. Since Merton's study in the 1940s (Merton 1948) and Rosenthal and Jacobson's study in the 1960s (Rosenthal and Jacobson 1968), it has been known that teachers' expectations of students tend to have an effect on students' achievement in school.

Another effect of representation is that it has an impact on how policies are formed. In the present restructuring of the Danish education system, the government has cancelled state support to mother tongue teaching, and instead supported the enrolment of ethnic minority children in Danish-speaking preschool institutions. This educational strategy can be characterised as 'compensatory education', a strategy that emerged in the USA in the mid-1960s (see e.g. Bloom, Davis and Hess 1965). Compensatory education builds on a deficit-based perception of ethnic minority students and an individualising version of the social inheritance theory. Compensatory education has since been discredited as ineffective by government-sponsored (McDill *et al.* 1969) and other studies (Campbell and Fry 1970). Nevertheless, the compensatory educational strategy is today a widespread strategy in the Danish school system as well as in the other Nordic countries (Skutnabb-Kangas 1990:127-135). Teachers' and politicians' deficit-views of ethnic minority children are not the sole causes of these initiatives, but they work as a part of the rationale behind them; these views prevent development and in-school implementation of alternative pedagogical approaches that take students' background and resources as their points of departure. When educational problems are located inside the ethnic minority students and their families by drawing on the individualising social inheritance discourse, it becomes logical to direct educational efforts at compensating for these problems. This situation calls for a thorough political and educational debate on schooling in the increasingly multi-ethnic Nordic countries. Instead of more or less consciously copying largely unsuccessful compensatory strategies, educators in the Nordic countries ought to look more into recent developments in multicultural education in places such as England (e.g. Lynch 1986, 1989; May 1999; Parekh 2000) and the United States (e.g. Banks 1995, 2003; Nieto 1996, 1999) and to reflect on and experiment with ways to adapt such pedagogical responses to ethnic and cultural diversity to a Nordic context. However empirically founded and theoretically advanced such studies are, pedagogy must be developed in the educational, social, and political context in which it is always embedded.

# 6

# Celebrating internationality: constructions of nationality at preschool

## Sirpa Lappalainen

### Introduction: Citizenship and education

This chapter explores ways in which nation, nationality, ethnicity and gender are constructed in a preschool context. My main concern is how nationality and ethnicity are manifested in social practices, how they are perceived, constructed and (re)negotiated and finally, how gender and nationalism are intertwined within the preschool context.

The Finnish schooling system has traditionally been based on an over-emphasised idea about cultural homogeneity. In the beginning of the 1990s, immigration gradually increased and began to challenge this belief. This change had implications for the curriculum and teachers' work. In the curriculum document of the National Board of Social Affairs (1984), tolerance in relation to other nationalities was mentioned as a goal of ethical education. In the 1996 document, the increased cultural diversity in Finland was discussed: 'Because cultural diversity is increased into our country we have to take care that gender equality and ethnic equality are put in practice' (NBE 1996, 13). Cultural diversity was implicitly mentioned as a challenge for gender equality, which illustrates the strength of the myth about Finland as a gender-equal society (cf. Lahelma and Öhrn in this book). The new preschool curriculum (NBE 2000) is characterised by ambivalence between national and multicultural ideology. On the one hand, special attention is paid to the education of cultural minorities and immigrant children while, on the other hand, Finnish national values (without specifying them) and cultural heritage are emphasised more than in previous documents (Lappalainen 2002a).

Schooling has been important in the construction of national representations and subjectivities of individuals (Meyer *et al.* 1997, 153). As such, education plays a major role in the conceptualisation of citizenship, whereby Carol Pateman (1988, 11) has problematised its universality. She argues, for example, that even though women possessed the same abilities and attributes as men they were, paradoxically, both excluded and included by a liberal concept of citizenship. A 'citizen' is a member of a nation state and has particular duties and rights. Notions of citizenship are not entirely static but in dynamic relation to the political atmosphere. Schools are expected to produce citizens in the nation state, familiar with a common culture, common language, common history and a sense of their joint future. Compulsory state-organised schooling has been important in the construction of nation states (Gordon *et al.* 2000a: 9-20). Because of the geopolitical location of and the political history in Finland, education has had special relevance in nation building (Gordon and Lahelma 1998: 258).

Nira Yuval-Davies (1997: 11) argues that, in principle, the most inclusive mode of joining a collectivity is state citizenship; it is the central criterion for membership in the national collectivity. But a myriad of rules and regulations concerning immigration and naturalisation usually ensure that access is easier for some categories of people than for others. T. H. Marshall (1950; see Yuval Davis 1997) defines citizenship as full membership in the community, encompassing civil, political, and social rights and responsibilities. But, Yuval-Davies (1997: 24) points out that the notion of citizenship is both gendered and Eurocentric. Katri Komulainen (2001: 40) notes that citizenship can best be understood as a cultural category, referring to contextually, historically, and materially produced membership of community. Independence is often said to characterise the modern citizen. Children, however, are referred to as dependent, in need of guidance and discipline. The national education system handles children as adults-to-be who need to be raised and educated to become 'proper' citizens, able to exercise their rights, duties and responsibilities in an acceptable way (Gordon *et al.* 2000a: 12).

My theoretical starting point has been the sociological theoretisations of childhood in which the agency of children is taken seriously. Allison James, Chris Jenks, and Alan Prout have identified the ways in which childhood and agency are brought together. In the notion of 'tribal child' children are seen as active and formative within their own social world of the peer group. The notion of 'social structural' or 'minority group' child locates children within the broader social structure. The potential membership of a marginal social grouping constrains their action within the majority group. (James *et al.* 1998; Wyness 2000). Berry Mayall (2002) suggests the view that childhood can be understood as a social position or category which is a permanent component of social order. She argues that generationing processes, specific to various societies, as well as gender, class and ethnicity shape children's lives.

Within such a framework I am influenced by poststructuralist and postcolonial feminist research. In poststructuralist theories society is seen as being constantly created and recreated through discursive practices. Individuals have multiple ways to position themselves within those practices, and to develop subjectivities both in concert with and in opposition to the ways in which others position them (Davies 1989: xi). By following the tradition of humanism, professional discourses of education used to emphasise and celebrate the idea of a coherent, stable, unified and rational identity (cf. St. Pierre 2000; Lappalainen: 2002a). This view is challenged by Elizabeth St. Pierre (2000: 502-503), who argues from a poststructural feminist perspective that a subject, when exhibiting agency, constructs itself by taking up available discourses and cultural practices, while at the same time is subjected and forced into subjectivity by those discourses and practices. The significant questions are who, in a particular discourse, in a particular practice, is allowed to be a subject, and who is not? One who is subjected can, at the same time, become an agentic, speaking subject.

The relevance of postcolonial theories in a context without a colonial past (such as Finland) has been questioned. Colonial reasoning and representations have, for example, been mediated through literature, art, and media (cf. McClintock 1995: 11-13). Therefore I argue that they have their influence on thinking, regardless of whether the national community has a colonial past or not (Lappalainen 2002b, see also Gordon and Holland in this volume).

Cultural heterogeneity was one important criterion when I sought out preschools within which to conduct my research. I assumed that constructions of nationality are more visible in the context in which Finnishness, as a taken-for-granted frame, becomes problematised in everyday interaction. In order to illustrate the constructions of nations and nationalities, I present episodes from everyday life in two preschools near Helsinki. My analysis is based on ethnographic fieldwork lasting for one year. The data include written fieldnotes, photographs, videotapes, and recorded unstructured or semi-structured interviews of children, teachers, and parents. This particular analysis draws on fieldnotes and the interviews of children.[1]

The constructions of being Russian are explored in the first subsection, and those of being Somalian in the second.

## The injured Finnish maiden

In ethnographic research in two secondary schools, the research group of Tuula Gordon and Elina Lahelma distinguished three layers of the school: the official school, the informal school, and the physical school (e.g. Gordon et al. 2000a). The official school consists of curriculum, lessons, formal hierarchies, and the disciplinary apparatus. The informal school includes informal hierarchies, application and interpretation of rules, and social interaction. The physical school consists of spatiality and embodiment.

In my analysis I concentrate on the official and the informal layers of (pre)school. In a preschool context these layers may even be more intertwined than at school, but it does not make this distinction less fruitful as an analytical tool. In the official school nationality is constructed, for example, through learning materials, speech in lessons, and school rituals. In the informal school, constructions of nationality occur in everyday interaction (Gordon and Lahelma 1998).

Before presenting the episodes, I introduce the main characters in them[2]. Meri is a teacher of the preschool class and Olga is the teacher's assistant. Olga defines

---

[1] The research is part of the project, *Inclusion/exclusion in educational process,* directed by Dr. Elina Lahelma (2000) and funded by the University of Helsinki and the Academy of Finland.
[2] All names appearing in the episodes, except mine, are pseudonyms.

herself as Russian. Marina, Zahra, and Samia are girls and Timo and Eero boys in the preschool group. Timo's background is in the former Soviet Union. Sometimes he defines himself as Ukrainian, sometimes as Russian and sometimes as Estonian. Zahra's mother is Finnish, while her father comes from Somalia. Zahra defines herself as Finnish. Samia's mother is Finnish, and her father is Moroccan. Samia defines herself as Finnish. Marina and Eero have a Finnish background.

> *Timo gets permission to take his lunch. Olga and Timo discuss quietly in Russian. Marina asks Meri (the teacher):* What language are those two speaking?
> *Meri explains:* Timo can speak Russian.
> *Meri asks Timo and Olga to tell how they say 'good morning', 'thank you' etc., in Russian.*
> *Eero turns to Olga, looks at her a moment and asks:* Can you speak Russian?
> *Olga smiles and says:* Yes, I can.
> *Eero:* Are you Russian?
> *Olga:* Yes, I am Russian. I come from Viipuri near the Finnish border. It's an old Finnish town.
> *Eero:* Russia is really a big country.
> *Olga:* That's true. If Finland is like this *(puts her thumb and forefinger together)*, Russia is like this *(puts her hands about 30 cm from each other).*
> *After that Olga takes a globe from the table and shows Eero.*
> *Olga:* Russia is here and Finland is here.
> *Eero:* Russia has conquered the arm of Finland.
> *Olga puts the globe back onto the table and takes her seat. She looks a little bit stressed.*

Marina's question about language is handled in a sensitive way by Meri and Olga. The capacity to be able to speak Russian is explained as a resource. The discussion between Eero and Olga continues with a focus on language and nationality to questions of territory. Eero seems to handle knowledge of Russian language as a resource that someone might have or might not have, regardless of nationality. Finland becomes constructed as a tiny territory next to the huge Russia.

A few weeks later, the preschool held an 'International week'. Children were asked to bring items from abroad (for example souvenirs) and the staff constructed an exhibition. Overhead transparencies on foreign countries were displayed. Some of the meals had a theme related to a specific country. For example Mexican, Russian, Somalian and Chinese food was offered and tables were decorated in 'national styles'. Immigrant parents were invited to present cultural heritage of 'their own'. One day Meri (the teacher) collected us together in the hall. One of the walls was covered by national flags and with pictures of children representing different families. We all sat quietly, and Meri started a discussion.

> *Meri:* Do you remember what flags we have here in the hall? The first one is the Finnish flag with a picture in which children row a rubber boat in a lake on a sunny day.
> *Meri continues:* What is this flag?
> *Chorus of children shouts:* Finland!
> *Meri:* What is the name of the state?
> *Zahra:* Finnish.
> *Joonas:* Helsinki.
> *Meri:* Is the name of the state Finland?
> *Chorus:* Yeah!
> *Meri:* What is the language spoken in Finland?
> *Chorus:* Finnish!
> *Meri:* Good, all of you knew. But let's make an agreement that we raise our hands. Well, what is our capital?
> *Someone:* Helsinki.
> *Meri:* What is our nationality?
> *Chorus:* Finnish.[3]

Finland is described as a homogeneous country. This construction excludes cultural diversity. Finnish is regarded as the only language spoken in Finland. Even Swedish, the other official language was not mentioned. Nira-Yuval Davies (1997) argues that the concept of the nation-state is based on an assumption of a complete correspondence between the boundaries of the nation and the boundaries of those who live in a specific state. This is a fiction which naturalises the hegemony of one collectivity and its access to the ideological apparatuses of both the state and the civil society. Minorities are constructed into assumed deviances from the 'normal', and excluded from important sources of power.

> *Then Meri asks the questions about language, state, nationality and capital concerning Estonia, but continues:* Timo, your granny or mummy was born in Estonia, wasn't she?
> *Timo:* I don't know.
> *When we discuss the Russian flag, Eero says with full-throated voice:* Damn, Russia has conquered the arm of Finland and little bit of its skirt.
> *Meri:* Yes, that was a long time ago.
> *Eero:* It's a damn stupid country.
> *Timo (with quiet voice):* Russia is stupid, there is nothing to do about it.
> *Meri:* Russia is the neighbour of Finland.
>
> *In the afternoon when we dress for outdoor activities, I ask:* Eero, I think I didn't understand what you said about Russia. Would you please explain it to me?

---

[3] Unfortunately, I did not manage to see or hear clearly enough whether all bilingual children shouted answers to Meri's question, at least Timo, who spoke Russia at home, did.

*Eero begins to draw a figure of Finland on the floor with his finger and starts to explain:* Look at this. This is Finland and. . .
*Meri:* You can show from the map.
*(There is a map of Finland on the wall.) Eero jumps up to the map and starts to explain again:* This is Finland and this is Russia. This is Finland's arm. *(He points at the most narrow part in the north.)*
*I break in:* Is this the other arm? *(I point at the other side in the north.)*
*Eero:* No, it's the head. This was the right arm but that stupid Russia conquered it, and a part of its skirt too. *(He points at the southeast of the country.)*
*Sirpa:* How do you know that?
*Eero:* My mum has told me.

Tuula Gordon and Janet Holland note (in this book) that nation space is not only physical but social and mental space as well. Eero's comment 'Russia has conquered the arm of Finland' does not make sense without thinking of Finland in terms of the metaphor of the Finnish Maiden. An attractive young woman acquired the place as a personification of Finland during its period as a Grand Duchy under Russian rule, and particularly during the 1870s as a manifestation of emerging nationalism and nation building (Paasi 1996). Seppo Knuuttila (1998) argues that metaphorically Finland used to be male, but that Finland in danger became a maiden whose bodily integrity must be defended by all men working together as one. The imagery of the injured Finnish Maid is still strong and lively even though almost six decades have passed since the war between Finland and Russia. From Eero's point of view, the correct borderline - the perfect body of a Finnish Maiden - was the boundary confirmed in the peace of Tartu in 1920.[4]

Every time Russia was discussed Eero raised his voice and mentioned the arm of Finland. The contrast between the sizes of the territories of Russia and Finland seemed to have preoccupied him. Once I saw Eero and Timo looking at a children's world map in which borders were marked not by concrete lines but by stereotypical representations of cultural artefacts. (For example the borderline between Finland and Russia was marked by an orthodox church and a ballet dancer). Eero was perfectly aware how far away to the east the territory of Russia extends. The boys compared both territories and pointed out how huge Russia is.

When I asked how Eero had formulated his concept concerning Finland and Russia, Eero mentioned his mother as a source of information. A few months later I interviewed Antti, a boy from the other preschool in my field-work. We talked about friends, and Antti mentioned Finnishness as one criterion for a good friend.

*Sirpa:* Well, we talked about friends, so how do you know then that someone is a Finn?

---

[4] After the Winter War (1939-40), Finland ceded areas from both the northeast and the southeast to the Soviet Union thus giving the current border its form.

*Antti:* Colour.
*Sirpa:* Colour?
*Antti:* Yes, the Colour of the skin.
*Sirpa:* The Colour of the skin? How about Swedes or Russians then?
*Antti:* I don't like Russians.
*Sirpa:* Really, why not?
*Antti:* Because Russia took a part of Finland.
*Sirpa:* Really, you know that story?
*Antti:* Yes I know.
*Sirpa:* How have you learnt it?
*Antti:* Because everybody has talked about it.
*Sirpa:* Was it here in preschool when there was some talk about the other countries?
*Antti:* No, they didn't mention Russia at all.
*Sirpa:* Hm, do you remember who told you about it, your mother...
*Antti:* (with a snort) Everybody has told me.
*Sirpa:* Everybody has told you it was quite a long time ago...
*Antti:* A nice friend is someone who gives free Pokemon cards.

Russia emerged into the discussion because of my attempt to problematise the idea about the strict connection between the skin colour and the nationality. Finnishness becomes constructed as whiteness (cf. Gordon 2001). Unlike Eero, Antti did not name any particular source of information and turned the discussion away from the theme when I tried to discuss more about it. The piece of land lost in the war a long time ago appeared to him as a legitimate reason to dislike Russian people.

In the preschool territories of Finland and Russia are discussed by boys. When analysing young people's reflections on military service Elina Lahelma (2001) has pointed out that the word 'fatherland' often has direct military connotations among young men. Benedict Anderson (1991) defines the nation as an imagined community. One of the strategies to imagine the modern nation is as a national narrative told by national histories, literature, media and popular culture (Hall 1999). Anssi Paasi (1996) argues that the boundary with Russia, or the Soviet Union, has been one essential ideological constituent in the historical construction of the grand narrative of Finnish nation building and the cultural 'semiosphere' of the state. Päivi Harinen (2000) suggests that the boundary with Russia forms a central part of a Finnish national narrative. Russia is narrated as a 'demon of history' and a self-evident threat. Finnishness is constructed by collective memory which includes the idea of a small and persistent community forced to defend itself against a bigger and more powerful one.

National narratives can be read as available discourses or resources in the process of subject formation. Máirtín Mac an Ghaill (1999) emphasises the importance of locating masculinity by examining the locally situated interplay between class, sexuality, 'race'/ethnicity and age, in order to comprehend fully how institutional contexts produce, normalise and regulate emerging forms of sexuality. The Finnish maiden in need of being defended is an established metaphor that works as a cultural device for naturalising hierarchies of gender (cf. Chambers 2001: 76). The metaphor constructs heterosexuality as a normal form of sexuality and in doing so strengthens the reproduction of the nation.

## Somalian clothes

During the international week we were familiarised with Somalian culture. First we could smell and taste spices. After that Meri (the teacher) showed us transparencies. Most of them were taken from the countryside. Domestic animals were a common visual illustration. One of the slides got special attention. In the following extract Riia and Tiina are girls and Juuso a boy with a Finnish background:

>*Samia:* Children with blankets.
>*Meri:* This is a Somalian school. *Some of the children laughed at the picture.*
>*Meri:* What is different here compared to a Finnish school?
>*Samia:* There are no seats and no walls.
>*Meri:* They don't need walls because it's so warm there.
>*Timo:* Why do they have those blankets then?
>*Meri:* In Somalia they use a different kind of clothes, robes.
>*Timo:* I don't ever want to go to Somalia.
>*Meri:* They are used to sitting on the ground.
>*Riia:* I would never like to go.
>*Samia:* Neither would I.

The next illustration was a town scene, with some houses and towers.

>*Juuso:* Is that one a jail? *(points to one of the houses with his finger)*
>*Meri:* No it isn't. It's an ordinary house. Those shutters are there because of heat.
>*Eight people of different ages had been photographed in the next slide. This slide got more attention.*
>*Meri:* This is a Somalian family. For Somalians the family is beloved, very important.
>*Tiina:* Look, she has a baby!
>*Samia:* She has a headscarf.
>*Meri:* Somalian women are used to wearing different clothes than us. You have seen this in Finland too. They have headscarves. Their hair and mouth are covered.
>*Samia:* Their hair is not allowed to be seen by men.
>*Meri:* That's true.
>*Samia:* Because of the men.

*Timo:* They are angry.
*Samia:* They aren't. They just look angry.
*Zahra comes and takes her seat.*
*Meri:* Zahra's father comes from Somalia.
*Zahra has a confused smile on her face.*
*Timo:* I come from Tallinn.
*Eero laughs and says:* I'm Russian! —no I' m not I'm Finnish.
*Timo:* Are you really Russian?
*Juuso grins and says:* I'm Chinese.

Applying the distinction between the layers of the school is particularly helpful when analysing a complex episode like this. Transparencies, Meri's speech and the way the activities are organised represent the official (pre)school. The countryside with domestic animals was a theme in most of the illustrations which emphasised the lack of material resources in the countries illustrated. However, preschool children were also directed to pay attention to differences. They were asked to identify what was different at school, and Samia paid attention to the absence of seats. Somalia became conceptualised as a poor and unpleasant place. When looking at a family portrait the baby was not discussed but the headscarf was, even though the headscarf covered only the hair of the mother. Children were told that Somalian women wear different clothes than we do. The variation between Somalian women was not discussed. One of the postcolonial critics has pointed out that in the multicultural approach all members of a minority group are assumed to be equally committed to that culture. The members of minority groups become easily constructed as homogeneous, speaking with a unified voice (Yuval-Davies 1997).

The representation of a Somalian woman constructed by Samia, Meri, and Timo was a woman with her face covered with a veil. The representation emphasised cultural difference more than the actual illustration: 'otherness' becomes established through an imagined veil. When saying 'they are angry' Timo expresses the idea about 'the other' as threatening. Samia takes a position as an interpreter of the culture. She explains the function of the scarf and makes sure that everybody understands. She expresses that she understands Timo's point of view. But she also corrects Timo's impression about the state of mind of Somalian women. Gender relations are discussed through embodiment and clothes: women are supposed to be protected by the veil against the contaminating gaze of men.

People take up and further develop various subject positions in their everyday lives (Søndergaard 2002). The last section of the above episode represents the informal (pre)school. Timo's parents are from the former Soviet Union. Sometimes he defines himself as Ukrainian, sometimes as Russian and sometimes as Estonian. In this situation it seems to be important to him to define himself as Estonian. My interpretation is that in this situation nationality becomes problematised and Timo emphasises a difference in relation to Somalia by choosing the position which he evaluates as the best one in this particular situation. Eero's joke 'I'm Russian' and Juuso's comment: 'I'm Chinese', undermine Timo's position. A social order between boys may be in the process of being negotiated through discussions about nationality.

## Gendered nationalism

When analysing texts concerning foreign policy in Finland, Outi Lepola (2000) suggests that a cultural image of Finland is developed by exaggerating conceptions of cultural homogeneity which marginalise ethnic minorities and cultural diversity. Anne McClintock (1995: 352-353) argues that all nationalisms are gendered, invented and dangerous. According to McClintock nations are historical practices through which social differences are invented and performed. Production of nationality is an issue in the preschool context too. In the official layer of (pre)school nationalism as a gendered phenomena is seen in crystallised form particularly in different kinds of celebrations, for example celebrations of Christmas or the Day of Independence (cf. Lappalainen 2002b). Nationalism is an issue in the informal layer of preschool as well. Among the six-year-old boys it took the form of territoriality. A potential threat often seems to be involved when boys discuss 'the other'. McClintock (1995) notes that there is no single narrative of nation. Different groups (genders, classes, ethnicities, generations and so on) experience the myriad of national formations in diverse ways. When analysing women's school memories from the 1930s, Katri Komulainen (2001) has traced ways of relating to Finnish national ideology as transmitted by schooling: Celebrations experienced as uplifting by Finnish women might have been experienced as fanatic patriotism, even as racism, by immigrant women. Many of the Finnish national representations draw on the territories lost in the last two wars.[5] National masculinity is constructed and the Finnish male becomes positioned as the defender of the arm and skirt of the Finnish maiden.[6] I suggest that the history of the conflicts with the former Soviet Union (1939-1944) has impinged upon the territorial identity and integrity of Finland, This concerns not only the project of nation building, but also the question of constructing a heterosexual masculinity which includes a continual readiness to defend Finland's territorial integrity against enemy attacks coming from the 'east' (cf. Harinen 2000). In other words Finnish national masculinity is characterised by territoriality.

The educational system is one way, but not the only way, of preparing children for interpreting some experiences as national (cf. Paasi 1998: 13). When studying young people in the eastern part of Finland, Anne-Mari Keskisalo and Sini Perho (2001: 81) have pointed out that the common idea about flexible and cosmopolitan youth is partly a myth. There are young people whose position is characterised by

---

[5] The history of the two wars between Finland and the Soviet Union (1939-1940) and (1941-1944).
[6] Discussion with Reetta Mietola, Katariina Hakala and Anu Åberg 22 August 2001.

resistance to cosmopolitanism. These young people are focused on tradition and the past instead of the future. The experiences of previous generations were mobilised when six-year-old boys in my research preschools discussed Russia. As Russians constitute the biggest single immigrant group in Finland (Statistics Finland 2001), national narratives, when marginalising them, are a challenge to education equality. When discussing Somalia the logic of exclusion is different: the covered hair and mouth of a Somalian woman became interpreted as hostile. The threat is based on something which is not seen. It assumes personification in the representation of a Somalian woman. Anna Rastas (2002: 14) notes that seeing difference is a cultural phenomenon: visual meanings are constructed discursively. Difference is not only considered as a characteristic which is seen, but also as a construction. The formation of the meanings attached to it influence the observer's ability to interpret what she/he sees within the various and cultural landscapes and catalogues. When studying Finnish young people who were considered to be non-white, Anna Rastas (2002: 13) has pointed out that some of those young people noticed fear in other people's gaze.

## Conclusions

International or multicultural weeks are common tools in preschool pedagogy. The international week in this preschool was organised with fantastic enthusiasm; there were events such as exhibitions, music, food and dance. But while observing, I began to wonder whether it would be possible to celebrate things shared, rather than celebrating differences. We were invited to compare cultures. Differences became emphasised, being constructed in relation to an eastern neighbour and a country in the southern hemisphere. We were not invited to talk about the Scandinavian 'life style', even though Finland has a common border with Sweden and Norway, and even though the number of Swedish people living permanently in Finland is far larger than the corresponding number of Somalian people (Statistics of Finland 2001).

In the social sciences, space is represented using images characterised by breaking, rupturing and disjunction, whereas nations, societies, and cultures are understood as unproblematic divisions of space. For example, the world is represented as a collection of 'countries', divided by different Colours into diverse national societies, each 'rooted' in its proper place (Gupta and Ferguson 1997: 33-34).[7] According to Anthony Giddens (1989), sociologists tend to define culture as a particular way of life, whether of people, a period, or a group. Such a way of life is constituted by the values, the norms, and the material goods created by the group. These ways of making sense of the world are intensively promoted in the official and physical layers of preschool. Children were encouraged to search for

---

[7] Problematisations concerning connections of nations, space and culture are mainly produced by postcolonial and feminist research.

differences between cultures, whereas similarities were not discussed. More than one wall in my research preschools was covered with maps. National symbols, for example national flags, were identified. During the international weeks families were encouraged to bring items from home to the preschool so that libraries and halls looked like an ethnographic museum. When studying young people's speech about immigrants, Leena Suurpää (2001) has pointed out that the social and cultural space for immigrants appears restricted in Finland: their activities can be intelligible and even welcome in controlled and predictable circumstances, for example, as presenters of their ethnic origin in multicultural events or as restaurateurs. These restrictions, continues Suurpää, concern people coming particularly from non-European societies. It is a concern for politics of equality if certain groups of people become conceptualised as a resource two weeks per year, and as a problem during the remaining 50 weeks of the year.

Stuart Hall (1999) argues that national culture is a discourse: It is a way to construct and arrange meanings which organise our action and help to construct our individual identity. National cultures acquire a strong feeling of their own identity by comparing themselves to other cultures (Hall 1999). In this sense, it may be that the celebration of internationality is thus experienced more as a celebration of Finnishness.

## Part III: Discourses and Practices
## 7

## The politics of time in educational restructuring

### Daniel Sundberg

*The Mock turtle went on:*
*'We had the best of educations – in fact, we went to school every day'.*
                        \*                    \*                    \*
*'And how many hours a day did you do lessons?' said Alice, in a hurry to change the subject.*
*'Ten hours the first day, 'said the Mock Turtle, 'nine the next, and so on'.*
*'What a curious plan!' exclaimed Alice.*
*'That's the reason they're called lessons,' the Gryphon remarked; 'because they lessen from day to day'.*
*'Then the eleventh day must have been a holiday?'*
*'Of course it was,' said the Mock Turtle.*
*'And how did you manage on the twelfth?'*
                from *Alice in Wonderland* by Lewis Caroll (1993, 55)

### Introduction

Time is, in educational restructuring, increasingly becoming a nexus for social control in education and schooling. I use the term restructuring here in a broad sense, meaning changed relations between societal fields such as education, the state, civil society and the market which also involve processes of *rescaling*, i. e. changed relations between global, national and local contexts (cf. Daun and Benincasa 1998). These social changes, I will argue, involve new modes of control in education concerning the social administration of time in schools. I use data on educational policy discourses in Sweden during the last decade and ethnographic data from an ongoing investigation of the reform of time frames in the Swedish comprehensive school emanating from the school reform *Without a national timetable in compulsory school* (Ds 1999:1) in order to conceptualise these changes. My purpose is to explore and investigate the educational consequences of the reform and to identify how new policy shifts discursively, for instance from outer-directed prescriptions (such as the national timetable) to inner-directed self-regulation, through the disembedding of time and space as a contested issue of power and control, or what Gordon, Holland and Lahelma (2000a) refer to as a differentiation of time-space paths in social institutions (also Giddens 1991; Harvey 1990). Popkewitz and Brennan (1998) refer to this as a radical reconception of space and time that 'shifts attention from notions of geographically bounded contexts that develop in chronological sequences' to notions of regions bounded by 'a discursive field and uneven time dimensions' (Popkewitz and Brennan 1998: 12). Although time is one of the most constitutive factors in teaching it is often neglected in educational research. An ethnographic approach is useful here, because it is context sensitive and provides multiple aspects of practice. Moreover, I argue, along with Fairclough and Chouliaraki (2000), that it is necessary to recognise the discursive elements of social change and adopt linguistic reflexivity. Timetables have been a part of the Swedish national curricula since the common compulsory school was established in the 1960s. They have worked to nationally regulate school time by providing a general frame as well as time allocations (syllabi) for different subjects. I use the reform of general time frames as an example of how the politics of time has moved from the state arena to the local school arena in educational restructuring. This, I will argue, is not merely a technical and organisational question, but also a political one. As Gándara suggests: 'Time is not just time, but a political resource as well. The use of time in schools requires that important decisions be made about how this resource will b:e distributed and who will wield the power over its distribution' (Gándara 2000: 7; cf. Adams 1995).

The point of departure of my investigation is based on a critical perspective on the question of reform. This perspective holds a notion of a dynamic view of change where the dialectics between social structures and agency interplay in every-day-action, language and practice (Fritzell 1996; Beach 1995, 2000) and requires a reconsideration of the scientific-technical rationality underpinned by an interventionist policy perspective. The critical perspective is concerned with the moral-political basis of change and asks what changes imply for school as an arena for democratic deliberation and learning (Hammersley 1994). Reforms are understood as non-linear and polyvocal. They contain struggle and disparate meanings and consequences. There is no straight progression from reform intentions and plans to change (implementation) and developments or outcomes. The ongoing restructuring processes are part of discursive dynamics, interlinked with economic competition and politics of globalisation (Stronach *et al.* 2002), recognised in specific social and cultural settings. Discourse analytical ethnography, as employed here, explores this interrelation between the discourse of restructuring policies and processes, and their contexts of enactment.

## Educational restructuring: from state regulation to self regulation

Social, economic, cultural and political changes in late modern society have interplayed with processes of restructuring in educational systems and governance during the 1980s and the 1990s in most European countries (Daun and Benincasa 1998; Lindblad and Popkewitz 2000b and this volume). This restructuring includes governance, organisation and regulation of school systems on a national level, as well as curriculum organisation and classroom practice. Even if there is local variation, some converging themes such as decentralisation, the introduction and reinforcement of choice possibilities and privatisation/reinforced support to private schools enable us to address these processes as transnational (Daun and Benincasa 1998; Daun 2002). Sweden, USA, UK and New Zealand are among the OECD-countries that have been most responsive to the globalisation trends and have started restructuring processes in the 1990s (Whitty et al. 1998; Daun and Benincasa 1998; Blomqvist and Rothstein 2000). The control of schools in these countries can be said to have undergone an epistemic shift corresponding to a movement from government to governance in education.

The wider implications of such an epistemic shift need to be placed in a historical context. The model of the comprehensive school became dominant during the second half of the twentieth century in all Nordic countries (Tjeldvold 1998). The establishing of the 9-year comprehensive school in Sweden (*grundskolan*) was to a large extent a product of rational modernity and thus characterised by a 'regime of visibility' (cf. Rose 1999: 135). Nationwide common contents and timetables, representing what was considered a homogenous culture, were compulsory for all students. Schools were organised in a rational and instrumental way – limited in scope as well as depth of focus. Detailed plans for activities, subjects, times and places were elaborated to reduce the complexities of social interaction. Through these plans conformity and deviation could be judged, coded, compared, ranked and measured. School life was temporalised in clearly defined modules, courses and lessons. Gordon, Holland and Lahelma (2000a) refer to these fixed time-space paths as constitutive of the institutional order of schools. They are crucial in the process whereby a child becomes 'a pupil' (Salo, this volume).

During the 1980s and the 1990s the assumptions of the rational-modernist school project became contested in Sweden and the long tradition of consensus in school reforms was broken. Cultural homogeneity was questioned because of immigration and increased international communication and technological development. The new economic situation, it was argued, called for a more innovative and effective school organisation. Political practice, from the 1990s, became increasingly a matter of alliances rather than unity around universal interests and identities (Fairclough and Chouliaraki 2000; Lindensjö and Lundgren 2000). Accountability, performativity and efficiency became keywords that implied a changing relationship between the state and the school as a response to the crisis of legitimacy of the welfare state and a massive new-right wing, neo-liberal criticism of cost ineffective centralised bureaucracy (Klette et al. 2000; Falkner 1997; Daun 1998). From having previously been centred round the 'regime of visibility', the curriculum in the 1990s began to follow principles of the 'regime of flexibility' (Sennett 2000).

Restructuring processes concern not only structural changes in the educational system (as flexibility and freedom of choice) but also ideological shifts that cause an intensified struggle between different policy discourses. A discourse of self-regulation is emerging in a tension between economic and democratic imperatives. There are shifts on the one hand towards local freedom, democracy and collegiality, and on the other hand towards managerialism, performativity and accountability. The question is whether this new discourse aids democratic participation and deliberation or represents a subtle form of disciplining in the interests of market rationalities (Beach this volume). It is not useful to presuppose a binary construction between policy and practice in answering this question, but instead to look at policy as discourse (Ball 1994). Policy does not operate at a level above the practice, but is constituted/reconstituted in discursive fields, locally as well as globally. It is a course of action (or inaction) where the defining and allocation of goals, values and resources (such as time) are discursively legitimated (Marshall and Peters 1999) and provide support for certain relationships and types of interaction but not others (Ball and Maguire 1994; Beach 2000).

## Equality vs efficiency

The establishment of the welfare state during the period of 1947-1975 raised questions of how to allow diversity in a united comprehensive system. The answer was sought for in rational planning and control. In the educational discourse of the 1950s and 1960s the question of differentiation was part of the modernist discourse of technocratic and rationalist concern of efficiency. It is, as Broadfoot, suggests, 'an odd irony that the assessment technologies were part of a reformist mission of justice through rationality' (1995: 174). The national timetable (NTT) played an important role in the first and second generation of comprehensive school reforms (Ds 1999:1) both as an administrative control over the input of curriculum resources but also as an instrument for creating equality. The bureaucratic structure and its rationalised way of looking at time are slowly transformed through a discursive construction of 'the self-regulated learner' based on individualisation, 'disciplinisation', goal-rationalisation, and decontextualisation. This development does not merely reflect a replacement of central state control but rather its transformation from direct to 'liberal' technologies of indirect control (Power 1997; Rose 1999). Self-regulation refers to an emerging mode of performativity-based regulation. The Swedish compulsory school as a 'school of modernity' was based on a principle of simple rather than complex equality (Walzer 1983). However, the idea of simple equality and centralised uniformity of educational provision has historically proved to be insufficient for achieving social justice. The underlying assumption behind this idea is potentially deterministic and stigmatising as it relies on classifying special needs of certain social groups (such as gender, ethnic, class, disability, rural, generation, and religion). Complex equality involves allocating different social goods according to criteria of difference. Thus, we face a dilemma: how do we know what counts as a relevant difference.

The third generation of reforms in the Swedish comprehensive school has to deal with this question in a quite different situation. The legitimacy of the national curriculum has been questioned and the autonomy of local schools has increased at the same time as decentralised governance has been introduced that no longer sets strong frames for action but rather works by 'demands on results' (Lindensjö and Lundgren 2000). This shift from a pre-active to post-active state steering can also be seen in the light of national tests, large-scale surveys and school ranking (also Lindblad and Popkewitz, this volume). The decentralisation of steering intertwines with a centralisation of strategies. The discourse of the self-regulated learner seems in this respect to have replaced the discourse of centralised egalitarianism. The values, purposes and procedures underlying new ways of organising the school curriculum involve an increasing concern with effectiveness and accountability rather than community and equality (Lindblad et al. 2002). The tension in educational restructuring between schooling for global competition in economic efficiency and schooling for democratic deliberation in public dialogue is becoming more salient not only in educational policy making but also in everyday school practice.

## The national timetable reform and the ethnographic study of Small Town High

The national timetable reform (the NTT-reform) was proposed by the Public School Committee in 1999 and initiated by Parliament as a five-year experiment in which about 20 percent of the comprehensive schools in different municipalities were permitted to freely decide the allocation and regulation of time, in relation to the goals of syllabus. To legitimise this experiment, quantitative measures were introduced for steering by goals, for individualisation and for local decision-making. There was very little discussion, however, about the goals that individualisation was aimed at. Means and ends are instrumentally defined to exclude qualitative, value related and internal changes.

Klette *et al.* (2000) have identified an ever-growing instrumentalism and managerialism in the Nordic countries during the process of restructuring. One significant feature of this is that, as Popkewitz suggests, common distinctions of individualisation and flexibility are often posited as 'means separate from ends' (Popkewitz 1991: 155). In the NTT-policy this instrumental reasoning and the decontextualisation of teaching is tangible (Ds 1999:1). First, it is stated that how equity is realised must be decided in every school, not by the state. Second, to manage this mission the school must be able to plan and use its resources in a flexible and goal rational way. Third, in this respect the national timetable is regarded as outmoded, unnecessary and as an obstacle for effective teaching and organisation (Ds 1999:1, 46). Fourth, the NTT-reform thus should be regarded as a tool in the elimination of obstacles in order to stimulate more desirable forms of schoolwork. The NTT-reform can be analysed as a prism of these changes. Time is an important question here. The linear conception of time has been replaced by a more dynamic, pluralistic and fragmented conception in the discourse of the self-regulated learner. The keywords of the restructuring policies – effectiveness, flexibility, goal rationality – are in fact temporal. This means that from the macro-aspects of restructuring, I have identified some general tendencies of new modes of control inherent in discourses of educational change. These aspects do not, according to Codd (1988 cited in Marshall and Peters 1999) work on a level above practice, but are encapsulated in daily encounters, as also Berlak and Berlak (1981: 125) suggest.

In order to understand how these changes influence the daily life in school I conducted ethnographic fieldwork in one school since the start of the experimental period. The school, 'Small Town High', participated in the aforementioned school experiment. The school is a year 7 through 9, (equivalent to UK 9 through 11) secondary school of about 300 students. Some 70 percent of students live in a periphery surrounding the school and go to school by bus. Because of the school bus, the time frame of the school day is from 8. 30 to 15. 00. The school has started an extensive process of changes in curriculum organisation and stated the following aims for giving up the timetable:

(i) to encourage management by objectives;

(ii) to stimulate inter-disciplinary/inter-subject thematic work;

(iii) to enable more individualisation and to respond to the diversity of students; and

(iv) to allow local conditions to play a more important role in the curriculum and teaching.

A school-based timetable was constructed to include class teaching in the morning and option-choice courses in the afternoon. About one third of the total time in school is thus open for the students' choices. A highly sophisticated course system was elaborated to respond to the needs of individual students. For example, to allow them to catch up in specific subjects, courses like 'German grammar' and 'More Math' were created. Students' interests were taken into account through integration of leisure and school activities, for example in subjects like 'Photo' and 'Hunting and fishing'. Finally, cross-subject, thematic schoolwork was planned in order to counteract tendencies toward balkanisation of the curriculum: 'The school newspaper' and 'The American lifestyle' are examples of these kinds of courses. The school year was divided into four periods with one 'buffer week' between each period, including extra time for re-examinations and a so called 'Open Time' for home work, unfinished work and unfinished courses.

During the fieldwork at the school I was aware of certain tensions and dilemmas in the processes of change. The majority of the teachers was positive about the reform and saw it as part of their development work at the school. However, there was also awareness—although seldom articulated—of the disadvantages of restructuring and feelings of loss, anxiety and struggle were voiced. Furthermore, alongside individualisation, choice and flexibility that the reform was supposed to fulfil, there was also intensification, enhanced stress and loss of control. Observation and follow-up interviews with teachers, students and principals, made it possible to understand the complexities involved in the implementation of the reform. Different stories of educational change involve both similarities and differences in motives and vocabularies between different subjects, teachers, students and principals.

The head teacher and deputy head deliberately chose a low profile in the restructuring and argued that the teachers must conduct the development work. They saw the territorial defence of subject time and the lack of time for common planning as the major dilemmas of change. Helen, the deputy head, commented as follows:

> I feel that subject teachers in secondary school live too much with watertight bulkheads between the subjects. There is much knowledge among the teachers, they are very competent, but a comprehensive view on students is lacking.

Internal evaluations carried out by the school suggest that students were generally satisfied with the opportunity to choose courses and with the open, less class-bound teaching. But they also experienced the limits of this optional freedom when they did not get the courses they chose, because of course collisions and problems with changes in schedules and locations. Small Town High has strong relations with the local community. To some extent this can explain how the discourse of the self-regulated learner has been incorporated in the development work in school. The local community is well known for its 'entrepreneurial spirit'. The local culture of 'coping on your own' and finding developmental ideas is also identifiable in the culture of the school.

## Reform implementation: ambiguities and responses of hybridisation

One significant difficulty inscribed in the NTT-reform is its supposed simplicity. Policy documents are constructed around flexibility, goal rationality and local freedom, and a national timetable is considered as a 'technical' obstacle for the desired change. At Small Town High this was the point of departure in implementing the reform and initiating organisational changes. The NTT-policy text was interpreted in congruence with the intentions of existing development work. High expectations were raised in creating a flexible organisation, built on student-centeredness. New organisational plans were elaborated and a new course system was introduced to promote students' own choices and influence. One of the main driving forces was Barbro, who has worked as a teacher at the school for a long time:

> *Daniel:* What was it primarily you wanted to change?

*Barbro:* It was to a large extent that the kids sit in the lessons doing the same things ... for you know, you acquire knowledge at a different pace. Some need to work a lot with basics, others have the requirements to enter deeply into subjects, and because you choose more freely it's funnier, even if it actually isn't funnier ...
*Daniel:* More individualised ...
*Barbro:* Yes ... to everyone according to their need ...
*Daniel:* By choice ...
*Barbro:* Yes... and at the same time [that] we as tutors try to steer those with problems for example in Swedish, English or maths, so they can work at a different pace, so they can work with time ... for basically, it's about time ... you don't acquire everything [at] the same pace ...

The process of implementation of the reform faced some difficulties in the culture of the school, as it involved changes in the embedded temporality of institutional order and life. Such institutional resistance is also identified by Cambone (1994) in a study of temporality in American public schools. As he demonstrated, the embedded temporality of the school involves identities, self-perceptions, status-relations between subjects, confidence and trust. When we speak about the culture of schools, we are speaking of cyclical time of schools. Cambone (1994) elaborates this further:

> The rhythm and tempo of school life shape ... activities and ... meaning ...
> It is not surprising that efforts to change those cycles – by lengthening teaching periods, instituting schools within schools, having teachers teach fewer classes, building in collaboration periods where there were none before – are met with difficulty.           (Cambone 1994: 1)

As social interaction in school becomes less centred and fixed, new ways of dealing with uncertainties are formed. In responding to changes and new conditions for teaching, signs of hybridisation of traditional and progressive discourses can be seen. The teacher, like Walter Benjamin's *Angelus Novus*, is drawn into the future – into the accelerated 'now-flux' of time – while s/he is all the time looking back. The written rules, the articulated need for more specified goals, performance indicators and fixed marking grades are included among reactions to new uncertainties.

Ann, who has been working as a language teacher at the school for three years, expresses the 'ambivalence of control' involved in the conception of the self-regulated learner:

> *Ann:* It's very difficult, I feel how it limps ... that you get what you need from the chosen course ... from some teachers you don't hear anything about how it has gone on the courses, they say nothing. So, we have a little form to fill in. If they have worked well, that's a plus, or worse, a minus, or in between, that's a zero.           (teacher interview)

Aware of this 'limping' Ann is drawn into the ambivalence of control, looking back while moving forward. She articulates this ambivalence by reference to her feelings ('I feel how it limps') but responds in an instrumental way. These new uncertainties among teachers about their work and their selves can be connected to dilemmas of the modern self that Giddens (1991) has identified (cf. Woods and Jeffrey 2002). Ann's ambivalence about control and her efforts to resolve this by using quantifiable assessment can be understood as efforts to 'sidestep the personal and local, putting emphasis on the abstract and the universal' (Woods and Jeffrey 2002: 97). This ambivalence of control is manifest in the curriculum: the compulsory part of subject teaching (morning lessons) is getting more traditional and the optional part of integrated curriculum courses (afternoon lessons) more progressive.

> *Ann:* [In the afternoon courses] we have more free work, if it's not a course for 'slow' learners. You can do your research and work independently in a lesson of 60 minutes. And it's also necessary that it is freer, because you cannot sit still 60 minutes and read English, there has to be variation. On class time you have 40 minutes in the language studies, so it is more of traditional bench-work, with tasks from the textbook. (interview)

For Ann, the self-perception of what it means to be a good, professional teacher is closely related to control. The more traditional class time is in this respect important for Ann's self-perception as a good teacher. The specific kind of hybridisation is a response to the concurring imperatives of the discourse of professionalism. These comprise internal criteria for actions, the discourse of accountability and performativity and external criteria on output measures (Jeffrey 1999). Ann feels trapped in between professional autonomy, on the one hand, and audit accountability on the other. A loss of control turns easily to feelings of guilt for not having lived up to self-perceptions of teacher professionalism:

> *Ann:* Well, yes—just about—I have some time [for planning], and I should cut something down to have time, but I have problems in cutting things down and still being satisfied ... it all depends on me. (interview)

The discursive construction of the learner in discourses of educational reform implies a move from the outer-directed to the inner-directed learner. One consequence of changes in our perceptions about the learner in school is that the collective endeavour, built on loyalty within groups, has been replaced by individualism. Where shame was a feature of norm anomalies in classroom interaction of the 1950s and 1960s (arriving late for lesson, for example), the norms of today are to a higher degree constructed around individual guilt (Hargreaves 1994). Through self-inspection, self-problematisation and self-monitoring students are to evaluate themselves according criteria provided by others. Despite the enforcement of inner-directed self-regulation at Small Town High, the students are still aware of the monitoring of school performances:

*Barbro:* Yes, there are students who are very afraid of not having done everything they need to do in order to be approved, or whether they have sufficient knowledge skills. But I think it is an exaggerated fear... You try to give them what is absolutely basic, but then it isn't just me who teaches them everything or that they do everything anyway, so ... it isn't as if everything we pour in stays ... unfortunately (interview)

Barbro evokes questions of equity and discusses the responses to self-regulation given by different students. It is obvious, though, that the discourse of equity and equality is not easily comprehensible within the discourse of the self-regulated learner. For Barbro, the conflicts and contradictions between the discourses of common good and instrumental reason may be felt but they are not articulated. The implementation of the reform seems to have intensified the underlying dilemma between 'collective self-direction' versus 'self-control'. The discourse of the self-regulated learner provides an inadequate vocabulary for collective self-direction. The previously highly structured time-space paths of institutional order seem to have been challenged by more loosely pre-structured and less visible paths as part of a new politics of time. Collective practices of regulation and negotiation of time in school have become salient.

## The politics of time in the processes of change at Small Town High

In the local processes of restructuring, the new politics of time concern not only the allocation of subject time between teachers, but also classroom time between teachers and students, as well as teaching and non-teaching time between teachers and head teachers. As time is an increasingly limited resource in school, due to the policy and information overload, the emergence of a new politics of time has become salient. The temporal frames of Small Town High have imploded and challenged the cultural borders between different subjects, as well as between teachers and policy makers/administrators, concerning teachers teaching time and non-teaching time. Helen, the assistant principal, points at this changed politics of time at the school:

*Helen:* Previously we followed the national timetable and the subjects fought over the space available. They submitted their requirements and the Head decided. This year the development group has a proposal which has been discussed in the working teams and which the Head thereafter confirmed. (interview)

The new politics of time in the implementation of the NTT-reform is not explicit and well defined. A major part of the micro-politics is implicit in school culture and embedded in time structures and routines. It is therefore part of the institutional life and includes a distribution of clock hours and struggles about status, roles and values (Ball 1987). Furthermore, the modes of control implicated in the discursive construction of the self-regulated learner include a number of inherent dilemmas that teachers felt required both intellectual and emotional energy to resolve. The changes in curriculum organisation were intended to increase the students' possibilities to choose and participate, and thus decrease the direct control of teachers. But choice also often means less time in the chosen and compulsory areas. Equity in choosing raises the question of how to deal with equity in the consequences of choices. Björn, a math teacher who has worked twenty years at the school, sees this as the downside of the new optional freedom:

> *Björn:* Well, we sat last term and cut a lot of stuff from the book, but it doesn't seem to work because I had already decided to run my working schedule and had cut a number of tasks. We are running after that ... and it turns out that it probably works because the others got into difficulties with the tests ... what should we include and what should we exclude ... but on the other hand the disadvantage was that it was very high speed ... because we've got less time. (interview)

The politics of time allocation in the national timetable is based on the egalitarian idea of sharing fairly between everyone. The starting point is that equality is constructed through collective sameness. The new politics of time has challenged this egalitarian idea because it has an individualistic point of departure based on difference, not on sameness. In responding to the enforced imperatives of individualisation and the required new skills of time management, forward planning is necessary. Barbro explains:

> *Barbro:* Well, I get notes from other teachers, and then it is above all the basic subjects Swedish, English and Math. Petter and Kalle should take math here, cause they need it, it is a course suitable for them. You always have to be alert [...] so that you don't come afterwards, when the pupil has already chosen, and state that you should have taken this course ... You've had so and so many hours in handicraft, so you can coax them in order to get them where you want. (interview)

Barbro articulates individualisation of time as something that is both reified and negotiable. You have to, as Barbro says, 'coax' the students. Thus time becomes a contested issue of power and control. As the infrastructure of the institutional time-space paths is more differentiated and invisible, there seems to be a demand for more time both by the teachers and students, so that they are able to define their positions, their subjectivity and their aspirations. The management of time, which can be seen as a significant qualification of the self-regulated learner, increasingly becomes an important institutional lesson to master. Österlind (1998) demonstrates succinctly how the strategic competencies of planning are also related to social class. The middle classes seem to have advantages over others in developing these strategic competencies. Ann and Barbro evoke these questions. But they also raise contradictory dilemmas, such as working with the common good, and yet also responding to imperatives of audit accountability and performance. The new politics of time in school seems critical for educationalists engaged in working for equity and equality.

## Concluding reflections

Three main issues emerge out of the ethnographic case study. The first is the conception of the self-regulated learner in policy-making. Choice, time management and flexibility are frequently addressed in official policy. However, the conception of the self-regulated learner is also embedded in a new common sense of restructuring at Small Town High and contains inherent dilemmas concerning the temporal organisation of teaching. The differentiation of time-space paths and the disembedding of time in social institutions (Giddens 1991) promote a new stratification of time, that is a new politics of time in school. The case study suggests that this is not an unproblematic implementation, but involves culturally embedded identities and self-perceptions. Stronach and colleagues (2002: 128) refer to this transformation as the 'Trojan Horse system of self-regulation', which offers managerially rather than professionally determined a priori categories and measures of performance. These new modes of control seem not only to be as powerful as the pre-active state steering but also subtler (Whitty, Power and Halpin 1998). The regime of flexibility and the construction of the self-regulated learner (multi-skilled, efficient, self-reliant, team-oriented, adaptable and flexible) are an increasingly dominant educational policy discourse. The wider implications and unintended side effects of these are yet to be realised.

The second issue is the question of time and modes of control. The temporal aspects of organising school knowledge and the change of these in school practice involve organisational conditions of education, but also have a dynamic interplay within schools. The timetable reform seems to have initiated a new form of micro-politics of time, where the modes of control inherent in the discursive construction of the self-regulated learner have new patterns. The embedded rhythm, pace and coordination of teaching cohere as discursive dynamics, and the hierarchical forms of control, regulations and legal prescriptions are rejected in favour of principles of self-regulation, in combination with 'ex-post corrections' (Woods *et al.* 1997). These new modes of control assume a variety of expressions in school practices and are institutionalised in diverse ways. Behind the rhetoric, in the 'backstage' of decentralisation, devolution and self-steering in Swedish official discourse, these new forms of control need to be investigated as a set of complex networks of control patterns. Critical ethnographic inquiries focusing on the processes of restructuring and teaching practice are most important in understanding school change not as linear, but as involving tensions and dilemmas. Change is specific rather than general, contextual rather than abstract, connected to concurring values rather than a specific norm and pointing at a lot of different solutions rather than to fixed prescriptions of right/wrong courses of action. It is important to question whether these new forms of discursive practices provide equal democratic deliberation and learning. It is necessary to ask how effective is this new politics of time concerning the questions of equity and equality.

Thirdly, the time horizon of curriculum reform and restructuring needs to be considered. The case study of Small Town High is an example of a time clash between policy intentions and the institutional grammar of the local school. A longitudinal perspective is necessary in mapping the career of restructuring policy and reforms in their local institutionalisation. It is not a plain route to realisation, but a complex trajectory into a lived school culture. As the hectic pace of school reforms seems to accelerate in global competition, unrealistic pressure is created for teachers and head teachers as well as students. A national timetable is part of an embedded temporality that has formed an institutional infrastructure for a long time (for example the school year, the subject-based week schedule, and the forty minutes lessons). Further explorations of restructuring policies and processes need to address not only short-term organisational and political (micro political and macro political issues of time in school) but also long-term social and cultural consequences in terms of educating for common good, equity and equality.

# 8

# Becoming a pupil

## Ulla-Maija Salo

*'I've had about enough,' Emma declared. 'You know nothing about the theatre, not the least bit. Less than nothing, and that's that. A theatre is the most important sort of house in the world because that's where people are shown what they could be if they wanted, and what they'd like to be if they dared to and what they really are.' 'A reformatory,' said Moominmamma, astonished.*

(Jansson 1971: 95).

### On the school borderlands

Every autumn new children go to school and become 'pupils'. In Finland they start school the year they reach seven. The start of school is a turning point in their lives, during which many of the school's practices become explicit objects that are wondered at, talked about and questioned. The entrants have a fresh perspective and the new situation prompts them to ask and to wonder out loud. Here, I endeavour to walk through the school door with the children on those first days, and to wonder as one of them.

The present chapter sets out to problematise school from within a more comprehensive social context. More precisely, I am interested in studying the social meaning of attending school from data I gathered in an ethnographic study during the beginning of Year One at a Finnish comprehensive school (Salo 1999). This start and my own first school days are separated by some three decades, and both of my own children have started school in the interim. Thus, in a way the present start is my fourth. However, I am inclined to argue that all those passing years and several repetitions have not made such a fundamental difference.

My analytic point of departure is interactionist. Social interaction in school is not defined directly by educational politics or curricula development as such. Rather, we should understand it in a context of a more comprehensive drama. For me ethnography is very much *ethno graphia* – the writing of culture. In this case, it is writing about dramatic episodes in which social meanings are constructed. My analysis is an effort to link thick ethnographic description (Geertz 1966) and Erving Goffman's (1963) dramaturgical approach to social reality, with a focus on the social dynamics of school interaction.

Studying children ethno-graphically is in many ways an extraordinary undertaking and one that is not without its surprises. Occasionally, I might even question my own adultness and act contrary to what I know 'best' as an adult, mother, researcher and former teacher. But I am convinced that there are a number of ways to be an adult. Perhaps it is quite significant, and relevant to educational policy, that adult resources might include the child within us and the ability to both doubt our own adultness and to challenge the normality of order within each of us. The social construction of a 'pupil' is not limited to a particular school, country, or time period (see Lindblad and Popkewitz in this volume).

Ethnographic analysis suggests a huge variety of new political issues. It challenges the basic discourses concerning the relationship between the child and the school. Traditionally in the field of education the dominating discourse has been that of developmental psychology. However, the liminal situation between the child and the 'pupil' cannot be understood within traditional concepts of that discourse. I argue that the complexity of social and cultural interaction is fundamental in analyses of the worlds of education and teaching. My analysis suggests that the reality constructed by the school is by no means indispensable or the only possible one, but is in fact contingent, conditional and chosen. The limits of school practices and degrees of freedom could also be negotiated in a different way.

The social order in school has been challenged from several macro perspectives. Marxist theories for instance often view the school order in terms of their functional relationships to the accumulation of capital. In this interpretation, abstract and indifferent ways of handling children are seen as socialising them to the world of alienated and instrumental wage labour (Ottomeyer 1978). The problem with this interpretation is that it can tend toward totalisation. The alternative (proletarian, polytechnic, non-alienated) is given without any analysis of the actual interaction in school institutions.

Basil Bernstein (1967) in an early article developed a rather optimistic insight into the growing, relative 'openness' of the social order in school. Bernstein saw an old order, based on 'closure' and public symbolism, as being challenged by a new order of private symbolism. This transition implies changes in the school division of labour. According to Bernstein the role of the teacher as well as time and space at school become less rigid and are not regarded as fixed referents. The authoritative teacher's role of yesterday gives way to the problem poser or the facilitator. As an achievement of modernity, we are to move in a world of openness with greater student choice and autonomy. This optimistic vision, however, is as totalising as the Marxist approach (see James, Jenks and Prout 1998). Chapters in this book suggest that Bernstein's vision has not been achieved (see Gordon and Holland and Sundberg in this volume). Rather than postulating a general and inevitable development we need a more specific ethnographic analysis of actual interactions and institutional changes. From this perspective the basic interests in school reform cannot be conceptualised at the level of macro processes as such.

The establishment of order has its own rationale, not much touched by changes in educational politics and policies. But this is not all. There seems to be an intimate relationship between 'the child' and the idea of social order (James, Jenks and

Prout 1998: 198). In fact, the volatility and fragility of the taken-for-granted adult order is challenged by children themselves. They offer an example of living in the margins of the social order by virtue of their constant promise of liminality.

## Oh almighty order!

I approach the school conceptually through the notion of order. The Finnish word for order, *järjestys,* goes back to the Karelian *järgi,* whose meanings include 'in order, in single file, in a row'. As a verb, the word has also traditionally meant placing things in a row or putting things in order. In the language of the Finnish school, 'order' appears in the words for schedule ('working order'), seating order, order of height and in many other activities found almost exclusively in the school. The original form of the word is *järki,* meaning 'reason', 'sense'. Everything in school is sense-making and should be done with reason. In assignments, rabbits, teddy bears, letters and numbers are usually in rows, lined up, written or drawn on lines and in a straight line. And these rows and lines have to be done as the teacher says, with everyone doing their work as neatly and tidily as they possibly can.

I suggested that in the field of education school pupils are usually viewed in terms of developmental psychology, but the many forms of order in the school are manifestly social in nature. In addition to their having numerous consequences for the pupils, these forms of order can be considered outcomes themselves. As Goffman (1963: 8) observes, 'a social order may be defined as the consequence of any set of moral norms that regulates the way in which persons pursue objectives. Social order, in other words, is a fundamental element of social existence – one of the features which define a society'. Sets of norms also specify the ways in which people strive to conform to norms. Taking Goffman's idea a bit further, one might ask for a description of the sets of norms whose outcomes pupils represent.

From an ethnomethodological perspective, order is ultimately something external, something taken more or less as natural; action is then *context-shaped,* or conforming to some order. But this is only part of the picture; action can also take shape in context and be *context renewing* (see Heritage 1989, 1996). This observation provides the motivation for my own research as well. For the pupils, the new schoolchildren, order seems to be an abstract and external sociosymbolic world, whose symbols are still alien to them. Or, with no explanations offered for the symbols, pupils have to come up with accounts themselves. This is how Mikko construes why children have to sit in their seats and be still:

'There ... It'd stir up dust and someone might have an asthma attack.'
(Interview)

Children have a distinct way of producing meaning for their everyday life in the school. All of us look at our world in established, routine ways and from the perspective of our own social and personal orders. The above excerpt from the interview shows how people arrive at socially sensible meanings in different ways. Or, as Garfinkel puts it: 'the activities whereby members produce and manage settings of ordinary everyday affairs are identical with members' procedures for making those settings accountable' (Garfinkel 1967: 1; Heritage 1989:179). The pupils have to deal with a situation in which the teacher is the only one who knows what to do.

The worlds of the school come to be questioned and doubted continually by the children. The school is constructed through speech, actions, texts, restrictions and opportunities (cf. Gordon, Holland and Lahelma 2000a). Things are renamed. Various ways of doing things are tried out, rules are created and school practices are reinforced. My particular research focus is on these processes of establishment, in which first encounters can offer a means of studying school practices. It may be beneficial for the researcher to collect her/his material in such first encounters, for it enables her/him to share in the knowledge of the subjects and – at least in part – their reality as well (Delamont and Galton 1986; Lahelma and Gordon 1997. See also Ball 1984; Draper 1993).

## A contingent reality

My point of departure in studying children is that they are active, living agents with their own familiar ways of making sense of the world and of producing a reality grounded in everyday life through their own thought and action (Berger and Luckmann 1966). This world includes children's conceptions of how to play, move, talk and laugh. Children have their own views on how the world is or is not.

The world of the school is a specific reality and, accordingly, is produced as separate functional orders. When children first start school, this world is a new space in which they act. It is a new order of objects and affairs which has been appropriately labelled for them before they come out on stage (cf. Berger and Luckmann 1994).66this sense, the worlds of the child and schoolchild might be considered in terms of double contingency: both worlds are real and both are possible, but at the beginning of school, also frequently contradictory and arbitrary. If a child is to capture the idea of being a school pupil, s/he must opt for selective reception.

The teacher sees school as work. She stresses this very often:

> Yes, yes, they get to play plenty in kindergarten, but now they're mature enough to know that this is work. This is work and they like to work. When they get right down to it (Interview).

The teacher does not hide her opinion that 'to dawdle around' is bad, and pupils know that they at least look as though they are working hard. Work and play start to become very different things. A boundary is set up. On one side is the more mature work, on the other the play that is now past. Small schoolchildren seem to be well aware of this. As Timo puts it on his sixth day in school: 'Kids in school study and kids in kindergarten are taught how to go to school' (Interview). Ville talks about school and draws a line marking a break with his past: 'School is not playing. We do schoolwork and stuff like that. School is nothing but *having to do things*' (Interview).

Orders can also be conceived of as functional frames in which different things can become possible or impossible. The frame determines the qualities, obligations and rights that the participants are implicitly understood to have with respect to one another (Peräkylä 1990: 160). In the context of the start of school, these obligations and rights are far from self-evident. The demands made are imposed from the outside. How do children coordinate change when they start school? And what does the new, institutional position of citizen-pupil require?

The following excerpt from observation data describes how new pupils understand a metaphor literally and begin to drum information into their heads. Everything that can be memorized is worth knowing and smacks of school knowledge. The teacher tells the pupils to look carefully at a picture in their book. Then they have to close their books and the teacher asks them what they remember about the picture.

>  *Mikko:* Do we have to remember everything?
>  *Teacher:* Yes. Put everything into your memory right up here (points to her head).
>  *Mikko:* But I can't remember!
>  *Teacher:* Oh, that's OK. (Fieldnotes)

The pupils begin looking at the picture in the book and begin drumming the information into their heads with their hands. The same drumming-in goes on for the duration of the lesson. And the teacher goes along with her own metaphor, asking at the end what the pupils have 'drummed' into their heads.

## Starting to feel like a pupil

Children are prepared for the start of school in many ways, with their parents, brothers and sisters, grandparents, godparents, neighbours and even 'the people my mother works with' getting involved. Jyrki says in all seriousness, sounding as though he has thought through everything very carefully: 'When you're seven you start feeling like school is where you really belong' (Interview). In this respect, I listen to the children in my recordings as though 'culture is speaking itself' through an individual story (cf. Riessman 1994: 69).

It is possible to be a proper pupil from the very first day. 'Yeah, yeah, I was already, on my first day of school, I was a good pupil' (Tuomo, Interview). This good behaviour can take many forms, but it necessarily involves some kind of self-control and an awareness of one's weaknesses.

*UMS:* How are you supposed to behave?
*Tuomo:* Decently, you know.
*UMS:* What does that mean that you're supposed to behave when you're in school?
*Tuomo:* You shouldn't horse around or play tricks on people.
*UMS:* Well what if you think of a trick you'd like to play on someone, what do you do?
*Tuomo:* I just don't do it. That's all. (Interview)

Many of the things connected with school are already familiar from the culture in which children live. This cultural dimension often takes the form of *cultural dating* (Thorne 1993) and children who are approaching school age are placed – as if through a mutual agreement – into ready storylines by highlighting 'things which a child in school should or has to do'. As suggested by the following interview, however, once in school, children have to look a lot farther ahead.

*UMS:* If you think you've been in school for seven days, have you had to change into a schoolgirl somehow... or somehow be different than you were before?
Anne: Yeah, things have changed a lot.
*UMS:* How? If you think about it...
*Anne:* Well, wait a minute, I feel like I am really big already. Like I'm already in the seventh grade or something.
*UMS:* What else. How does it feel to be big?
*Anne:* You start to, start to become an adult.
*UMS:* Is this school adult life or children's life?
*Anne:* Children's.
*UMS:* What? If this is children's life, how do you grow up and become an adult this way?
*Anne:* Well, you first get confirmed and then you go to vocational school.
*UMS:* But what if you think if you're grown up, big, then haven't you had to change somehow?
*Anne:* A little bit.
*UMS:* How?
*Anne:* Like, you start developing, get bigger and then...
*UMS:* What if you think just about being in school, what is the one most important thing? How should someone in school act? What's expected of you in school?
*Anne:* You're supposed to act like an adult.
*UMS:* Do you feel like you have to act like an adult here in school?
*Anne:* I don't feel like that but when it's time to get confirmed, then that's when it starts feeling like you should. (Interview)

Anne is looking for her position and basic cultural codes as she talks. She thinks about my questions, talks thoughtfully and carefully – constructing at the same time the worlds of her narrative and the order of those worlds. Anne says she feels *like she's already grown up* and being grown-up seems rather abstract but inevitable as well. To her, *confirmation and vocational school* seem to act as thresholds to adulthood. Children in school are expected to act like adults or, paradoxically, like adults and children at the same time. As the day-to-day routine of the school takes shape in 'your class' and desk, 'your spaces', things also take on an order of their own. The pupil's things are renamed and labelled using the pupil's own name (ownership) (see Salo 1999: 77–90). The way in which school things are handled is part of teaching; it implements order and, consequently, what is right and wrong:

> *Teacher:* You sort of have the pencil in the wrong hand and you're holding it funny. This is the way to do it. This is the way you hold it.
> *(Teacher shows to Jyrki how to hold the pencil)* Yeah, try to change. It's not too good to do it that way...
> *Timo:* Look, Jyrki. This is how you do it!
> *Teacher:* Yes! Now you got it!
> *Anne:* This is the way I always hold it. *(Anne shows the teacher)*
> *Pia:* Hey, teacher! Do we always start these [letters] from the top?
> *Teacher:* Yes. From the top towards the bottom. That's the way it's done!
> 
> (Fieldnotes)

In school, things are done in a particular way. The expectations, hopes and pressures directed towards children are often abstract. It is hard for the children to grasp these pressures; they have to concretise them in their thoughts and reconcile them with their own bodies; that is, they have to take a certain position with regard to school. Here, my data falls into an intermediate space, in which the children wonder about things, talk about them, name them and construct them – looking for the right position: *stories are told in being lived and lived in being told* (Kemp 1989: 72). The intensity and range of the pupils' experiences can be seen in their narratives:

> *UMS:* Have you had to change somehow, now that you're in school?
> *Ville:* I haven't exactly changed all that much. Got my hair cut a little bit.
> 
> (Interview)

### Child-like and school-like

Learning and teaching spaces are sites of the first encounters in which pupils are told what is right and wrong, where right and wrong are constructed and the border between right and wrong is drawn. When the teacher tells the pupils how things are *supposed* to be done in school, it paves the way for the children's own methods of producing pupilhood. School knowledge proves to be stronger, more serious and more certain than one's own, especially when one's own thoughts seem to be incomplete and insecure (Davies 1993).

There appears to exist an already-written script for many things in school; it is written in the textbooks and workbooks. But often scripts and their organization may be guessed at beforehand.

> *Sini:* What should I do here?
> *Teacher:* You should do the same as it says. Put a three in every second square. (Fieldnotes)

The children learn to ask questions 'like they're in school'. They use words like *should*, *must* and *as you're told*. The way of knowing in school is absolute; it does not admit of alternatives, which is alien to the idea of play. In play, intention becomes focused continuously according to what one would like to be or what one would like to become. This way of thinking is alien to the school. In school there is generally only one way of knowing something correctly. Information becomes abstract and external, with the knower either hiding or putting her/himself aside (Salo 1999).

> *Jussi:* Can I guess wrong, teacher?
> *Teacher:* Go ahead, but they'll be marked wrong. They'll be wrong. But go ahead and guess if you really want to. (Fieldnotes)

School has its very own signs for right and wrong as well as for not knowing. Similarly, textbooks have their own colours; assignments are in blue, extra assignments in green – and red is naturally reserved for the teacher, who uses it to separate right from wrong. The marks for 'wrong', 'right', and 'don't know' are constructed socially as having meanings; that is, these accounts are loose and become fixed in particular social contexts (see e.g., Handel 1982; Kasanen and Räty 2002). In school, the construction of accounts is also bound to the other structures and the order that prevails there – to a script, as I prefer to see it.

For example, ladybirds have to be coloured in red and black, and flowers have their own right' colours. Just like it really is.

> *Mikko*: What do we do when we've coloured everything in?
> *Teacher:* Colour it red, so it's easier to see. Make it the colour it really is. (Fieldnotes)

Play ends when school begins. Textbooks and answering questions are part of the formal frames of school, where play has no real place. Classroom talk produces school-based understandings (Davies 1993: 24, 56, 129; Rhedding-Jones 1996).

> *Teacher:* Timo, why don't you take out your book, too? Let's put all the toys away and start answering questions! Take out your crayons and raise your hand when you know the answer.

*Teacher (to the pupils):* Everyone has to raise their hand. How many yellow butterflies are there on page ten? (Fieldnotes)

Being in school starts to shape the children's ways of being at home. School makes children pupils outside of the school as well; the pupil space extends to the home and can be seen in everyday life there. Many pupils tell how their rooms, their space, at home have changed. I've only got two baskets of toys left' (Saara). 'We've bought desks, book shelves, cupboards and whatnot' (Pekka). In the children's talk, their social space, the spaces of the home, their own subjective and mental space all overlap, and they begin to move in all of the spaces simultaneously. The pupil begins to occupy the space of the child:

*Hannu:* I don't play so much anymore at home.
*UMS:* Why don't you play?
*Hannu:* Well, I have all that homework to do, so I don't really care too much. (Interview)

Hannu is talking about how being in school can be seen in concrete terms at home: 'Well, Mum notices when I've been sitting at the school table and drawing. She can tell from whether my clothes get dirty' (Interview). The pupil works at a desk, sits, draws, and writes. His mother can see this from his dirty sleeves. Being in school carries obligations. This can be seen in the following episode. In addition to doing one's homework and behaving oneself, you cannot be a *little kid* anymore:

*Anne:* Mum said that I have to do my homework when I come home from school.
*UMS:* How can people tell at home that you're in school except that you have to do your homework?
*Anne:* Well, I can't anymore... I *can't* be a little kid. I can't start crying for nothing, stuff like that.
*UMS:* I see.
*Anne*: And I don't cry, either.
(Interview)

The children provide both sad and vivid accounts about how their childhood is coming to an end. We see the same sentiment in *Winnie the Pooh* through the voice of Christopher Robin. After he starts school, Christopher Robin can only go back to his make-believe friends when he's doing 'nothing' (Milne 1999).

## The teacher's tests

On the very first days of school, the pupils' subjectivities begin to be built through learning and teaching. The concept 'pupil agenda', coined by Bronwyn Davies (1983), describes this facet of the pupils' activities. This agenda embraces the pupil's curriculum-based skills, and, generally, it is the curriculum that in fact spells out the skills pupils must master.

In my data, the teacher gives the pupils various tests (cf. Kasanen, Räty and Snellman 2003), but the 'results' and 'points' she talks about are completely meaningless to the children themselves. Likewise, the symbols for 'right answer' and 'wrong answer' and 'don't know' are confusing to the pupils.

> *Teacher (to pupils):* You've got to work all the time. Here you have to work, do as much as you can. What you don't finish, you have to do at home.
> *Teacher (to boys):* No laughing or fooling around, now! Get to work there! (...) Boys! Come on up here from the back, now! There's no need for everyone to be sharpening their pencils back there when each of you has your own pencil sharpener. You're just playing around ... and you still have the hard problems to do! (Fieldnotes)

Children learn to distinguish work from play surprisingly fast. Yet in the interviews they have a hard time saying what they do in school: the words 'mathematics' and 'Finnish' do not mean anything to them. The pupils' general comment when they come from recess is something like 'What do we do now?' 'Teacher, what next?' However, 'keeping busy' – part of the school agenda – seems to have become part of the pupils' agenda as well.

Pupils are starting to take school seriously From the very start of school the teacher gives various tests in which the pupils have to fill in tasks that have been prepared. A number of these 'measurements', as the teacher calls them, are done during the first few days (see also Kasanen, Räty and Snellman 2003). The teacher explains to the pupils that the reason she is giving them the test is that 'I can see what kind of skills you have so that I can give different tasks to different people' or 'I can see what level of development you're at' (fieldnotes). One important aspect of the start of school seems to be to determine what students already know when they get there.

> *Teacher:* Now, this is important, a pretty important thing we're going to do now. Listen carefully. It's early in the morning so you're wide awake, take out your nice sharp pencils and two coloured wooden pencils, a blue one and a red one.
> *Saara:* Kirsti (teacher), I sharpened all my pencils yesterday!
> *Teacher:* Good. (Fieldnotes)

Saara's comment can be seen as an attempt to win the teacher's favour, and here she is doing what girls can often be seen to do in my data. They put themselves in the teacher's world, side with the teaching, sympathise with the teacher, and show this through obedience. They may well forget themselves and their own experiences in entering the 'good girl' category. They can even do this to their own disadvantage (See Davies 1993: 53–56)

## What am I going to be when I grow up?

On his seventh day at school, I asked Jyrki how it felt to be in school. He could not say specifically. However, after thinking for a while, he answered: 'Can't you tell I'm a pupil now?' (Interview). Jyrki spoke in a low voice, seriously and unemotionally. He rocked back and forth in his chair as he spoke, as if trying to get a feel for the situation and for his own body. I still remember the expression on his face: serious, big brown eyes looking right into mine, as if he were wondering: 'You mean you can't tell I'm already a schoolboy, or at least that I'm trying to be?'

It is typical of the children's accounts that they do not talk much about or comment on the past; in contrast, the future is almost present, quite close (cf. Labov and Waletzky 1967/1973) 'I am here and now but, at the same time, I am also in the future, as if in an already thought of world' (interview). Starting school, their first school experiences, things heard from others who are more experienced as well as imaginary tales also clearly prompt children to think about the unknown to come. The question usually asked of children – 'What are you going to be when you grow up?' – is an obvious one, although I never asked it explicitly:

> Saara: I'm, I'm gonna be a florist, someone who paints jewellery, who makes jewellery, ohhhhh a singer and hmmmm what was it I was supposed to be ... a cook.
> UMS: Mhmma.
> Saara: Yeah, a ... someone who ... a nanny.
> UMS: A nanny.
> Saara: Yeah.
> Saara: And, if I have time, and can fit it all in: a TEACHER (Interview)

Saara imagines her futures, and decides on the possible occupations and identities without any doubt. All are available, here and now. The children's portrayals go beyond the normal, adult-like conventions of narrating.

Timo leaves his story and future open but, as if having thought about it and considered different alternatives, he says: 'Well, I'll become whatever I become' (Interview). I begin to wonder how much space there is to join in these common narratives, the shared orders. Does all of this really happen in the name of education and teaching? The orders pursued by the school and the children's own purposeful activity, their accounts and questions, may often indicate a possible change. Perhaps a change in a new direction, *what people could be if they wanted, and if they dared to*.

# 9

# Mathematics goes to market

## Dennis Beach

Neo-liberal support for the corporatisation of the welfare state is apparent in education in at least two ways. It is apparent firstly in education planning. Neo-liberal education planners suggest that there is no gaping hole between market logic and good education and that the two can be 'run together'. It is apparent secondly in the curriculum, where even though this fact may be disguised, a form of investment logic dominates daily talk and practices in school classrooms and staffrooms (Beach 1999a, b, 2001).

Based on an ethnographic investigation of efforts to reform upper-secondary schooling in Sweden in the 1990s (Beach op. cit.), the present chapter problematises aspects of the infusion and disguise of neo-liberal interests in education in a specific case comprised by the first two mathematics courses on an upper-secondary school natural sciences programme at one upper-secondary school. Talk and behaviour inside mathematics classrooms are examined and a correspondence between school and society (specifically termed a market value relationship) is identified. This relationship is related to the infiltration of education by the neo-liberal value-programme of market capitalism (also Allman 1999; McMurtry 1998; Brosio 1994; Gee *et al.* 1996). It is problematic for education because the ideological elements of market capitalism are antagonistic toward good education as they encourage the value practices of schooling to become fetishised.

The empirical and analytical foundations of the research are based on one year of participant observation that combined conventional ethnography with critical discourse analysis (cf. Fairclough 1995). This has led to a strong concentration on the language of classroom interaction and a strong contextualisation of this linguistic dimension. Three developments in the use of language are focussed on in particular. These are the ways in which text and talk are oriented, vary according to social context and are used for controlling, monitoring and naming social interaction and education products.

### Education from civil commons to commodity form

Education in Sweden and the other Nordic countries is still part of the civil commons of the welfare states that emerged in the 1940s and 1950s. The welfare state became known as the 'folk-home' emphasising it as the home of all citizens. Keynesian economic planning, full employment, full health insurance and comprehensive education for all characterised the folk-home (Lindblad 1994;

Carlén 1999). However, since the mid-1980s, this concept has come increasingly under fire from the political right for undermining cost effective services and individual responsibility, and a new welfare discourse has emerged that is now in ascendancy. This neo-liberal discourse describes a new form of welfare that celebrates a decentralised, entrepreneurial form of welfare as a commodity with a price that can be set for profitability. Market ideas and economic incentives become the new structuring principles for a welfare provision controlled by welfare agencies and economic relations in a welfare society (Dale 1997; Lindblad 1994).

The replacement of the folk-home concept of welfare by a commodity form has consequences for education provision. Some of these are already visible in the Nordic countries, even though they are less preponderant there than elsewhere. Instead of a collectively owned and supported national education system for all, what is developing is an emphatic privatisation of the means of education production, the provision of a market for private sector involvement in education, the introduction of management based on an economic rationalist model (called new-managerialism), an exodus of middle class students from schools in poorer areas and an increase in the competitiveness and privatisation of learning, where people and organisations become inauthentic toward their own values and experiences so as to be successful in the new market situation. The education to market relationship in Nordic countries is not yet about direct takeovers by external corporate agents. It is about updating the requirements of what has long determined modern formal education in favour of the prevailing societal economic system in a way that seriously threatens education democracy and equality (Hill 2001).[1]

## Education restructuring and a new school vision

Government Proposition 1990/91: 18 expressed that the traditional way of controlling education by state regulation should end, and that control should be exercised by Parliament stating education objectives and frameworks and handing over the responsibility for their execution to the municipalities (17). The aim was to help create new schools that emphasise self-regulation and life-long learning for tomorrow's knowledge society and a new national curriculum with loosely set national objectives was introduced in 1994, reflecting these ambitions (Lindblad 1994; Lundahl 2001; Zackari 2001; Lindblad and Popkewitz this volume). The

---

[1] Welfare state ambitions peaked in Nordic countries during the third quarter of the previous century. They included comprehensive education, good housing, unemployment and sickness benefits, healthcare and an adequate pension for the elderly and infirm, regardless of occupation and income, and according to need. These needs were balanced against those of the capitalist economy. However, neo-liberalism marks the beginning of the end of such ambitions through the exposure of welfare to the economic power of private property and the interests of an abstract and parasitic form of capital (finance capital) that dominates capitalism in its phases of decline. It opposes welfare as a public commons, as everything has to be owned and sold in the interests of capital accumulation. So although the former welfare state did not transform and equalise class society (cf. Offe 1996: 63-64), in comparison to market control in the interests of a disequilibriating capital there were favourable aspects to it.

result was expressed as follows by the headteacher at the main research site in my study:

> We have since the decentralisation and introduction of a new curriculum been given the opportunity to live out pedagogical ambitions for a new school... This school gives lots of individual responsibility and freedom of choice to students and teachers, who will take responsibility for the curriculum by controlling content from within a system of choice options. However, we are not just offering simple choices but choices within choices. Through the study period system students can determine where and when they learn... Teachers and pupils together form the key to school improvement... Minimum standards for matriculation will be possible within any elected study option... We have moved from governing by rules to goals. Our aim is to help students to be motivated, alert, inquiring, self-governing and flexible users as opposed to just recipients of knowledge. It is in their best interests but demands their responsibility as well... We need self-motivated learners in the knowledge society (and) must organise situations to reinforce these qualities... We need a strategic competence in order to identify and overcome obstacles in the drive toward... creativity and self-discipline... This can be done if we learn to recognise that all students can be active and creative and that successful learning is accomplished actively and creatively...

The 1994 curriculum reform worked in tandem with the School Development Agreement (SDA) of 1995. In the SDA individual salary setting and regulated work time were introduced and the local reorganisation of schools and teaching methods were emphasised in an attempt to give greater autonomy to local schools. Team teaching, collaborative planning and co-operation were extended and professional freedom, it was claimed, was to replace steering by regulations. Municipal districts, local schools and teachers obtained, at least theoretically, possibilities for defining learning, stipulating educational goals, selecting content and methods and formulating goals, grading criteria and the basic format of evaluation (Sundkvist 2000; Carlgren 2000). However, these changes can also be seen in economic terms. They were initiated after the sale of state owned enterprises by a former right-wing coalition government and in the aftermath of a national economic crisis brought about by a massive growth in the national debt incurred by that same government. Furthermore, the changes can also be seen in terms of their lack of effect. For the most part things still go on in schools in much the same way as before, but under intensified conditions of labour. For instance, the formality of key subjects has not decreased since the reform, and self-determined learning has not increased. As before, there are formal accountability measures formed by examinations, homework, spot-tests and national equivalence examinations and university entrance requirements which are still appropriated for grading and evaluating student performances and for separating students for differential treatment on the basis of their performance. In relation to maths teaching these 'continuities' were suggested in my field journal in ways like the following:

> Teachers say they are under more stress now... and have more to do in less time. However, there is also a consistent pattern to maths... Students listened to the teacher during an introduction and followed instructions about what work they should do. This work involved mundane things rather than highly theoretical content. Many repetitive calculations were made each lesson and students remained within the classroom to work. They talked about specific questions from their books interspaced with questions like 'what did you get', 'what about this', 'is this how it should be', 'I don't really get it', 'is this right'. The teacher corrected them if so needed... Furthermore... students and teachers prolonged a dependency relation by regarding subject knowledge as an externally established truth contained in text-books, by seeing teachers as authorities on subject knowledge and student performances, and by regarding student ability and motivation as the force behind student success... Students were graded, controlled and separated on the basis of their different performances according to standardised performance criteria...

Upper-secondary school maths is normally described in terms of its relations to a parent discipline, as concerned with complex formulae, difficult theories and demanding cognitive activities. However, in the present study maths content comprised mundane algorithms to be completed under time-pressure and, rather than reflecting abstract knowledge and complex formulae, getting right answers to concrete algorithms and completing work in time in order to get good grades was stressed (Dahland 1998; Beach 1999 a,b,c, 2001). These aspects seem to typify school maths from early years all the way through the compulsory school in Sweden according to for instance Gustafsson (2002) and Bentley (2003) and into the upper-secondary school (Dahland 1998; Beach 1999 a,b, 2001). The importance of good grades is suggested in the following fieldwork diary extract:

> The results from the first maths test came back today. Most students had at least a distinction. They still bickered. This upset Liz who expressed how they want even more instruction now... They are worried about grades and are blaming Liz for them not getting a top grade... As one of them put it, they need good grades to be competitive toward university entrance requirements... In the A course you need at least a distinction they say, as without it 'you have no chance of getting into the best courses at uni..'. The A course is all about getting things done and grafting things in. The workload and work rate is a challenge but they need to do the work to be competitive and get the results... Students and teachers engage in practices whereby answers to pre-set problems are developed and swapped in

examinations to obtain good school grades and university places. And these principles are major forces conditioning the social practices of the education.

What is described above is a concept of banking education (cf. Allman 1999) and something of the way in which potentially educative relationships are transformed into relationships that reflect the characteristics of accumulation and exchange in competitive and privatised learning processes. An accumulation of grades with a high symbolic and exchange value condition interactions in this educational context. In the Communist Manifesto of 1848, Marx and Engels' describe this kind of development as commodification, the reification of aspects of social life as natural objects with a fetishised economic value form. Such fetishisms help to constitute the market value relationship spoken on earlier. I observed them in my field-notes and teacher interviews in ways like the following:

This job is about helping students recognise their abilities and... make the best of what they have... Joint abilities to maximise output sets limits on any return that can be made from education for those involved in it.

If only there were more time... we could give them the attention they need... All of them have ability. I have to help them ...find ways of being effective and make the best of their abilities and what they have to offer as learners...

There is an amount of ability, time, available resources and a set of demands. It is a simple equation of optimising availability and effort to get a good result... These students are all potentially capable ones... I have to help them become effective learners as well... They bring what they can to the work. I do what I can to help them get a good return on their ability and effort...

The working form of banking education is in many senses against the new school vision and the school curriculum, where maths is said to be about 'helping participants to develop understandings of themselves, the subject, their situation and the relationship between this situation and broader society (particularly higher education), so they may be able to take responsibility for their learning' (Liz). Maths as practiced has another logic - a market logic. Within it teachers accept student performances as being based on a distribution of individual abilities and levels of motivation for making the most of available resources and they objectify the students working relationships within the education in relation to standardised performance criteria. The contradiction is illustrated somewhat in the table below, contrasting teachers' visionary discourse with their talk about actual education outcomes:

| **Visionary discourse** | **Talk about actual outcomes** |
|---|---|
| My preferences are for getting them to a good level of understanding… Understanding is what is important… | I will move on and cram for tests to help students get better grades… Understanding (is) sacrificed for coverage… |
| We want them to get a feel for the subject…I would rather not have a book… They can all achieve. We should help all…to attain full understanding…and become independent, self-motivated, self-monitoring learners. Having a book obstructs this to a degree… | The examination tests book content. It has to be covered to prepare for the exam…They have different abilities. The examinations can identify these…We have to help them to the right level …Grading and testing are important in generating a fair signal system… |
| We have created a new school environment and organise resources to support students as they take charge of their own learning… And we have done everything in our power to make sure that there is access and provision for everyone in the new inclusive school… They can all be successful… | There is…an ideal and then there is reality…They don't all have the ability or motivation needed to be successful in a demanding subject like maths given the competition at this level. They don't all recognise the need to invest. This shows in the end…The sooner the better really for all concerned… |

The above table suggests not only how the principle of banking education predominates in talk about actual education transactions, but also what banking education inevitably leads to in competitive circumstances; differentiation. Differentiation is normalised in teacher talk about education outcomes. Aims like free choice and understanding are claimed but contradicted and abandoned, whilst aims like covering the syllabus or textbook in time are upheld, so that selections of individuals for further investment processes in economically rationalist cycles of education can be made. However, like banking education, differentiation also runs counter to the logic of the new school vision and new curriculum, as it encourages teachers to see students as 'separated from the outset by differential capabilities… that will finally always show themselves, no matter what' (Liz, teacher). As another teacher put it:

> There are different kinds of problems with different groups … With the good groups we have to find out who has the problems… The weaker students need less frustrating work to occupy them to keep them off my back… There is special help (for bright kids) and special support (for slower learners)… We help them… to find their own levels and spaces… to make use of resources… to the best of their abilities… Some are worth an extra effort because of their extra-ordinary abilities and interests… We

can help them go far... Others, not science students but... the new clientele who don't want to be here in the first place, are more of a burden... They need to be occupied with something, anything, so we can get on with the job of helping those who want to and have the ability to do well.... (Brian: Teacher)

It would be easy to blame teachers for the differentiating outcomes of education Teachers compare and grade student performances and treat students as investment objects on the basis of how they use the resources and consume the mathematical activities that are given to them (Beach 2001; Boaler 1996), but this is not only a decision made by individual teachers. It is a consistent feature of education systems in capitalist countries (cf. Bowles and Gintis 1976; 1988 a, b; Brosio 1994). Thus, whilst teacher understandings of the distribution of student ability and their acceptance of the liberal attainment ethic are culpable factors in the accommodation of new principles for relating learning outcomes to old ideas about meritocracies, teachers do not fully control the procedures by which capitalist interests are reproduced inside the education system. It is true that economic principles of investment that teachers condone and support resonate better with education practices than formal aims do, in that students do the same things at the same time and are then compared and graded according to their performances against a given standard. Students become objects in an education market place whose intrinsic worth is based on calculations of an objectified investment value based on the results from privatised and repetitive calculations and the attainment of measurably correct answers to identical problems that can be exchanged for school grades. Students are assessed, graded and selected against a performance standard, over which they have little control, in practices that reproduce and inscribe the capitalist hallmark of domination. But this 'commoditised ideal' is also stabilised by its external relations to long-standing production relations in wider society that are internalised and accepted as normal by *both* students and teachers alike in this investigation. Students have to internalise performativity and investment values to be successful, and they know that resistance correlates with counter productive tendencies. What we are seeing are outcomes of new ideas within a specific context. They aren't inevitable! They are cultural and contingent. They represent the formation of objective forms of education capital as described in Bourdieu's work (e.g. Bourdieu 1997) and are key aspects of education in class society. However, they are also directly denied by those involved. This denial suggests one further characteristic of the conditions of capitalist markets as they appear in education, the lack of authenticity.[2]

[2] Although produced within the school context the ideas expressed here are resonant with dominant cultural understandings of the distribution of ability, individual limitation and investment thinking and are thus reproductive beliefs that support a view of good education involving effective accommodation to objective demands. In the end successful students have to do repetitive calculations and exams to accumulate education capital and have to act towards this situation as if it was an inevitable and natural one where ability, genuine commitment, solid directions and practice make the perfect student, and where success is taken to confirm

## Articulation, interdiscursivity, hegemony and opposition

The concept of hegemony describes a potential to constitute the world in line with the interests of a specific group through the common and unquestioned adoption of a logic that determines what is generally understood to be true and is a question of the alliances by means of which a leading class assumes a position of leadership over others, often by 'guaranteeing' them certain benefits (Gramsci 1971; Beach 1995, 1997, 1999b, d, 2000; Bernstein 1990). However, as the guarantee is usually false, hegemony also becomes a question of an articulation of interests, not through a guarantee of reward, but through a fusion of economic, political, intellectual and moral leadership brought about by groups that have the ability to articulate the interests of others to their own by means of ideological struggle. The education system studied seems to have the characteristics of hegemony. However, when I say this I do not mean to assert that the education institutions I have studied are monolithic entities. On the contrary, they are not. There is always incompleteness, contradiction and the space within them for creativity and pluralistic struggle (Willis 2000), even when the organisation of resources and practices in the routinisation of daily work suggest a constant tendency. This applies even in the present instance. For example some teachers tried actively to break the concept of banking education in mathematics and some students openly expressed the view that the maths they experienced represented a boring, repetitive, crypto-capitalist, money-to-money investment logic that was played out in everyday life, with negative effects on those exposed to it. A good question to ask therefore is what happened to this opposition? This was investigated and framed in my fieldwork journal writing as follows:

> Teacher opposition to banking education was restricted, localised and essentially reproductive. 'Alternative maths was a motivational device and soft option for weaker groups' (Brian: Teacher). It was used first after differentiation had been accomplished... Student opposition obtained an even worse fate. Either it was ignored as 'an inconsistency that everyone goes through' (Liz: Teacher), or it was turned back on students as a means of suggesting that they, not the maths, were the learning problem. 'Jon simply didn't have the metal for maths' (Brian: Teacher).

On closer observation there were two different levels of criticism from students to consider. The most common one had a basic symmetry with the working hegemony. Typical here was a criticism that maths was 'high pace and repetitive', tough, but that if you 'have a head for numbers and are set on a good career you'll get by' (student). This symmetry is visible also with respect to teachers' understandings of the demands posed on students. 'Students have to accommodate

the value of the learner as an investment object. However, whilst what is normal to maths is sitting still and engaging in repetitive activities toward the determined ends of being assessed and selected by an external power, the importance of this compliance is often denied.

to find the best solution to a problem. Maths can be experienced as repetitive and boring (but) there is no other way. They simply have to buckle down to it'.

The symmetrical criticisms and views of the difficulties of maths above can be contrasted to what I termed as asymmetrically critical views. This is done in the table below, which also presents typical responses from teachers to these more difficult criticisms. Again there is a normalisation tendency in these responses, in that the criticism is absorbed into a dominant discourse of limited supply and dominant ideas about the need of effort and ability to achieve. Once again common concepts about maths being a special subject that requires special ability and a commitment to work are reproduced, as is a normative understanding that student performances will always reflect these qualities. A pathological view of oppositional students also becomes apparent:

| **The criticism of maths** | **Teacher comments on criticisms** |
| --- | --- |
| There is no time for opposition and debate. There is only time to learn the (facts) for solving the problems... If you stop to question what you are doing or why, the others (are) gone and you (are) behind. Once you get behind ...it is never ending... | X seemed to be a good student and was cheerful. But he didn't want to buckle down to the real hard work of maths at this level. I've seen this so many times before. He will cope much better in the social sciences where the pace (and) demands are less emphatic... |
| You find other things to do... But teachers make you feel both dumb (and) lazy... It doesn't matter what you do. Some of them say it straight out... But they can't do anything (and) take criticism personally... | The good ones persevere! We don't have finances for smaller classes to cater for differences. We have ...max 2 minutes per individual... There is a syllabus... I can do so much (the rest) is up to them... |
| I started off trying but got sick about half way through...I couldn't concentrate... When I came back I was... tired (but) did try. However, I was behind and the pace was too high... I fell further and further back... I thought of changing programmes but my parents convinced me to take some time off and start again (otherwise) I'd have quit. | I explain (things) in the time that we can give (after that) you just have to move on... Some of them can't keep pace. They lack ability or effort usually. The good ones are aware of their goals... and buckle down to the job of learning... Interest, commitment and ability... separate good (from) mediocre performers... and science students... from most others... |

The responses teachers make to asymmetrical criticism is counter to the 'new' curriculum where critical reflection is to be encouraged and so again maths becomes a living contradiction of the values espoused for it. They suggest that teachers accept prevailing ideological understandings of rational individualism that have their roots in utilitarian philosophy and they mediate the idea that all students are involved in their education solely (or at least primarily) in order to maximise educational credentials and qualifications and will invest as hard as they can for these reasons. The concept of maximisation of self-interests is important within the liberalist concept of the market and is reproduced and reinforced within the present educational arrangement. Maths is not about the freedom to learn, authenticity, fair rights of negotiation, broadened involvement, the realisation of an intrinsic value as a learner and the promotion of life-long learning, as in the idealism of the new school vision. It is a fetishistic and commoditised system of relations where competitive exclusion and ideological reproduction prevail. Maths is a competitive subject. But it even makes the procedures of performance related differentiation seem fair; even to those who have their educational life chances damaged by them. Maths education in this sense again forms a structural and cultural correspondence with the ideological and confirmatory needs of a capitalist investment system (cf. Bowles and Gintis 1988a, b; Brosio 1994).

## On agency and structure

The suggestions made in the chapter have bearing on the structure versus agency debate in educational research. This is because what is being suggested is that there are formations of power operating in relation to maths education that limit agency because they have a common ancestry in, structural similarity with and common moral foundation inside a market value programme. This constrains individual freedom and the development of the post-Fordist educational vision of the upper-secondary reform. This applies because even though agency exists more than just hypothetically within the researched contexts, the researched education still favours commoditisation and the reproduction of fetishistic values inside its everyday practices, and does so despite agent aspirations and desires rather than simply because of them. So although it is currently assumed that teachers and students have extensive agency to reform education practices, my suggestion is that this agency is severely limited in modern schools as these are both ideological and repressive in the senses spoken on by Althusser (1971). I support this claim via the descriptions in the present chapter of the way banking concepts of education have developed and been maintained within the current attempts to reform education, even against the expressed aims of its active agents.[3]

3. A reminder of the points made about the meaning of marketisation for education could be reasonable here from which to assess the levels of creativity and agency and those of reproduction (cf. Ainley 2000; Allman op. cit.; Hill 2001). Just specifically an emphatic competitiveness and privatisation of learning seem to be developing where people and organisations are becoming inauthentic in their practices toward their own values and experiences so as to be successful. The current education to market relationship in recent school reforms in Sweden is not yet about direct takeovers by external corporate agents but is about reproducing the conditions necessary for a prevailing societal economic value system.

Banking education is clearly the dominant (hegemonic) education form in maths according to the present investigation. This form of education is antithetical to the concepts of education expressed in the new school vision as it contributes (materially and ideologically) to the suppression of forms of autonomous, oppositional thought, sets foundations for the development of a capitalist structure of inter-subjectivity (both through its inter-discursive articulations and incentives of control) and enables a consistent interpellation of market discourses at individual levels that allow a market value programme to be actively supported even by those who are oppressed by and would otherwise only be made subject to it. The window of resistant agency is tightly closed if not fully shut. Structuring education according to the logic of the market means structuring it against values of equity, social inclusion, social justice and critical reflection. These things are materially repressed and ideologically devalued in the world of the market. As Brosio (1994), Ainley (2000), Hill (2001), Allman (1999) and McMurtry (1998) point out, the values of a good education and market values are antithetical because of a contradiction between their respective logics of practice and what it means to positively attain in them.

## On contradictions of values

The antithesis signalled by McMurtry (1998: 188) regarding the respective logics of the market and (good) education is an important point in relation to the present chapter. In good education, practices of autonomous co-determination predominate, where people become creative, critical thinkers and doers, whilst in markets dependency relations and the possibilities of exploitation prevail, where people pay to consume and come to depend on the products and services of others. This latter description fits practice in the present situation. It suggests that whilst the idealism of formal education policy and education restructuring expresses that there is no gaping hole between market logic and good education, the case is the reverse. Inside a market programme the value-practices of education are not about living out progressive democratic principles or helping students understand themselves, their position or their subjects, they are about reproducing the conditions of reproduction for a (globalised) market discourse within local forms of work where individuals are graded according to their choices and performances with respect to contents and ideas that are acted towards as fixed and ready made. In this way they become supporters of a neo-liberal ideology that works against common values and reduces the effective agency of education managers, teachers and learners. This reactionary agency is very evident in mathematics education, which, lest we forget, is also the key social class, ethnic and gender cleaver in schools according to Svensson (2001), Beach (1999a,b, 2001) and Papanastasiou (2000). Education control and selection are accomplished in discursive, ideological and material practices through consensus rather than overt force and though practices that deploy rituals that indoctrinate individuals in market thinking and submissive behaviour by hegemonic means.

## Conclusion

The suggestions of the present chapter fit in with Marcuse's (1968) ideas about culture as a historically identifiable unity with two dimensions - the common sense constructs and cultural categories that articulate experiences within complicated social processes and the existing modes of economic production. Marcuse uses the term *affirmative culture* with respect to this duality. Within the presently affirmed education culture, educational change does not as yet consist of overt takeovers by corporate enterprises, as in common 'linear' understandings of education restructuring, but of an updating of the moral determination of education subjects by the economy and an abdication of responsibility for the plight of these 'self-determined' learners by their teachers and ultimately the state. This is in accordance with a decreased dependency of capital on the value form of production labour inside the Nordic countries and the exportation (i.e. globalisation) of this production labour (as a labour relation and form of work) to the formerly non-industrialised nations to the east and south. However, the reproductive tendencies of the economic system within education do not stop at this. In the same sense as within economic privatisation more broadly, inside the new education system, when market interests override issues concerned with equity and equality, the educationally rich get richer and the children of the people 'at the bottom' of the socio-economic ladder are also found at the bottom of the education ladder (Svensson 2001; Eriksson and Jonsson 2003). This common 'global' problem has also been focused on recently by the Hillcole Group (1997). In their account, as in the present chapter, emphasis on the market in education has led to an accentuation of inequalities and a growth of distress (18). These things may become ever more common within Nordic education systems.

# 10

# Changes in teacher students' knowledge by changes in technologies of freedom and control

## Inger Anne Kvalbein

This chapter deals with issues of restructuring in Norwegian teacher education through an analysis of two extensive ethnographic projects. The focus is on how teacher students pursue their studies at college, how they learn and what they consider as relevant knowledge and appropriate conduct in their preparation to become teachers. This is in accordance with the view that teacher education is a political tool to develop teachers fit to meet the demands of the compulsory school. However, whilst reforms in teacher education are usually felt to follow reforms in the compulsory school, during the last decade reforms in Nordic teacher education have been more frequent than those in school. For instance, teacher education in Sweden has been the subject of two reforms and one substantial revision in the last twenty years (Beach 2000) whilst the school has only been reformed once. The same applies to Norway where teacher education has been restructured by a new national curriculum three times in the past eleven years (in 1992, 1998 and 2002) whilst schools have only had one big reform during this period. This suggests that reforms in teacher education are not only caused by developments in compulsory school, but also by other initiatives.

The main political objectives for the teacher education reforms in Norway in the latter half of last century have been to create a more coherent education, foster more student responsibility and initiative and get students more engaged in their total educational project. Lack of student engagement has been a general complaint from authorities and teacher educators in Norway, as it has in Sweden (Beach 1995, 1996, 2000; Carlgren 1992; Emsheimer 2000; Riksdagsuttryck 1984/85: 122; SOU 1999: 63).

In Norway two successive National Laws have been passed to help the traditional higher educational institutions gain more freedom to establish and implement their own courses, to help them 'stay attractive in the education market'. Reforms have aimed to restore the full time student and at the same time reduce the demands for formal attendance in the educational activities. This is in accordance with new policies of restructuring, which not only demand accountability and control, but also presuppose citizens to be self-motivated and self-responsible actors striving to reach the determined goals. Teacher education has, however, until the last reform to be implemented from August 2003, been strictly regulated by detailed national curricula. Some special national regulations connected to the general reforms have nevertheless spilled over to teacher education. Mandatory attendance to most classes has for instance vanished, giving the students freedom to pursue their study interests more independently. Recent research suggests, however, that these efforts have not had desired outcomes. Teacher students use only a fraction of their time for studying compared to other students in higher education (Dæhlen 2001; Teigen 1997).

Two comparable ethnographic studies were carried out with an interval of eight years; the data were collected in 1993/1994 and 2000/2002. I examined how teacher students emphasise some forms of knowledge more than others when they fulfil institutional requirements and achieve certification. Students engage in strategic activities that foster special kinds of learning and knowledge and develop attitudes through participation in specific interaction embedded in dominating local norms, values and concepts of reality (also Emsheiner 2000; Beach 1995, 1996). The present story is about how teacher students and teacher educators in Norway have adapted their teacher education practises and knowledge production to new policies of restructuring.

## Trends in Norwegian teacher education

Norway has a history of roughly 170 years of public teacher education, but reforms in this education have taken place with increased frequency in recent decades. As in other Nordic countries, these reforms have mostly concerned the duration and content in teacher education. For instance, initial teacher education has been extended from three to four years, mandatory subjects have been altered and increased and the curriculum has gained a more binding status. General aims have been to adapt teacher education to reforms in primary and lower secondary school and to develop an improved, integrated teacher education. According to national policy documents, professional orientation, student activity, responsibility and engagement should characterise teacher education (NOU 1996: 22, NOU 1988: 32, UFD 2002a; see Beach 1995, 1996, 2000; Carlgren 1992; Emsheimer 2000; Riksdagsuttryck 1984/85: 122; SOU 1999: 63 for descriptions of similar developments in Sweden).

Formal teacher education in Norway started, as did most teacher education in the Nordic countries, in the first half of the 19th century in what were called teacher seminaries. These were usually placed in rural surroundings to keep students away from the temptations of the city (Kvalbein 1999). Teacher education was not an academic education. It recruited bright students with basic schooling and prepared them for work in compulsory schools. Through the years, teacher education expanded and demanded more educated students but it remained a professional education until 1975 when entry requirements were raised and it became part of formal higher education. In 1994 teacher colleges became part of state colleges of higher professional education in a region. Most of teacher education is based in the colleges. Teaching practice in compulsory schools is spaced in between, and covers approximately half a year of the total education.

Today teacher education may be extended up to master degrees and some faculties in regional colleges also grant doctoral degrees. Teacher education has become recognised as academic, even though it still has some unique norms and values because of its special traditions and history as a professional education. A strong culture regulates positions and responsibilities in everyday college life and indicates what is considered natural, normal and right in teacher education. Traditions and local culture have usually limited the impact of Acts of Parliament on how students work and learn. This applies even though educational models have been frequently changed.

## The new restructuring turn—issues of freedom and control

Contemporary western policies of restructuring show tendencies towards accountability and closer links to economic life, but also towards individual freedom. The latter takes place through self-managed behaviour of citizens who, by their own choice and commitment, should engage in activities to further societal values and ethics. Neo-liberal societies are governed and deliberated in balance between public administration and individual management (Rose 2000). People operate within webs of independence and regulation and conduct themselves as free and autonomous individuals and as producers of expected objectives and social functions at the same time (Giddens 1998, Hultqvist 1995, Rose 2000). There has been a shift from government to governance, as Lindblad and Popkewitz (this volume) have expressed it.

Bourdieu (1979) and Foucault (1975) have identified disciplinary power and disciplinary technologies that influence how modern society—through expertise and symbolic power—individualises and normalises citizens who internalise appropriate values, beliefs, sentiments and conceptions of reality. In the British social democratic 'third way', the state conceives itself as the enabling state, or the state as animator to further change of responsibilities from national collective bodies to communities, institutions and individuals. The state will no longer answer all society's needs. Individuals, firms, organisations, localities, schools, parents, hospitals and others will take on a portion of responsibility, which they then interpret as a gain in freedom (Rose 2000). There is a new discourse at play. In this discourse:

> Populations that were once under the tutelage of the social state are to be set free to find their own destiny. Yet, at the same time, they are to be made responsible for their destiny and for that of society as a whole. Politics is to be returned to society itself, but not longer in a social form; in the form of individual morality, organisational responsibility, and ethical community (Rose 2000: 4).

This accentuation of freedom for institutions and individuals implies use of sophisticated tools to assure that the coveted virtues are developed and maintained.

Government bodies will have greater need for evaluation, and instruct institutions to account for institutional practice of high quality. Freedom and control coexist in the organised society, though in varying degrees. They are not constituted as binaries or poles on a one-dimensional scale. Rather they are strategic webs interacting at the same plane in societies and institutions. The neo-liberal turn, accompanied by different emphases on freedom and control, may be seen as backdrop for the changes in teacher education through reforms at the end of the last century.

I focus on ways in which these policies are played out in everyday life, and how the new regimes of freedom and control transform teacher education. In accordance with Humboldt's declaration at the start of the 19$^{th}$ century, European universities have had a great degree of freedom for learning and teaching. University education has demanded that students exercise self-discipline and responsibility, find appropriate courses to attend and choose suitable working methods needed for passing the exams. In this respect, universities have practised politics of freedom and control for centuries.

The ethics of teacher education institutions in the Nordic countries, however, differ from these principles. General teacher education in the Nordic countries did not become part of the universities until the last part of the previous century. It also has been conceived as exceptional due to its societal importance for future generations and has been closely regulated by national legislature and directives for admission, extent, content, curriculum, teaching methods and examinations, at times in detail. Since being promoted to part of or comparative to the university system at the end of last century, teacher education has received special parliamentary attention, particularly in Norway and Sweden.

## Ethnographic studies of teacher education

In ethnographic studies, educational institutions are analysed as local cultures with dominant cultural content and common cultural symbols (e.g. Geertz 1966, Willis 2000). In the present investigation the dominant values, norms and concepts in practices of teacher educators and teacher students have been identified through interviews and observation. Their actions and attitudes have been interpreted according to meaning attached to them in interactions within the social and cultural relationships of the educational institution.

Two ethnographic projects have informed my analysis. Both have been case studies of a teacher education institution as local culture. Through participant observation of teacher students and semi-structured interviews with teacher educators, I have endeavoured to meet the actors on their own terms and in their own territory. The analytic questions I have posed can be phrased as follows: What are the people doing when they engage in everyday teacher education and why? What kinds of knowledge and attitudes are developed?

Before commencing the field study I mapped out the history and traditions of general teacher education through literature reviews. I also examined the relevant curricula and policy documents. In addition, my long experience as a teacher educator gave access as an insider as well as an outsider. Continuous reflection and attention to an array of theories and methods was practised in order to ensure that as many relevant perspectives as possible were given adequate attention.

During the data collection in 1994, I spent six months in the field with the teacher students and their educators. Half of this time I observed first year students, the other half students in their last year of teacher education. I arrived at the college when it opened in the morning and attached myself to the first students who arrived. The rest of the day was spent with the class, as a whole and in smaller groups, in lessons, breaks, meetings and in places the students spent their time at the college, until the last student left in the afternoon.

The aim of the field study was to help me to understand the local culture that evolves in interaction between students and teacher educators in the everyday discourse – the discourse that constitutes what is regarded as valid teacher education knowledge and approved ways of acting (Beach 1990; Carlgren 1992). I focused on how students perceived their positions related to study content and ways of work. This had great importance for their relationships and for ways in which the learning processes were played out in everyday life. These perceptions regulated the students' use of time and energy to their studies and their understanding of the kind of knowledge they should produce or reproduce. They also had an impact on how knowledge should be displayed and how students in general should behave 'as good student teachers' (ibid.).

I spoke extensively with about a third of the teacher educators engaged in general teacher education. I conducted semi-structured interviews about their understanding of their tasks as teacher educators. They spoke about their relationships to students and their subjects, their responsibilities in the educational processes and their relations to teaching as work in compulsory schools (see also Carlgren 1992). From the field study and the interviews the predominant cultural core—prevalent values, main norms and dominant concepts of the realities of teacher education—could be identified. Issues that at first seemed strange could be understood as rational and effective, even though they were not always desirable according to national or local guidelines for the education.

Pertinent cultural symbols in the teacher education institution convey values and norms and inflict discipline and self-discipline. Central symbols closely connected to the cultural core include various actors' positions in time and space, the architecture that regulates possible interactions and actions, the hierarchy, the organisation and the disciplining technologies (Beach 1995, Foucault 1975). These aspects were also given attention in my field studies. I did not primarily focus on how the rhetoric of policy documents had filtered through into everyday teacher education practises or whether the teacher educators practised what they preached in the interviews. The challenge was to find the salient features and cultural symbols of the dominant local culture, and examine how and what kind of knowledge is constructed through practise by student teachers in this context (Olesen and Whittaker 1968).

The second study was undertaken at the turn of the millennium after an extensive teacher education reform in 1998. The focus was still on how teacher students construct their teacher education knowledge, but under new conditions after the reform. This project also put special emphasis on how knowledge related to the teacher profession is handled. Methodologically this study replicates the former, but this time students at all levels have been included in the field study that lasted about one study year, autumn 2001 and spring 2002. Interviews with teacher educators were conducted in autumn 2000.

## Teacher education 1994—disintegration of the seminary contract

The teacher education institution studied in 1994 appeared in many respects to be similar to basic schools. Students were grouped in classes of the same size as in compulsory schooling, attendance at lectures and other educational activities at the college was mandatory, the curriculum was divided into mostly the same subjects as in compulsory schools, and usually classes had one teacher in each subject. Students were required to follow schedules with most of the subjects given for each year, though as in lower and upper secondary schools, there was some room for elected subjects. The classes of about 30 students stayed together for three of the four years' education. There were not many, if any, cultural symbols in the organisation of every day college life signalling that the institution expected different behaviour from the student teachers than what students experience in compulsory schools.

Teacher colleges have been characterised since the beginning by the 'seminary contract' (Kirkhusmo 1983; Kvalbein 1999). This concept refers to the special culture that is described as an unwritten contract, implying that teacher students renounce freedom in their education in favour of close relationships in a social community that considers itself responsible for their education and qualifications. Teacher educators take the responsibility to select and transmit the necessary knowledge for students to pass the exams, they initiate various processes to help students learn, and take care of their students. The students' main part of the bargain is to attend and participate at the college. Teacher educators create a supportive social climate and lead students through mandatory subjects and educational activities. Through the last two centuries teacher students have usually spent much of their time at the colleges, both in classes and in various social activities in the afternoons, evenings and weekends.

Teacher educators and teacher students still expected this relationship in 1994. Teacher educators considered their work as a rather comprehensive educational project, comprising responsibility for students' development in both professional and personal terms, even though they were mostly concerned about transmitting subject knowledge. They wanted to arrange stimulating learning processes and to promote healthy actions and attitudes among students, at the same time as they were striving to teach them basic knowledge in their subjects through lectures and assignments. Exams dealt usually with questions thoroughly covered in the class (see also Carlgren 1992; Beach 1990). The following statements from interviews are typical:

> I think that our main concern is that we shall not frighten the students with tough demands during teacher education. ... I will say that the main aim is to make the students enjoy the subject and want to work with it as teachers.
> (Female teacher educator, spring 1994)

> The students do not read much, we cannot expect that they read and learn the content of the few books we have on our reading list. And at times I don't agree in the way the books present the topics. That might be a problem. So, the teacher educators collect information from different sources and teach it to the students. We hope the students manage to grasp what they need for the exams. And we are very thorough!
> (Male teacher educator, autumn 1993)

Teacher educators endeavoured to make the students feel secure and successful in their education. They often developed close personal relationships with their students and avoided authoritarian conduct and rigorous demands in the class. As one teacher educator said:

> ... this issue of confidence is of utmost importance. We try to make the students feel secure. They must be confident with their teacher, they must be able to talk about everything. Particularly related to the subject, of course, but everything... (Male teacher educator, spring 1994)

Teacher educators expressed more commitment and responsibility towards their students than they did toward the students' future students. This influenced the ways students were assessed. Positive responses and considerate marking of papers, tests and exams were the rule. Students, who entered teacher education and stayed there the required time, succeeded. In evaluating exams, teacher educators regarded themselves as their students' defenders. External examiners have felt pressured to give better marks than they intended.

In everyday teacher education, the teacher educators controlled student attendance (which was mandatory) and graded their work, albeit most often in a fairly student friendly way. Teacher educators' pastoral disciplinary techniques acted at times as buffers against centralised national regulations and control. Teacher educators had the everyday control and the responsibility, and they might also adjust the national curriculum and angle the exams to focus issues they found most important in their subjects. In this situation, students were able to take work demands lightly if they kept their end of the bargain by being present and maintaining positive relationships with their teachers.

Student teachers expected the teacher educators to take the responsibility for education. But something changed in the seminary contract in 1994. Students became less willing to spend most of the day sitting in a classroom. They now started to regard their teacher education project as just one of many elements in their life. Social obligations to families and friends, work, special interests, travel and other activities seemed to have more importance for this generation of students and demanded more of their time. Students attended the college in the required mandatory hours and then went on to other places to experience new events. The amount of learning taking place at the college itself was dramatically reduced.

In transactions with their educators' comprehension of teacher education, student teachers prolonged their own well-known 'student' role (Kvalbein 1999). They regarded the knowledge they were supposed to develop during teacher education as certain and set. They saw their teacher educators as the main source for given knowledge. They understood their educational challenge as participation, adaptation, reception and reproduction, and considered that to be educated was to be taught. This is illuminated by an excerpt from the field notes:

> Two weeks before exam the students in the class confront the teacher with questions about the content of his lectures this year. They think he has talked much about topics outside of what some of them just now have discovered to be in their textbooks. They want to know what the topics for the exam will be. Issues from his lectures or from the textbooks? The teacher tries to calm them, saying that he has covered textbook stuff, but in a more comprehensive way. He says that the college teachers of the subject will compose the exam together, and it will cover four main themes; all in the textbooks and all lectured on. Students murmur loudly and discontentedly. One student says: 'I think you alone shall formulate our exam! Here we come and listen to you, and if you don't give us exam questions from what you have been talking about, there is no reason why we should attend your lectures!' Other students give supporting sounds and exclamations. The teacher promises to talk with his colleagues. And this class gets their own exam questions, especially geared towards the teacher's lectures.   (Field notes from the graduating class, spring 1994)

Student teachers often described themselves as 'students' and the college as 'school'. They swiftly discovered that education at the college did not demand daily preparations, and that the all-important issue was to be present. Learning strategies used by most students were to satisfy teachers' demands with the least possible effort. Social practices in the institution studied encouraged students to accommodate to the college and to the teacher educators. In contradiction with the aims of the new policies, students developed few choices in and little responsibility for their education.

A common opinion among student teachers in the second half of last century was that they had a nice social time during their teacher education, but that they did not learn much. A great part of their lessons was repetition of subjects they had covered in primary and secondary school. Everyday life at the college was more conditioned by various school subjects than by the future profession (Kvalbein 1999; Jacobsen 1989). The concept of the 'seminary contract' became less relevant in 1994. However, it was not fully abandoned. Through the mandatory attendance, most students spent at least sixteen hours a week at the college, in social interaction with their teacher educators and fellow students. In these hours they could listen to their teacher educators as preparation for exams, or engage in discussions and planned activities. Pastoral control and the freedom now desired by the students, presented few challenges to seriously reflect on future professional demands.

## Teacher education 2002 – more freedom to the students

During the interval between the two research projects, new national reforms changed teacher education. Management by objectives and decentralisation were on the national political agenda in general but, paradoxically, the national teacher education reform in 1998 showed little evidence of these ideas. The number of compulsory subjects was increased; detailed curriculum reinforced and forms of exams regulated. Succession and placing of subjects in the different study years were more fixed, and the students' possibility to elect subjects more limited than before. The national curriculum was in all subjects as detailed as before, if not more so. Students were still organised in established classes with one main teacher in each subject. The evaluation and examination procedures were not much altered.

Organisational changes in educational institutions do not necessarily imply significant changes in institutional, communicative practice and learning. Reforms in the organisation of teacher education, for instance, may not alter ways that knowledge and attitudes are constituted and displayed in the everyday college arena (Beach 1995, 2000; Kvalbein 1999). Still, a different teacher education culture was observed in 2001/2002. The national construction of teacher education had become more rigid, and the teacher education institutions had implemented the new organisational model. However, whilst everyday teacher education and the daily work at the college was much the same as in 1994, relationships between teacher students and teacher educator had changed. Students had attained new and freer positions. What had happened?

A year before the reform, the Norwegian Ministry of Education lay down new rules for student participation in higher education in general, and these rules were in line with the new restructuring turn. Students were given freedom to decide whether to attend lectures or other educational activities at their institutions or not. They could only be required to attend arrangements at the colleges or universities that provided information they could not obtain from books and that could not be tested in exams. It is here that a neo-liberal understanding of students as independent, self-motivated and self-managed appears and begins to characterise the new disciplining regime. The regulations cohered with a shift in responsibility for education from the educators to the students themselves, even if this is not explicitly stated. At the same time a new national regulation for evaluation in teacher education was decreed from the Ministry. It was stated that external examiners should determine all final grades, and these should be based on final exams only, not on a compound made up of marks given by teacher educators during study and grades on final exams as before.

These regulations changed the former disciplinary technologies in teacher education and positioned students and teachers in a new relationship to each other, to course work, and to curriculum activities at the educational institution. The teacher educators, who should no longer give counting grades, had lost a powerful position. The students' freedom to avail themselves of the educational offering or not, implied the final breach of the seminary contract. Teacher educators and students experienced the 'offers of discursive meaning' provided by the college (Englund 1998) differently from before.

Teacher educators mostly regretted the new regulations (Michelsen 1999). They valued the seminary contract and initially tried to keep the same relationships with their students as earlier. But interviews in autumn 2000 suggest that many teacher educators have become more resigned. They have realised that they no longer know all their students, some of whom they hardly see at the college. Excerpts from interviews illustrate this:

> Our teacher students have made a big splash in the newspapers this spring, criticising teacher education. They say that teacher education at the college is not satisfactory. I think I have these students on the list for my class, but I have never seen them at the college!
> (Female teacher educator, autumn 2000)

> Often only half of the class is present at lectures. It is hard ...to keep the motivation for work high when the students don't show up.
> (Male teacher educator, autumn 2000)

New disciplinary techniques are surfacing. Teacher educators become more preoccupied by the mandatory work they are allowed to expect the students to conduct during the study year. They use the possibility to control the quality of these assignments. Local variations of the national curriculum in all subjects now list mandatory student work that has to be completed and approved before students may take exams. Teacher educators are not as lenient as before when it comes to demanding work within deadlines, and they are not as apt to accept substandard work as when the seminary contract prevailed and the personal relationships to students was stronger. More students now fail at exams. Teacher educators' former solidarity with students in most occasions is declining:

> Last year hardly half of the class participated in my literature seminars. I required them to read before the class, and the rest did not find time to do that. At the end of the term, students questioned if it was legal to keep students out of class with such requirements. I think we have the right to demand serious work from the students.
> (Female teacher educator, autumn 2000)

Participating in activities and processes at the college has diminished in importance for the students, and teacher educators have lost much of their status as main sources for relevant knowledge. Many students' main concern is how to effectively acquire the necessary curriculum content from the textbooks. They know it is the exams that count. Still, teacher students do participate in the educational activities offered at the college and roughly half of a class usually shows up. Quite a few of these are better prepared and take a more active part in teacher-invited dialogues in class than before. Students are more likely, however, to regard college attendance as a shortcut to pick up the most relevant in the syllabus for exams. If they find that issues modestly featured in textbooks dominate the lectures, many of them just get up and leave, while the teacher educator is still lecturing. Students interpret the college's offer as a market from which to pick the necessary goods:

> Around 70 students out of 220, comprising the whole class, are seated in the auditorium for the weekly double lecture, this week on educational planning. The teacher educator is talking about curriculum in compulsory school in certain subjects, illustrating his points with transparencies on the overhead projector. From my place in the back I hear after 20 minutes that students on the two last rows whisper to each other, wondering if this is relevant for the exam. Apparently, they don't think it is, six students get up and leave while the teacher is talking in front. After 45 minutes the teacher takes a break, 15 minutes! When he starts again, the number of students has diminished to 40.
> (Field notes from the graduating class, winter 2001)

Students, who do not attend classes or turn up at irregular intervals, make joint work and planned student contributions uncertain and difficult to plan for. Collective processes are occasionally focused in some mandatory group tasks in a few subjects, but most work and preparations are individual. The students' main concern is to individually be able to reproduce what they regard as textbook knowledge in assignments and exams. It seems that this might be the most rational way if the intention is to go through teacher education with least time and effort. Demands are modest. According to recent data (SPS 2002) only 10% of the teacher students in autumn 2001 felt motivated to study during the study year, compared to 21% in 1997.

Teacher education processes have become subordinate to the educational products, particularly the assignments and exams. Freedom of the individual students has undermined earlier collective processes. Valuable knowledge, attitudes and actions for future teachers, developed through daily collective processes and practices, have been strongly reduced. Last minute cramming and reproduction of given subject substance at given times is seen as constituting teacher education at the college by more students than before. Teacher educators' interpretations and critical reflections on central themes in lectures have lost importance in relation to textbooks. Processes featuring verbal communication give way to written products. Communicative patterns seem to fall short of fostering student self-motivation and responsibility for comprehensive knowledge development and professional preparation. The new freedom has not helped students develop a creative responsibility for their education.

## Teacher education in the future

A further new reform of Norwegian teacher education is to be implemented from autumn 2003. Again, there are no recent changes in the schools that teachers should be educated for. This persistent flow of teacher education reforms may be seen as an indicator of how hard it is to effect desired changes in teacher education culture (Beach 2000). Thoroughgoing changes in teacher students' and teacher educators' attitudes and patterns of actions seem to be hard to obtain. Cultural traditions have their own conditions for reproduction and they keep their strength and legitimating power as long as they furnish adequate interpretation systems (Habermas 1973). The research reviewed in this chapter shows, however, that transformations occur when disciplining technologies are changed.

The 2002 reform in teacher education opens it up for more student freedom, but also more control. Elected subjects constitute half of general teacher education from 2003, and the students will be taught in smaller groups and in closer contact with their teacher educators. Every student will sign an individual study contract with the institution. Guidance, frequent feedback and assessment of work during study is supposed to replace final exams. External examiners will no longer be required. The national curriculum will be short and modestly detailed, open for extensive institutional initiatives. This will, however, not happen without national control. A new agency, The National Agency for Quality in Education (NOKUT), has been established to handle approvals of advanced studies and to evaluate all higher educational institution every sixth year to secure that they offer high quality education (UFD 2002b). If institutions do not perform up to standards, which are to be decided, they may have to shut down.

The last reform illustrates the new policies of restructuring; expanded individual freedom and intensified procedures for accountability and control. Within reforms in tune with neo-liberalism and the third way, the institutions will have increased freedom and responsibilities for organisation, curriculum, assessment and financing, but will also have to fulfil governmental demands on national standards.

New rules about financing have also emerged recently. These rules may, however, endanger what has been called The Quality Reform (UFD 2002a). Higher educational institutions will from 2003 be allocated annual funds according to how many graduate students they produce whilst until now they have been granted money according to how many students they have accepted each year. The new financial routines put pressure on institutions to let as many students as possible pass. If so, the demands must not be severe.

## Conclusions

Teacher educational institutions are encountering challenges to develop consumer and market oriented approaches. They must be efficient in candidate production, popular among students and show economic success to gain public approval. Successful neo-liberalism or 'the third way' in higher education implies a balance between traditional scholarship, the enterprising individual, and market culture (Ling 2000). But as suggested by Beach (this volume), the alignment of ideological elements of (good) education and the market are normally heterodoxical and antagonistic, and the value practices of (good) education are usually fetishised within the processes of value *liquidation* implied by marketisation.

The current trend of control has led towards a form of student freedom from the demands of a strictly regulated and centralised education. The question is whether the technologies of freedom and control that have been used to bring this development about can be deliberately employed so as to place students in positions and relationships where they will take an active part in learning communities and find answers to unsolved questions related to their future profession. The last reform does not give clues about how this can be accomplished.

# Bibliography

Aapola, S. (1997) Mature girls and adolescent boys? Deconstructing discourses of adolescence and gender, *Young*, 5 (4): 50-68

Aapola, S., Gordon, T. and Lahelma, E. (2003) Citizens in the text?—International presentations of citizenship in school textbooks, in Torres, C. A. and Antikainen, A. (eds) *The international handbook on the sociology of education: An international assessment of new research and theory*, Lanham, Boulder, New York and Oxford: Rowman and Littlefield Publishers

Adams, B. (1995) *Timewatch—the social analysis of time*, Cambridge: Polity Press

Ainley, P. (2000) *From earning to learning: What is happening to education and the welfare state*, London: the Tufnell Press

Alanen, L. (2001) Explorations in generational analysis, in Alanen, L. and Mayall B. (eds) *Conceptualising child-adult relations*, London: Routledge Falmer

Alexiadou, N., Lawn, M. and Ozga, J. (2001) Educational governance and social integration/exclusion: The cases of Scotland and England within the U.K., in Lindblad, S., and Popkewitz, T. (eds) *Education governance and social integration and exclusion: Studies in the powers of reason and the reasons of power*, (Uppsala Reports on Education no. 39), Uppsala: Department of Education, Uppsala University

Allen, M., Benn, C., Chitty, C., Cole, M., Hatcher, R., Hirtt, N. and Rikowsi, G. (1999) *Business, business, business: New Labour's education policy*, London: the Tufnell Press

Allman, P. (1999) *Revolutionary social transformation: Democratic hopes, political possibilities and critical education*, Westport: Bergin and Garvey

Althusser, L. (1971) Ideology and ideological state apparatuses, in Althusser, *L. Lenin and Philosophy and Other Essays*, London: New Left Books

Anderson, B. (1991) *Imagined communities: Reflections on the origin and spread of nationalism*, London and New York: Verso

Apo, S. (1996) Suomalaisuuden stigmatisoinnin tradition [The tradition of stigmatising Finnishness] in Alasuutari, P. and Ruuska, P. (eds) *Elävänä euroopassa: Muuttuva suomalainen identiteetti [Living in Europe: Changing Finnish identity]*, Tampere: Vastapaino

Apple, M. W. (2001) Creating profits by creating failures: Standards, markets, and inequality in education, *International Journal of Inclusive Education*, 5 (2/3): 193-118

Arnesen, A. L. (2000a) Cultural tensions in social practices: Marginalisation, inclusion and exclusion processes in a Norwegian school, in Walraven, G., Parsons, C., van Veev, D. and Day, C. (eds.) *Combating social exclusion through education: Laissez-faire, authoritarianism or third way?*, Lueven, Apeldoorn: Garant

Arnesen, A. L. (2000b) Masculinities and ethnicities at play: A discourse analysis of conflict in a Norwegian classroom, *Pedagogy, Culture and Society*, 8 (2): 157-172

Arnesen, A. L. (2002) *Ulikhet og marginalisering med referanse til kjlonn og sosial bakgrunn. En etnografisk studie av sosial og diskursiv praksis i skolen* [Difference and marginality in relation to gender and social background. An ethnographic study of social and discursive praxis at school], University of Oslo: Unipub Forlag

Arnot, M. and Gordon, T. (1996) Gender, citizenship and marketisation: A dialogue between Madeleine Arnot and Tuula Gordon, *Discourse: Studies in the Cultural Politics of Education*, 17 (3): 377-388

Atkinson, P., Coffey, A., Delamont, S., Lofland, J. and Lofland, L. (2001) Editorial introduction, in *Handbook of ethnography,* London, Thousand Oaks and New Delhi: Sage

Bakhtin, M. (1981) *The dialogic imagination: Four essays* (Trans. C. Emerson and M. Holquist), Austin, Texas: University of Texas Press

Ball, S. (1984) Initial Encounters in the classroom and the process of establishment, in Hammersley, M. and Woods, P. (eds) *Life in school: The sociology of pupil culture,* Milton Keynes: Open University Press

Ball, S. J. (1987) *The micro-politics of the school: Towards a theory of school organization,* London: Methuen

Ball, S. J. (1994) *Education reform: A critical and post-structural approach,* Buckingham: Open University Press

Ball, S. J. and Maguire, M. (1994) Discourses of educational reform in the United Kingdom and the USA and the work of teachers, *British Journal of In-service Education,* 20 (1): 5-16

Banks, J. A. (2003) *Multicultural education: Issues and perspectives,* New York: John Wiley and Sons

Banks, J. A. and Banks, C. M. (eds) (1995) *Handbook of research on multicultural education,* New York: Macmillan

Baratz, S. S. and Baratz J. C. (1974) Indgriben 0i barnets tidlige udvikling—Det socialvidenskabelige grundlag for institutionel racisme [Intervention in early child development—the foundation of institutional racism in social science], in Gregersen F., Jakobsen, K. S., Olesen, H. S., Pedersen, A. S. and Rasmussen, P. (eds), *Klassesprog, Sociolingvistik og uddannelse: en antologi* [Class language, socio-linguistics and education: An anthology] København: Borgen/Basis

Beach, D, (1996) Socio-material structuration and education change, *Nordisk Pedagogik,* 16 (4): 203-213

Beach, D. (1990) *Policy making: A study of policy development in contemporary teacher education,* Göteborg: Institutionen för Pedagogik och Didaktik, Report 1990: 02

Beach, D. (1995) *Making sense of the problems of change: An ethnographic study of a teacher education reform,* (Göteborg Studies in Educational Research 100), Göteborg: Acta Universitatis Gothoburgensis

Beach, D. (1997) *Symbolic control and power relay: Learning in higher professional education,* (Göteborg Studies in Educational Research 119), Göteborg: Acta Universitatis Gothoburgensis

Beach, D. (1999a) Om demokrati, reproduktion och förnyelse i dagens gymnasieskol [On democracy and reproduction in the modern upper-secondary school], *Pedagogisk Forskning i Sverige* [Pedagogic Research in Sweden], 4 (4): 349-365

Beach, D. (1999b) Matematikutbildningens politik och ideologi [The politics and ideology of mathematics], *Nämnaren,* 26: 56-60.

Beach, D. (1999c) Alienation and fetish in science education, *Scandinavian Journal of Education Research,* 43 (2): 157-172.

Beach, D. (1999d) The problems of education change: Working from the ruins of progressive education, *Scandinavian Journal of Education Research,* 43 (3): 231-247

Beach, D. (2000) Continuing problems of teacher education reform, *Scandinavian Journal of Education Research,* 44 (3), 275-291

# Bibliography

Beach, D. (2001) Alienation, reproduction and fetish in Swedish education, in G. Walford (ed.) *Ethnography and education policy*, (Studies in education ethnography Vol. 4), Amsterdam, London and New York: Elsevier

Bentley, P-O. (2003) *Mathematics teachers and their teaching: A survey study*. (Göteborg Studies in Educational Research 191), Göteborg: Acta Universitatis Gothoburgensis

Berger, P. L. and Luckmann, T. (1966) *The social construction of reality: A treatise in the sociology of knowledge*, Harmondsworth: Penguin

Berggren, I. (2001) *Identitet, kön och klass: Hur abetarflickor formar sin identitet* [Identity, gender and class: How working class girls shape their identity], (Göteborg Studies in Educational Research 157), Göteborg: Acta Universitatis Gothoburgensis

Berlak, A. and Berlak, A. (1981) *Dilemmas of schooling*, New York: Methuen

Bernstein, B. (1967) Open schools—open society, *New Society*, 14 September, 351-3

Bernstein, B. (1990) *Class, codes and control Vol. 4: The structuring of pedagogic discourse*, London: Routledge

Bhabha, H. K. (1990) Introduction: Narrating the nation, in Bhabha, H. K. (ed.) *Nation and narration*, London: Routledge

Billig, M. (1995) *Banal nationalism*, London: Sage

Bjerrum-Nielsen, H. and Larsen, K. (1985) *Piger og drenge i klasseoffentligheden* [Girls and boys in the public classroom], Universitetet i Oslo, Pedagogisk Forskningsinstitut, Report No. 2

Blomqvist, P. and Rothstein, B. (2000) *Välfärdsstatens nya ansikte: demokrati och marknadsreformer inom den offentliga sektorn* [The new faces of welfare states: Democracy and market reforms within the public sector], Stockholm: Agora

Bloom, S. B., Davis, A. and Hess, R. (eds) (1965) *Compensatory education for cultural deprivation*, New York: Holt, Rhinehart and Winston

Boaler, J. (1996) Learning to lose in the mathematics classroom: A critique of traditional schooling practices in the UK, *International Journal of Qualitative Studies in Education*, 9 (1): 17 - 34

Boli, J. and Ramirez, F. (1986) World culture and the institutional development of mass education, in Richardson, J. (ed.) *Handbook of theory and research for the sociology of education*, New York: Greenwood Press

Bourdieu, P. (1979/1984) *Distinction*, Cambridge: Harvard University Press

Bourdieu, P. (1997) The forms of capital, in Halsey, A., Lauder, H., Brown, P., and Stuart Wells, A. (eds) *Education, culture, economy, society*, Oxford: Oxford University Press

Bourdieu, P. (1999) *The weight of the world*, Cambridge: Polity Press

Bowles, S and Gintis, H. (1976) *Schooling in capitalist America*, New York: Basic Books

Bowles, S and Gintis, H. (1988a) Schooling in capitalist America: A reply to our critics, in M. Cole (ed.) *Bowles and Gintis revisited: Correspondence and contradiction in educational theory*, London: Falmer Press

Bowles, S and Gintis, H. (1988b) Contradiction and reproduction in educational theory, in M. Cole (ed.) *Bowles and Gintis revisited: Correspondence and contradiction in educational theory*, London: Falmer Press

Brenner, N., Jessop, B., Jones, M. and Macleod, G. (eds) (2003) *State/space: A reader*, Oxford: Blackwell Publishing

Broadfoot, P. (1995) *Case studies in educational change 1, International perspectives on educational reform and policy implementation*, London: Falmer Press

Brosio, R. A. (1994) *A radical democratic critique of capitalist education*, New York: Peter Lang Publishing

Bruner, J. (1996) *The culture of education*, Cambridge: Harvard University Press
Burgess, R. G. (1984) *In the field: An introduction to field research*, London: George Allen and Unwin
Cambone, P. (1994) The multiple meaning of time for teachers, in Cambone, P. *Time for teachers in school restructuring*, www.ed.gov./pubs/
Campbell, D. T. and Fry, P. W (1970) The implications of learning theory for the fade-out of gains from compensatory education, in Hellmuth, J. (ed.) *Compensatory education: A national debate*, Disadvantaged Child Vol. 3, New York: Brunner/Mazel
Carlén, M. (1999) *Kunskapslyft eller avbytarbänk? Möten med industriarbetare om utbildning för arbete* [Adult education initiative or the substitutes bench? Meeting industrial workers in relation to education for work], (Göteborg Studies in Educational Research 144), Göteborg: Acta Universitatis Gothoburgensis
Carlgren, I. (1992) På väg mot en enhetlig lärarutbildning? En studie av lärarutbildares föreställningar i ett reformskede [Toward a cohesive teacher education? An investigation of the mind sets of teacher educators in a reform period], Uppsala: Pedagogiska Institutionen, Uppsala University,
Carlgren, I. (2000) The implicit teacher, in Klette, K. and Carlgren, I. (eds) *Restructuring Nordic teachers: An analysis of policy texts from Finland, Denmark, Sweden and Norway*, University of Oslo, Institute for Educational Research, Report No. 10
Carrington, S. and Elkins, J. (2002) Comparison of a traditional and an inclusive secondary school culture, *Inclusive Education*, 1 (6): 1-16
Carroll, L. (1993) *Alice in wonderland*, Ware: Wordsworth
Castells, M., Flecha, R., Freire, P., Giroux, H., Macedo, D. and Willis, P. (eds) (1999) *Critical education in the new information age*, Boulder, Colorado: Roman and Littlefield
Castells, M. (1996) *The rise of the network society: The information age, Economy, society and culture Vol. I*, Oxford: Blackwell
Castells, M. (1998) *End of millennium*, Oxford: Blackwell
Castells, M. (1999) Flows, networks and identities: A critical theory of the informational society, in Castells, M., Flecha, R., Freire, P., Giroux, H., Macedo, D. and Willis, P. (eds) *Critical education in the new information age*, Boulder, Colorado: Roman and Littlefield
Chambers, D. (2001) *Representing the family*, London, Thousand Oaks and New Delhi: Sage
Chouliaraki, L. and Fairclough, N. (1999) *Discourse in late modernity: Rethinking critical discourse analysis*, Edinburgh: Edinburgh University Press
Clifford, J. and Marcus, G. (eds) (1996) *Writing culture: The poetics and politics of ethnography*, Berkeley: University of California Press, Introduction
Codd, J. A. (1988) The construction and deconstruction of educational policy documents, in *Education Policy*, 3 (3): 235-247, cited in Marshall, J. and Peters, M. (1999) *Education Policy*, Cheltenham: Elgar Reference Collection
Coffey, A. (1999) *The ethnographic self: Fieldwork and the representation of identity*, London, California and New Delhi: Sage
Cohen, M. (1998) 'A habit of healthy idleness': Boys' underachievement in historical perspective, in Epstein, D., Elwood, J., Hey, V. and Maw, J. (eds) *Failing boys? Issues in gender and achievement*, Buckingham and Philadelphia: Open University Press
Connell, R. W. (1987) *Gender and power: Society, the person and sexual politics*, Cambridge: Polity Press

Connolly, P. (1998) *Racism, gender identities and young children: Social relations in a multi-ethnic, inner city primary school*, London: Routledge

Connolly, P. and Troyna B. (eds) (1998) *Researching racism in education: Politics, theory and practice*, Milton Keynes: Open University Press

Cruikshank, B. (1999) *The will to empower: Democratic citizens and other subjects*, Ithaca, NY: Cornell University Press

Dæhlen, M. (2001) *Usikre, dedikerte, engasjerte og distanserte* [Unsure, dedicated, engaged and aloof], Oslo: HiO-rapport nr. 12

Dahland, G. (1998) *Matematikundervisning i 1990-talets gymnasieskola* [Mathematics teaching in the 20th century upper-secondary school], Göteborg, Institutionen för Pedagogik och Didaktik: Rapport 1998: 05

Dale, R. (1997) The state and the governance of education: An analysis of the restructuring of the state-education relationship, in Halsey, A., Lauder, H., Brown, P. and Stuart Wells. A. (eds) *Education, culture, economy, society*, Oxford: Oxford University Press

Daun, H. (ed.) (2002) *Educational restructuring in the context of globalization and national policy*, London: Routledge/Falmer Press

Daun, H. and Benincasa, L. (eds) (1998) *Restructuring education in Europe—four country studies*, Stockholm: Institute of International Education, Report no. 109

Davies, A-M., Holland, J. and Minhas, R. (1992) *Equal opportunities in the new ERA*, London: the Tufnell Press

Davies, B. (1983) *Life in the classroom and playground: The accounts of primary school children*, London: Routledge and Kegan Paul

Davies, B. (1989) *Frogs and snails and feminist tales: Preschool children and gender*, Sydney: Allen and Unwin

Davies, B. (1993) *Shards of glass: Children reading and writing beyond gendered identities*, New Jersey: Hampton Press

Delamont, S. and Atkinson, P. (1995) *Fighting familiarity: Essays on education and ethnography*, Cresskill, N.J: Hampton Press

Delamont, S. and Galton, M. (1986) *Inside the secondary classroom*, London: Routledge and Kegan Paul

Denzin, N and Lincoln, Y. S. (1994) *Handbook of qualitative research*, London and New Delhi: Sage

Donald, James (1992) *Sentimental education: Schooling, popular culture and the regulation of liberty*, London and New York: Verso

Draper, J. (1993) We're Back with Gobbo: The re-establishment of gender relations following a school merger, in Woods, P. and Hammersley, M. (eds) *Gender and ethnicity in schools: Ethnographic accounts*, London and New York: Routledge

Ds (1999) *Without a national timetable—with an unchanged mission*, Ministry of Science and Education, Stockholm: Fakta Info Direkt

Dyson, A. (1994) Towards a collaborative, learning model for responding to student diversity, *Support for Learning*, 9 (1): 53-60

Education Group, Centre for Contemporary Cultural Studies (1981) *Unpopular education: Schooling and social democracy in England since 1944*, London: Hutchinson

Edvardsen, E. (1998) Fravær som er til stede [Absence that is present], in Klette, K. (ed.) *Klasseromsforskning på norsk* [Classroom research in Norway] Ad Notam Gyldendal

Eisenhart, M. (2001) Changing conceptions of culture and ethnographic methodology: Recent thematic shifts and their implications for research on teaching, in Richardson, V. (ed.) *Handbook of research on teaching* (Vol. 4), New York: Macmillan

Ejrnæs, M. (1999) Afskaf begrebet den social arv [Abolish the concept of social inheritance], *Social Forskning, Nyt fra Socialforskningsinstituttet,* 2 (July)

Emanuelsson, I. and Fischbein, S. (1986) Vive la difference? A study of sex and schooling, *Scandinavian Journal of Educational Research,* 30 (1): 71-84

Emerson, R. M., Fretz, R. I. and Shaw, L. L. (1995) *Writing ethnographic fieldnotes,* Chicago: University of Chicago Press

Emsheiner, P. (2000) *Lärarstudenten som subjekt och objekt—kritiskt tänkande och disciplinering i lärarutbildning* [The student teacher as subject and object—critical thinking and disciplining in teacher education], (Stockholm Studies in Education Science 24), Stockholm: HLS Förlag

Englert, C. S., Tarrant, K. L. and Mariage, T. V. (1992) Defining and redefining instructional practice in Special Education: Perspectives on good teaching, *Teacher Education and Special Education,* 15 (1): 62-68

Englund, T. 1998: *Teaching as an offer of (discursive) meaning?,* in Gundem, B. and Hopman, S. (eds) *Didaktik and/or curriculum,* New York: Peter Lang

Epstein, D., Elwood, J., Hey, V. and Maw, J. (eds) (1998) *Failing boys? Issues in gender and achievement,* Buckingham and Philadelphia: Open University Press

Eriksson, R. and Jonsson, J. O. (2003) Varför består den sociala snedrekrytering [Why does socially uneven recruitment continue] *Pedagogisk Forskning i Sverige* [Pedagogic Research in Sweden], 7, (3): 210-217

Fairclough, N. (1995) *Critical discourse analysis,* London: Longman

Fairclough, N. and Chouliaraki, L. (2000) *Discourse in late modernity,* Edinburgh: Edinburgh University Press

Falkner, K. (1997) *Teachers and the restructuring of school—an encounter between political intentions and compulsory school teachers' perspective of school change in Sweden,* Uppsala: Cta Universitatis Upsaliensis, no. 71

Fielding, S. (2000) Walk on the left!: Children's geographies and the primary school, in Holloway, S. L. and Valentine, G. *Children's geographies: playing, living, learning,* London: Routledge

Fisher, D., Roach, V. and Frey, N. (2002) Examining the general programmatic benefits of inclusive schools, *Inclusive Education,* 1 (6): 63-78

Foucault, M. (1975/1979) *Discipline and punish,* Harmondsworth: Penguin

Frimodt-Møller, I. and Ingerslev, G. H. (1993) Nye piger i gymnasiet [New girls in upper secondary school], in Nielsen, A. M., Stormhøj, C., Søndergaard, D.M., Frimodt-Møller, I., Grønbæk Hansen, K. and Eriksen, T. R.(eds) *Køn i forandring* [Gender in change], Copenhagen: Forlaget Hyldespjæet

Fritzell, C. (1996) Pedagogical split vision, *Educational Theory,* 46 (2): 203-216

Gándara, P. (2000) *The dimension of time and the challenge of school reform,* New York: State University of New York

Garfinkel, H. (1967) *Studies in ethnomethodology,* Englewood Cliffs, NJ: Prentice Hall

Gee, J., Hull, G. and Lankshear, C. (1996) *The new work order: Behind the language of the new capitalism,* St. Leonards: Allen and Unwin

Geertz, C. (1966) *The interpretation of cultures,* New York: Basic Books

Giddens, A. (1985) Time, space and regionalisation, in Gregory, D. and Urry, J. (eds) *Social relations and spatial structures,* London: Macmillan

Giddens, A. (1989) *Sociology,* Cambridge: Polity Press

Giddens, A. (1991) *Modernity and self-identity: Self and society in the late modern age,* London: Polity Press

Giddens, A. (1998) *The third way: The renewal of social democracy*, Cambridge: Polity Press
Gillborn, D. (1993) *Race, ethnicity and education: Teaching and learning in multiethnic Schools*, London: Unwin Hyman
Gillborn, D. and Gipps, C. (1996) *Recent research on the achievements of ethic minority pupils*, London: HSMO
Gimbel, J. (1992) *Modersmål og andetsprog: Tosproget undervisning for tosprogede elever* [Mother tongue and second language: Bilingual education for bilingual students], København: Mellemfolkelig Samvirke
Goffman, E. (1963) *Behaviour in public places: Notes on the social organization of gatherings*, New York: The Free Press
Gordon, T. (1986) *Democracy in one school? Progressive education and restructuring*, London, New York and Philadelphia: Falmer Press
Gordon, T. (1992) Citizens and others: Gender, democracy and education, *International Studies in Sociology of Education*, 2 (1): 43-56
Gordon, T. (2000) Tears and laughter in the margins, *Nordic Journal of Women's Studies*, 8 (3): 149-159
Gordon, T. (2001) Kuka voi olla suomalainen?—erot ja yhteisyys 'muihin' nuorten naisten ja miesten rakentamina [Who can be a Finn?—Differences and belonging to 'others' constructed by young women and young men], *Nuorisotutkimus* [The Finnish Journal of Youth Study], 19 (1): 25-38
Gordon, T. (2002) Kansallisuuden sukupuolittuneet tilat [The gendered spaces of nationality], in Gordon, T., Komulainen, K., Lempiäinen, K. (eds) *Hei hei Suomi-neitonen hei: Kansallisuuden sukupuoli* ['Finnish Maiden, hello:' Gendered nationality], Tampere: Vastapaino
Gordon, T. and Lahelma, E. (1998) Kansalaisuus, kansallisuus ja sukupuoli [Citizenship, nationality and gender], in Alasuutari, P. and Ruuska, P. (eds) *Elävänä Euroopassa: Muuttuva suomalainen identiteetti* [Alive in Europe: Changing Finnish identity], Tampere: Osuuskunta Vastapaino
Gordon, T. and Lahelma, E. (2001) Who wants to be a woman? Young women's reflections on transitions to adulthood. Paper at the Gender and Education Conference, London 4-6 April
Gordon, T. and Lahelma, E. (1996) 'School is like an ants' nest': Spatiality and embodiment in schools, *Gender and Education*, 8 (3): 301-310
Gordon, T., Hynninen, P., Metso, T., Lahelma, E. and Palmu, T. (1999) Learning the routines: 'professionalization' of newcomers in secondary school, *Qualitative Studies in Education*, 12 (6): 689-705
Gordon, T., Holland, J. and Lahelma, E. (2000a) *Making spaces: Citizenship and difference in schools*, London: Macmillan
Gordon, T., Holland, J. and Lahelma, E. (2000b) Friends or foes? Interpreting relations between girls in school, in Walford, G. and Hudson, C. (eds) *Genders and sexualities in educational ethnography* (Studies in educational ethnography, Vol. 3), Amsterdam, New York, Oxford, Shannon, Singapore and Tokyo: JAI, Elsevier Science
Gordon, T., Holland, J. and Lahelma, E. (2000c) 'From pupil to citizen: A gendered route', in Arnot, M. and Dillabough, J-A. (eds) *Challenging democracy: International perspectives on gender, education and citizenship*, London: Routledge

Gordon, T., Holland, J. and Lahelma, E. (2000d) Moving bodies/still bodies: Embodiment and agency in schools, in McKie, L. and Watson, N. (eds) *Organizing bodies: Policy, institutions and work*, London: Macmillan

Gordon, T., Holland, J. and Lahelma, E. (2001) Ethnographic research in educational settings, in Atkinson *et al.* (2001) *Handbook of ethnography*, London, Thousand Oaks and New Delhi: Sage

Gordon, T., Lahelma, E., Tolonen, T. and Holland, J. (2002) Katseelta piilossa: hiljaisuus ja liikkumattomuus kouluetnografin havainnoissa [Hidden from gaze: silence and immobility in school ethnographer's observations], in Aaltonen, S. and Honkatukia, P. (eds) *Tulkintoja tytöistä* [Interpretations about girls], Helsinki: SKS

Gramsci, A. (1971) *Selections from the prison notebooks*, New York: International Press

Gulbrandsen, L. M. (1994) Blant hester og gorillæer i skolegården: Utvikling i en kjønnet kultur [Among horses and gorillas in the playground: Development in a gendered culture], *Psyke and Logos*, 15 (1): 109-124

Gupta, A. and Ferguson, J. (1997) Beyond 'culture': Space, identity and the politics of difference, in Gupta, A. and Ferguson, J., *Culture power place; Explorations in critical anthropology*, Durhan and London: Duke University Press

Gustafsson, J. E. (2002) Händelser vid vatten—de världsomspännande försöken att privatisera en kollektiv nyttighet [Events by water–World wide efforts to privatise a collective value], *Clarte*, 2002 (3): 56-64

Habermas, J. (1973) *Legitimationsprobleme im Spätkaitalismus* [Problems of legitimisation in late capitalism], Frankfurt: Suhrkamp

Hall, S. (1992) Race, culture and communications, *Rethinking Marxism*, 5 (1): 10-18

Hall, S. (1996) New ethnicities, in Morley, D. and Chen K. H. (eds), *Stuart Hall: critical dialogues in cultural studies*, London: Routledge

Hall, S. (1997) *Representations: Cultural representations and signifying practice*, London: Sage/The Open University

Hall, S. (1999) *Identiteetti*, Tampere: Vastapaino [Identity. A collection of articles translated into Finnish.]

Hamilton, D. (1990): *Learning about education: An unfinished curriculum*, Buckingham: Open University Press

Hamilton, D. (1999) 'The pedagogic paradox (or why no didactics in England?)', *Pedagogy, Culture, and Society* 7 (1): 135-52

Hammersley, M. (1994) Ethnography, policy making and practice in education, in Halpin, D. and Troyna, B. (eds.) *Researching education policy: Ethical and methodological issues*, London: Falmer Press

Handel, W. (1982) *Ethnomethodology: How people make sense*, Englewood Cliffs, New Jersey: Prentice-Hall

Hargreaves, A. (1994) *Changing teachers, changing times: Teachers work and culture in the postmodern age*, Toronto: The Ontario Institute for Studies in Education

Harinen, P. (2000) *Valmiiseen tulleet—Tutkimus nuoruudesta, kansallisuudesta ja kansalaisuudesta*, Nuorisotutkimusverkosto and Nuorisotutkimusseura [Young citizens—arrivals at the given: A study of youth, nationality and citizenship] Helsinki: Network of Youth Research and Society of Youth Research, publications 11

Harvey, D. (1990) *The condition of postmodernity: An enquiry into the origins of cultural change*, Oxford: Blackwell

# Bibliography

Haug, P. (1999) *Spesialundervisning i grunnskulen: Grunnlag, utvikling og innhald* [Special Education in compulsory school: Basis, development and content], Oslo: Abstrakt Forlag

Heritage, J. (1984)/(1989) *Garfinkel and ethnomethodology,* Cambridge: Polity Press

Heritage, J. (1984)/(1996) *Harold Garfinkel ja etnometodologia,* Helsinki: Gaudeamus

Hey, V. (1997) *The company she keeps: An ethnography of girls' friendships,* Buckingham and Philadelphia: Open University Press

Hill, D. (1990) *Something old, something new, something borrowed, something blue: Schooling, teacher education and the radical right in Britain and the USA,* Hillcole Group, Paper 3, London: the Tufnell Press

Hill, D. (1999) *New Labour and education: Policy, ideology and the third way,* London: the Tufnell Press

Hill, D. (2001) State theory and the reconstruction of schooling and teacher education: A structuralist neo-Marxist critique of postmodernist, quasi-postmodernist and cultural neo-Marxist theory, *British Journal of Sociology of Education,* 22 (1): 135–155

Hillcole Group (1997) *Rethinking education and democracy: A socialist alternative for the twenty first century,* London: the Tufnell Press

Hirst, P. and Thompson, G. (1999) *Globalization in Question,* Cambridge: Polity Press. (2nd edition. 1st edition published 1996)

Hjort, K. (1984) *Pigepædagogik—?* [Pedagogy for girls—?], Copenhagen: Gyldendals Pædagogiske Bibliotek

Holland, J., Ramazanoglu, C., Sharpe, S. and Thomson, R. (1998) *The male in the head: Young people, heterosexuality and power,* London: the Tufnell Press

Holmen, A. (1993) Dansk som andetsprog [Danish as a second language: learning and teaching], in Skutnabb-Kangas, T., Holmen, A. and Phillipson, R. (eds) *Uddannelses af minoriteter* [Education of minorities], København: Danish Pedagogical University

Holmen, A. and Normann Jørgensen, J. (1993) *Tosprogede børn i Danmark—En grundbog* [Bilingual children in Denmark: a reader], København: Hans Reitzels Forlag

Hultqvist, K. (1995 (ed.) *Foucault,* Stockholm: HLS Förlag

Hunter, I. (1994) *Rethinking the school,* Sydney: Allen and Unwin

Hvinden, B. (1994) Tvetydighetens sosiologi: Fattigdom og sosial integrasjon i et simmelsk perspektiv [The sociology of ambivalence: Poverty and social integration in Simmelian perspective], *Sosiologisk Tidsskrift,* 2 (2): 112-124

Jacobsen, B. (1989) *Fungerer lærerutddannelsen?* [Does teacher education function?], København: Undervisningsministeriet

James, A., Jenks, C. and Prout, A. (1998) *Theorizing Childhood,* Cambridge: Polity Press

Jansson, T. (1955)/(1971) *Moominsummer madness,* London: Puffin Books

Jeffrey, B. (1999) Side-stepping the substantial self: the fragmentation of primary teachers' professionality through audit accountability, in Hammersley, M. (ed.) *Researching school experience: Ethnographic studies of teaching and learning,* London: Falmer Press

Jensen, I. (1998) *Interkulturel kommunikation i komplekse samfund* [Intercultural communication in complex societies], Roskilde: Roskilde Universitetsforlag

Jonsson, G. (1967) *Delinquent boys, their parents and grandparents,* Copenhagen: Munksgaard

Julkunen, R. (1997) Naisruumiin oikeudet [The rights of the female body], in Jokinen, E. (ed.) *Ruumiin siteet: Tekstejä eroista, järjestyksistä ja sukupuolesta* [The binds of the body: Texts on differences, orders and gender], Tampere: Vastapaino

Kallós, D. and Lindblad, S. (eds) (1994) *New policy contexts for education, Sweden and United Kingdom*, (Educational Reports 42), Pedagogic Institute, Umeå University

Kasanen, K. and Räty, H. (2002) 'You be sure now to be honest in your assessment': Teaching and learning self-assessment, *Social Psychology of Education*, 5 (4): 313-328

Kasanen, K., Räty, H. and Snellman, L. (2003, in press) Learning the class test, *European Journal of Psychology of Education*

Kehily, M. J. and Nayak, A. (1997) Masculinities and schooling: Why are young men so homophobic? in Steinberg, D. L., Epstein, D. and Johnson, R. (eds), *Border patrols: policing the boundaries of heterosexuality*, London: Cassell

Keith, M. and Pile, S. (eds) (1993) *Place and the politics of identity*, London: Routledge

Kemp, P. T. (1989) Toward a narrative ethics: A bridge between ethics and the narrative reflection of Ricoeur, in Kemp, P. T. and Rasmussen, D. (eds) *The narrative path: The later works of Paul Ricoeur*, Cambridge: The MIT Press

Kenway, J. and Epstein, D. (1996) Introduction: The marketisation of school education: feminist studies and perspectives, *Discourse*, 17 (3): 301–314

Kenway, J. and Willis, S. (with Blackmore, J. and Rennie, L.) (1998) *Answering back. girls, boys and feminism in schools*, London and New York: Routledge

Keskisalo, A. and Perho, S. (2001) Taistelua tilasta Joensuussa Rasismi paikallisten nuorten neuvotteluvälineenä [Struggle for space: Racism as a negotiation tool of local youth], in Suutari, M., (ed.) *Vallattomat marginaalit—yhteisöllisyyksiä nuoruudessa ja yhteiskunnan reunoilla* [Communalities in youth and in margins of society], Helsinki: Network of Youth Research and Society of Youth Research Publications 20: 77-102

Kirkhusmo, A. (1983) *Akademi og seminar* [Academy and seminary], Trondheim: UiT, Norges lærerhøgskole

Klette, K., Carlgren, I., Rasmussen, J., Simola, H. and Sundkvist, M. (eds) (2000) *Restructuring Nordic teachers: An analysis of policy texts from Finland, Denmark, Sweden and Norway*, University of Oslo, Institute for Educational Research, Report No. 10

Knudsen, F. (1998) *Integrationsdebatten i Danmark og Frankrig—Mellem universalisme og partikularisme* [The integration debate in Denmark and France: Between universalism and particularism], Esbjerg: Sydjysk Universitetsforlag

Knuuttila, S. (1998) Paikan synty suomalaisena ilmisnä [The birth of the place], in Alasuutari, P. and Ruuska, P. (eds) *Elävänä Euroopassa: Muuttuva suomalainen identiteetti* [Alive in Europe: Changing Finnish identity], Tampere: Osuuskunta Vastapaino

Komulainen, K. (2001) 1930-luvun suomalainen oppikoulu kansalaisuuden näyttämönä [1930s Finnish secondary school as a stage of nationality], *Nuorisotutkimus* [The Finnish Journal of Youth Study] 19 (1): 39-54

Krag, H. (1992) *Minoriteter—En grundbog* [Minorities: a reader], København: Spektrum

Kryger, N. (1990) Drengepædagogik? [Pedagogy for boys?], in Jacobsen, H. and Højgaard, L. (eds) *Skolen er køn* [School is gendered], Copenhagen: Ligestillingsrådet

Kvalbein, I. A. (1999) *Lærerutdanningskultur og kunnskapsutvikling* [Teacher education culture and knowledge development], Oslo: HiO-rapport nr. 15

Labov, W. and Waletzky, J. (1967)/(1973) Narrative analysis: Oral versions of personal experience, in Helm, J. (ed.) *Essays on the verbal and visual arts. Proceedings of the 1966 Annual Spring meeting of the American Ethnological Society,* Seattle and London: University of Washington Press

Lahdenperä, P. (1997) *Invandrarbakgrund eller skolsvårigheter? En textanalytisk studie av åtgärdsprogram för elever med invandrarbakgrund* [Migrant background or school difficulties? A text analytical study of intervention programs written for students with immigrant backgrounds], Stockholm: HLS Förlag

Lahelma, E. (1992) *Sukupuolten eriytyminen peruskoulun opetussuunnitelmassa* [Gender difference in the curriculum of the comprehensive school], Helsinki: Yliopistopaino

Lahelma, E. (2000) *Inclusion/exclusion in educational process,* Research plan for the University of Helsinki.

Lahelma, E. (2001) Going into the army: A gendered step in transition to adulthood, *Young: Nordic journal of Youth Research,* 8 (4): 2-15

Lahelma, E. (2002a) Peruskoulu, tytöt ja tekninen osaaminen [Comprehensive school, girls and knowledge in technology], in Smeds, R., Kauppinen, K., Yrjänheikki, K. and Valtonen, A. (eds) *Tiede ja tekniikka—Missä on nainen?* [Science and technology—where is the woman?], Helsinki: Tek

Lahelma, E. (2002b) Gendered conflicts in secondary school: Fun or enactment of power? *Gender and Education,* 14 (3): 295-306

Lahelma, E. (2002c) School is for meeting friends: Secondary school as lived and remembered, *British Journal of Sociology of Education,* 23 (3): 367-381

Lahelma, E. and Gordon, T. (1997) First day in secondary school: Learning to be a 'professional pupil', *Educational Research and Evaluation,* 3 (2): 119-139

Lähteenmaa, J. and Näre, S. (1992) Tyttötutkimuksen palmikoita punomassa [Girls' studies: Braiding the strands], in Näre, S. and Lähteenmaa, J. (eds) *Letit liehumaan: Tyttökulttuuri murroksessa* [Shake your hair! Girls' culture in the process of change], Tietolipas 124, Helsinki: SKS

Lappalainen, S. (2002a) 'Eskarissa eurokuntoon'—Esiopetus (suomalais) kansalisena projektina [Becoming 'Euro' citizen—Preschool education as a national project], in Gordon, T., Komulainen, K. and Lempiäinen, K. (eds) *Hei hei Suomi-neitonen hei: Kansallisuuden sukupuoli* ['Finnish Maiden, hello:' Gendered nationality], Tampere: Vastapaino

Lappalainen, S. (2002b) A day before the independence day: Constructions of nationality, gender and citizenship at preschool, in Komulainen, K., *Sukupuolitetut rajat—Gendered borders and boundaries,* University of Joensuu, Department of Psychology, publications 22

Larkin, J. (1994) Walking through walls: The sexual harassment of high school girls, *Gender and Education,* 6 (3): 236-306

Lavers, P., Pickup, M. and Thomson, M. (1986) Factors to consider in implementing an in-class support system, *Support for Learning,* 1 (1): 32-35

Lefebvre, H. (1991) *The production of space,* Oxford: Basil Blackwell

Lepola, O. (2000) *Ulkomaalaisesta suomenmaalaiseksi: Monikulttuurisuus, kansalaisuus ja suomalaisuus 1900-luvun maahanmuuttopoliittisessa keskustelussa* [From foreigner to Finlander: Multiculturalism, nationality and the Finnish identity in the political debate on immigration during the 1990s], Helsinki: SKS

Lindblad, S. (1994) Notes on post-welfare education: Towards a new-liberal education reform in Sweden?, in D. Kallos and S. Lindblad (eds) *New policy contexts for education: Sweden and United Kingdom* (Educational Reports 42), Pedagogic Institute, Umeå University

Lindblad, S. (1997) Imposed professionalization: On teachers' work and experiences of deregulation of education in Sweden, in Nilsson, I. and Lundahl, L. (eds) *Teachers, Curriculum and policy: Critical perspectives in educational research,* Umeå: Umeå Press

Lindblad, S. and Popkewitz, T. (eds) (2000) *Public discourses on education and social integration and exclusion: Analyses of policy texts in European contexts*, (Uppsala Reports on Education no. 36), Uppsala: Department of Education, Uppsala University

Lindblad, S. and Popkewitz, T. (eds) (2001) *Education governance and social integration and exclusion: Studies in the powers of reason and the reasons of power*, (Uppsala Reports on Education no. 39), Uppsala: Department of Education, Uppsala University

Lindblad, S. and Popkewitz, T. (2002) Education governance in transition: Stories of progress and denials and dissolutions of policy conflicts. A draft to the symposium 'Controversies in Education Restructuring' at the EERA 2002 meeting in Lisbon, September 11-14

Lindblad, S. and Sahlström, F. (1999) Gamla mönster och nya fränser: Om ramfaktorer och klassrumsinteraktion [Old patterns and new fashions: On frame factors and classroom interaction], *Pedagogisk Forskning i Sverige* [Pedagogic Research in Sweden], 4 (1): 73-92

Lindblad, S., Johannesson, I. A. and Simola, H. (2002) Education governance in transition: an introduction, in *Educational Research*, 46 (3): 237-245

Lindblad, S., Johannesson, I. and Simola, H. (2002) Education governance in transition, *Scandinavian Journal of Educational Research*, 46 (3): 237-245

Lindensjö, B. and Lundgren, U. P. (2000) *Utbildningsreformer och politisk styrning* [Education reform and political control], Stockholm: HLS Förlag

Lindroos, M. (1995) The production of 'girl' in an educational setting, *Gender and Education*, 7 (2): 143-155

Ling, L. (2000) *Places where teachers learn: Places where universities sell knowledge*, Barcelona: Papers of the 25th ATEE Annual Conference: 173-181

Lundahl, L. (2000) A new kind of order: Swedish policy texts related to governance, social inclusion and exclusion in the 1990s, in S. Lindblad and T. Popkewitz, T. (eds) *Public discourses on education and social integration and exclusion: Analyses of policy texts in European contexts*, (Uppsala Reports on Education no. 36), Uppsala: Department of Education, Uppsala University

Lundahl, L. (2001) Governance of education and its social consequences. Interviews with Swedish politicians and policy makers, in Lindblad, S. and Popkewitz, T. S. (eds) *Listening to education actors on social integration and exclusion*, (Uppsala Reports on Education no. 37) Uppsala: Department of Education, Uppsala University

Lynch, J. (1986) *Multicultural education: principles and practice*, London: Routledge and Kegan Paul

Lynch, J. (1989) *Multicultural education in a global society*, London: Falmer Press

Mac an Ghaill, M. (1988) *Young, gifted and black*, Milton Keynes: Open University Press

Mac an Ghaill, M. (1994) *The making of men: Masculinities, sexualities and schooling*, Buckingham: Open University Press

Mac an Ghaill, M. (1999) 'New' cultures of training: Emerging male (hetero)sexual identities, *British Educational Research Journal*, 25 (4): 427-443

Marcuse, H. (1968/1988) *Negations: Essays in critical theory*, London: Free Association Books

Marshall, T.H. (1950) *Citizenship and social class*, Cambridge: Cambridge University Press

Massey, D. (1993) Politics and space/time, in Keith, M. and Pile, S. (eds) *Place and the politics of identity*, London: Routledge

Massey, D. (1998) The spatial construction of youth cultures, in Skelton, T. and Valentine, G. (eds) *Cool places: Geographies of youth cultures*, London and New York: Routledge
May, S. (ed.) (1999) *Critical multiculturalism: Rethinking multicultural and antiracist education*, London: Falmer Press
Mayall, B. (2002) *Towards a sociology of childhood: Thinking from children's lives*, Buckingham and Philadelphia: Open University Press
McClintock, A. (1995) *Imperial leather: Race, gender and sexuality in the colonial context*, New York and London: Routledge
McDermott, R. P. and Varenne, H. (1995) Culture as disability, www.ameranthassn.org/caepubs.htm *Anthropology and Education Quarterly*, 26: 324-348
McDill, E. L., McDill, M. S. and Sprehe, J. T. (1969) *Strategies for success in compensatory education*, Baltimore/London: The John Hopkins Press
McDowell, L. (1999) *Gender, identity and place: Understanding feminist geographies*, Minneapolis: University of Minnesota Press
McMurtry, J. (1998) *Unequal freedoms: The global market as an ethical system*, Toronto: Kumarian Press
McRobbie, A. (1996) The Es and the anti–Es: New questions for feminism and cultural studies, in Ferguson, M. and Golding, P. (eds), *Cultural studies in question*, London: Sage
Melkas, T. (2001) *Tasa-arvobarometri* [Barometer of equality], Statistics—Finland
Merton, R. (1948) The self-fulfilling prophecy, *Antioch Review*, 8: 193-210
Meyer, J. W., Boli, J. and Thomas G. M. and Ramirez Francisco, O. (1997) World society and nation state, *American Journal of Sociology*, 103 (1): 144-181
Michelsen, S. (1999) *Lærerutdanningen under høgskolereformene* [Teacher education under the higher education reform], Oslo: Norges forskningsråd
Miller, J. and Glassner, B. (1997) The 'inside' and the 'outside': Finding realities in interviews, in Silverman, David (ed.) *Qualitative research: Theory, method and practice*, London, Thousand Oaks, New Dehli: Sage
Milne, A. A. (1999) Nalle Puhin mietekirja [The Pooh Book of Quotations], Helsinki: WSOY
Ministry of Education, Research and Church Affairs (1997) *The Curriculum for the 10-year compulsory school*, Norway
Ministry of Education, Research and Church Affairs (2000) *Act relating to Primary and Secondary Education (Education Act)*, Norway
Mirza, H. S. (1992) *Young, female and black*, London: Routledge
Mirza, H. S. (1997) Black women in education: A collective movement for social change, in Mirza, H. S. (ed.), *Black British feminism*, London: Routledge
Mørch, Y. (1998) *Bindestregs-Danskere—Fortællinger om køn, generation og etnicitet* (Hyphened-Danes: Narratives about gender, generation and ethnicity), København: Samfundslitteratur
Murphy, E. and Dingwall, R. (2001) The ethics of ethnography, in Atkinson, P. *et al.* (2001) *Handbook of ethnography*, London, Thousand Oaks and New Delhi: Sage
National Board of Social Affairs (1984) *Framework Curriculum for six year old children*, Helsinki: National Board of Social Affairs
NBE (2000) *Framework Curriculum for the Preschool*, Helsinki: National Board of Education
NBE (1996) *Framework Curriculum for the Preschool*, Helsinki: National Board of Education

Neumann, I. B. (2001) *Mening, materialitet, makt: En innføring i diskursanalyse* (Meaning, materiality, power: an introduction to discourse analysis), Bergen: Fagbokforlaget

Nieto, S. (1996) *Affirming diversity: The sociopolitical context of multicultural education*, New York: Longman

Nieto, S. (1999) *The light in their eyes: Creating multicultural learning communities*, New York: Teachers College Press

NOU (1988) *For et lærerrikt samfunn* [Towards a Learning Society], Oslo: Statens Forvaltningstjenesten

NOU (1996) *Lærerutdanning* [Teacher Education], Oslo: Statens Forvaltningstjeneste

Nóvoa, A. (2001) Texts, images, and memories: Writing 'new' histories of education, in Popkewitz, T. S. Franklin, B. M. and Pereyra, M. A. (eds), *Cultural history and education: Critical essays on knowledge and schooling*, New York: Routledge Falmer

Nóvoa, A. and Lawn, M. (eds) (2002) *Fabricating Europe: The formation of an education space*, Dordrecht: Kluwer

OECD (1998) *Education at a glance: OECD indicators*, Paris: OECD/CERI

Offe, C. (1996) *Modernity and the state*, Cambridge: Polity Press

Öhrn, E. (1990) *Könsmönster i klassrumsinteraktion: En observations-och intervjustudie av högstadieelevers lärarkontakter* [Gender patterns in classroom interaction: Observations and interviews concerning students' interactions with teachers in grade nine of the comprehensive school], Göteborg: Acta Universitatis Gothoburgensis

Öhrn, E. (1993) Gender, influence and resistance in school, *British Journal of Sociology of Education*, 14 (2): 147-158

Öhrn, E. (1997) *Elevers inflytande i klassrummet* [Students' influence in the classroom], rapport 1997: 05, Institutionen för Pedagogik och Didaktik, Göteborgs universitet

Öhrn, E. (1998) Gender and power in school: On girls' open resistance, *Social psychology of Education*, 1 (4): 341-357

Öhrn, E. (2001) Marginalization of democratic values: A gendered practice of schooling? *International Journal of Inclusive Education*, 5 (2/3): 319-328

Öhrn, E. (2002) *Könsmönster i förändring? En kunskapsöversikt om unga i skolan* [Changing gender patterns? A review of research on young people in school], Skolverket

Oinas, E. (1998) The sexy Woman and the smart girl—embodied gender identity and middle-class adolescence, *NORA—Nordic Journal of Women's Studies* 6 (2): 1-11

Olesen, V. and Whittaker, E. (1968) *The silent dialogue*, San Francisco: Jossey-Bass

Österlind, E. (1998) *Disciplining via freedom: Independent work and student planning*, Uppsala: Acta Universitatis Upsaliensis, Dissertation

Ottomeyer, K. (1978), Människan under kapitalismen [A human being under capitalism], Göteborg: Röda Bokförlaget AB

Paasi A. (1996) *Territories, boundaries and consciousness—The changing geographies of the Finnish-Russian border*, Chichester: John Wiley

Paasi, A. (1998) Koulutus kansallisena projektina—'Me' ja 'muut' suomalaisissa maantiedon oppikirjoissa ['We' and the 'others' in Finnish textbooks of geography], in Alasuutari, P. and Ruuska P. (eds) *Elävänä Euroopassa muuttuva suomalainen identiteetti* [Alive in Europe—Changing Finnish identity], Tampere: Vastapaino

Papagiannis, G. J., Easton, P. A. and Owens, J. T. (1992) *The school restructuring movement in the USA: An analysis of major issues and policy implications*, Paris: UNESCO

Papanastasiou, C. (2000) Internal and external factors affecting achievement in mathematics: Some findings from TIMMS, *Studies in Educational Evaluation*, 26 (1): 1-7

Parekh, B. (2000) *Rethinking multiculturalism: Cultural diversity and political theory,* Basingstoke: Palgrave
Pateman, C. (1988) *The sexual contract,* Cambridge: Polity Press
Peräkylä, A. (1990), *Kuoleman monet kasvot: Identiteettien tuottaminen kuolevan potilaan hoidossa* [Many faces of death: Identity formation in taking care of a dying patient], Tampere: Vastapaino
Phil, J. (2001) Paradoxes of inclusion and exclusion in Norwegian educational reforms in the 1990s, *Nordisk Tidsskrift for Spesialpedagogikk,* 79 (1): 14-33
Phoenix, A. (1997) Youth and gender: New issues, new agenda, *Young,* 3 (3): 2-19
Popkewitz, T. (1991) *A political sociology of educational reform,* New York: Teachers College Press
Popkewitz, T. (1998a) Dewey, Vygotsky, and the social administration of the individual: Constructivist pedagogy as systems of ideas in historical spaces, *American Educational Research Journal,* 35 (4): 535-570
Popkewitz, T. (1998b) *Struggling for the soul: The politics of schooling and the construction of the teacher,* New York and London: Teachers College Press
Popkewitz, T. S. (2000a) *Educational knowledge: Changing relationships between the state, civil society, and the educational community,* New York: SUNY Press
Popkewitz, T. (2000b) Reform as the social administration of the child: Globalization of knowledge and power, in Burbules, N. C. and Torres, C. A. (eds) *Globalization and education: Critical perspectives,* New York: Routledge
Popkewitz, T. (in press) Governing the child and pedagogicalization of the parent, in Bloch, M., Holmlund, K., Moqvist, I., and Popkewitz, T. (eds) *Governing children, families, and education: Restructuring the welfare state,* New York: Palgrave Press
Popkewitz, T. and Brennan, M. (1998) *Foucault's challenge: Discourse, knowledge and power in education,* New York: Teachers College Press
Popkewitz, T. and Pereyra, M. (1993) An eight country study of reform practices in teacher education: An outline of the problematic, in Popkewitz, T. (ed.), *Changing patterns of power: Social regulation and teacher education reform,* Albany, NY: State University of New York Press
Popkewitz, T., Tabachnick, B., and Wehlage, G. (1982) *The myth of educational reform: A study of school responses to a program of change,* Madison: University of Wisconsin Press
Power, M. (1997) *The audit society: Rituals of verification,* Oxford: Oxford University Press
Rastas, A. (2002) Katseilla merkityt, silminnähden erilaiset: lasten ja nuorten kokemuksia rodullistavista katseista [Visibly different, marked by gazes: Children's and young people's experiences of receiving racist stares], *Nuorisotutkimus* [The Finnish Journal of Youth Study], 20 (3): 3-17
Rhedding-Jones, J. (1996), Researching early schooling: Poststructural practices and academic writing in an ethnography, *British Journal of Sociology of Education,* 17 (1): 21–37
Riessman, C. K. (1994) Making sense of marital violence: One woman's narrative, in Riessman, C. K. (ed.) *Qualitative Studies in Social Work Research,* Thousand Oaks, London, New Delhi: Sage
Riksdagsutryck (1984/85: 122) Regeringsproposition om en lärarutbildning för grundskolan och kommunal vuxenutbildning [Teacher education for the

compulsory comprehensive school and municipal adult education], (Swedish) *Government Proposition 1984/85: 122*

Roman, L. (1993) Double exposure: The politics of feminist materialist ethnography, *Educational Theory*, 43 (3): 279–308

Rose, N. (1999) *Governing the soul: The shaping of the private self,* London: Free Association Books

Rose, N. (2000) Community, citizenship and the third way, in *The American Behavioral Scientist,* 43 (9): 1395-1411

Rosenthal, R. and Jacobson, L. (1968) *Pygmalion in the classroom,* New York: Holt, Rinehart and Winston

Ryan, W. (1986) How to blame the victim, in Lindenfeld, F. (ed.), *Radical perspectives on social problems: Readings in critical sociology,* New York: General Hall

Sætersdal, B. and Heggen, K. (eds) (2002) *I den beste hensikt?: 'Ondskap' i behandlingssamfunnet* [With the best intention? 'Evil' in pastoral care societies], Oslo: Akribe

Salo, U-M. (1999) *Ylös tiedon ja taidon ylämäkeä: Tutkielma koulun maailmoista ja järjestyksistä* [Up the hill of knowledge and skill: The worlds and orders of the school], Acta Universitatis Lapponiensis 24 Rovaniemi: University of Lapland

Schram, S. F. and Neisser, P. T. (eds) (1997) *Tales of the state: Narrative in contemporary U. S. politics and public policy,* New York: New York University Press

Schultz Jørgensen, P. (1990) Er en ændret pigeroll på vej? [Is a new female role on its way?], in Jacobsen, H. and Højgaard, L. (eds) *Skolen er køn* [School is gendered], Copenhagen: Ligestillingsrådet

Sennett, R. (2000) *The corrosion of character: The personal consequences of work in the new capitalism,* Stockholm: Atlas

Skeggs, B. (1997) *Formations of class and gender,* London: Sage

Skeggs, B. (2001) Feminist ethnography, in Atkinson, P., Coffey, A., Delamont, S., Lofland, J. and Lofland, L., *Handbook of ethnography,* London, Thousand Oaks and New Delhi: Sage

Skolverket (1999) *Läroplanerna i praktiken* [Curriculum in practice], Report no 175, Stockholm: Liber

Skrtic, T. M. (1991) The Special Education paradox: Equity as the way to excellence, *Harvard Educational Review*, 61 (2): 148-206

Skrtic, T. M. (ed.) (1995) *Disability and democracy: Reconstructing (Special) Education for postmodernity,* New York, London: Teachers College Press

Skutnabb-Kangas, T. (1990) *Minoritet, sprog og racisme* (Minority, language and racism), København: Tiden

Smith, D. E. (1990a) *The conceptual practices of power: A feminist sociology of knowledge*, Boston: Northeastern University Press

Smith, D. E. (1990b) *Texts, facts and femininity: Exploring the relations of ruling,* London and New York: Routledge

Smith, D. JE. (1987) *The everyday world as problematic: Feminist sociology,* Toronto: University of Toronto Press

Smith, N. and Katz, C. (1993) Grounding metaphor: Towards a spatialised politics, in Keith, M. and Pile, S. (eds) *Place and the politics of identity,* London: Routledge

Soja, E. (1985) The spatiality of social life: Towards a transformative theorisation, in Gregory, D. and Urry, J. (eds) *Social relations and spatial structures,* London: Macmillan

Søndergaard, D. M. (2002) Poststructuralist approaches to empirical analysis, *Qualitative Studies in Education*, 15 (2): 187-204

SOU (1999) *Att lära och leda. En lärarutbildning för samverkan och utveckling* [Learning and leading: A teacher education for co-operation and development] Lärarutbildningskommitténs slutbetänkande, Stockholm: Utbildningsdepartementet

SOU (1990) *Demokrati och makt i Sverige: Maktutredningens huvudrapport* [Democracy and power in Sweden: Main report from the Swedish Commission on Power], Stockholm: Allmänna Förlaget

Spencer, J. (2001) Ethnography after postmodernism, in Atkinson, P. *et al.* (2001) *Handbook of ethnography*, London, Thousand Oaks and New Delhi: Sage

Spradley, J. P. (1979) *The ethnographic interview*, Orlando: Harcourt Brace Jovanovich

Spring, Joel, H. (1972) *Education and the rise of the corporate order*, Boston: Beacon Press

SPS (2002) *StudData rapport* under arbeid [Statistical report on student behaviour and attitudes, work in progress], Oslo: HiO

St. Pierre, E. A. (2000) Poststructural feminism in education: An overview, *Qualitative Studies in Education*, 13 (5): 477-515

Staberg, E-M. (1992) *Olika världar, skilda värderingar* [Different worlds, different values], Pedagogiska Institutionen, Umeå Universitet

Statistics of Finland (2001): http://statfin.stat.fi/statweb/

Staunæs, D. (2003) *Etnicitet, køn og skoleliv* [Ethnicity, gender and school life], Roskilde: Roskilde University, Department of Journalism, Communication and Computer Science

Steinberg, D. L., Epstein, D. and Johnson, R. (eds) (1997) *Border Patrols: Policing the Boundaries of Heterosexuality*, London: Cassell

Stronach, I., Corbin, B., McNamara, O., Stark, S. and Warne, T. (2002) Towards an uncertain politics of professionalism: Teacher and nurse identities in flux, *Education Policy*, 17 (1): 109-138

Sundkvist, M. (2000) Analyses of steering documents for compulsory school in Sweden during the 1990s: What is a teacher supposed to know and do? in Klette, K. and Carlgren, I. (eds) *Restructuring Nordic teachers: An analysis of policy texts from Finland, Denmark, Sweden and Norway*, University of Oslo, Institute for Educational Research, Report No. 10

Suurpää, L. (2001) Foreigners as a Strategic constructions, in Helve, H. and Wallace, C., *Youth, Citizenship and Empowerment*, Aldershot, Burlington, Singapore, Sydney: Ashgate

Svensson, A. (1998) *Hur lyckas eleverna i den nya gymnasieskolan?* [How students succeed in the new secondary high school?], Institutionen för Pedagogik och Didaktik, rapport 1998: 07, Göteborgs Universitet

Svensson, A. (2001) Består den sociala snedrekrytering? Elevens val av gymnasieprogram hösten 1998 [Student upper-secondary school programme choices 1998], *Pedagogisk Forskning i Sverige* [Pedagogic Research in Sweden], 6 (3): 161-182

Taylor, S. (2002) Researching the social: An introduction to ethnographic research, in Taylor, S. (ed.) *Ethnographic research: A reader*, London, Thousand Oaks and New Delhi: Sage

Teigen, K. (1997) *Studievaner blant allmennlære-og ingeniørstudenter* [Study habits of teacher and engineer students], Oslo: NIFU skriftserie 22/97

The Hillcole Group (1997) R*ethinking education and democracy: A socialist alternative for the twenty-first century,* London: the Tufnell Press
Thorne, B. (1993) *Gender play: Girls and boys in school,* Buckingham: Open University Press
Tjeldvoll, A. (1998) *Education and the Scandinavian welfare state in the year 2000: Equality, policy and reform,* New York: Garland
Tolonen, T. (1995) Controlling body and space: Encounters at school, in Aittola, T., Koikkalainen, R. and Sironen, E. (eds) *'Confronting strangeness': Towards a reflexive modernisation of the school,* Department of Education, University of Jyväskylä, Finland
Tolonen, T. (2001) *Nuorten kulttuurit koulussa: ääni, tila ja sukupuolten arkiset järjestykset* [Voice, space and gender in youth cultures at school], Helsinki: Gaudeamus
Tomlinson, S. (1996) Conflicts and dilemmas for professionals in Special Education, in Christensen, C. and Rizvi, F. (eds) *Disability and the dilemmas of education and justice,* Buckingham and Philadelphia: Open University Press
Troyna, B. (1993) *Racism and education,* Buckingham and Philadelphia: Open University Press
Troyna, B. and Hatcher, R. (1992) *Racism in children's lives,* London: Routledge
UFD (2002a) *Stortingsmelding nr. 16 (2001-2002) Om ny lærerutdanning* [On new teacher education], Oslo: Ministry for Education and Research
UFD (2002b) Press Release: National Agency for Quality in Education, Oslo
Utbildningsdepartementet (1993) *Visst är vi olika!* [We certainly are different!], Stockholm: Utbildningsdepartementet
Utbildningsdepartementet (1994) *Vi är alla olika* [We are all different], Stockholm: Utbildningsdepartementet
Vidich, A. J. and Lyman, S. M. (1994) Qualitative methods: Their history in sociology and anthropology, in Denzin, N. and Lincoln, Y. S. (eds) (1994) *Handbook of qualitative research,* London and New Delhi: Sage
Walkerdine, V., Lucey, H. and Melody, J. (2001) *Growing up girl: Psychosocial explorations of gender and class,* Houndmills: Palgrave
Walzer, M. (1983) *Spheres of justice: A defence of plurality and equality,* Oxford: Robertson
Weis, L. (1990) *Working class without work: High school students in a de-industrializing economy,* New York: Routledge
Wernersson, I. (1977) *Könsdifferentiering i grundskolan* [Gender differentiation in the comprehensive school], Gothenbourg Studies in Educational Sciences 22, Mölndal
Westwood, S. and Phizacklea, A. (2000) *Trans-nationalism and the politics of belonging,* London and New York: Routledge
Whitty, G. (1989) The New Right and the national curriculum: State control or market forces? *Education Policy,* 4 (4): 329–41
Whitty, G., Power, S. and Halpin, D. (1998) *Devolution and choice in education: The school, the state and the market,* Buckingham: Open University Press
Willis, P. (1977) *Learning to labour,* Farnborough: Saxon House
Willis, P. (1999) Labour power, culture and the cultural commodity, in Castells, M., Flecha, R., Freire, P., Giroux, H., Macedo D. and Willis, P. (eds) *Critical education in the new information age,* Boulder, Colorado: Roman and Littlefield
Willis, P. (2000) *The ethnographic imagination,* Cambridge: Polity Press
Willis, P. and Trondman, M. (2000) Manifesto for ethnography, *Ethnography,* 1 (1): 5–16

Woods, P. and Jeffrey, B. (2002) The reconstruction of primary teachers identities, *British Journal of Sociology of Education*, 23 (1): 89-106

Woods, P., Troman, G. and Boyle, M. (1997) *Restructuring schools, reconstructing teachers: Responding to change in primary schools*, Buckingham: Open University Press

Wright, C. (1992) *Race relations in the primary school*, London: David Fulton

Wyness, M. G. (2000) *Contesting childhood*, London and New York: Falmer Press

Young, R. (1995) *Colonial desire: Hybridity in theory, culture and race*, London: Routledge

Yuval-Davis, N. (1997) *Gender and nation*, London: Sage

Yuval-Davis, N. (2003) Citizenship, territoriality and the gendered construction of difference, in Brenner, N., Jessop, B., Jones, M. and Macleod, G. (eds) *State/space: A reader*, Oxford: Blackwell

Zackari, G. (2001) Swedish school actors about education governance changes and social consequences, in Lindblad, S. and Popkewitz, T. (eds) *Listening to education actors on governance and social integration and exclusion*, (Uppsala Reports on Education 37), Uppsala: Department of Education, Uppsala University

Printed in the United Kingdom
by Lightning Source UK Ltd.
9788100001B/76-84